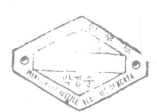

MINISTRY INTSKE DEP. OF KOREA

DIRECCION SEG. ESTADO
-FRONTERAS-
04. 9. 98.    189
SALIDA
A
MAHON

DEPARTMENT OF IMMIGRATION
PERMITTED TO ENTER
AUSTRALIA.
24 APR 1986
on
For stay of 12 Month
SYDNEY AIRPORT 54

IMMIGRATION DIVISION BANGKOK THAILAND
A
72
DEPARTED
- 6 FEB 1988
SIGNED

IMMIGRATION & ETHNIC AFFAIRS
..........Person
30 OCT 1989
DEPARTED
AUSTRALIA
SYDNEY   32

中华人民共和国
广东省公安厅

上陸許可
ADMITTED
15. FEB. 1986
Status: 4-1-    4
Duration:    90 days
NARITA(N)
№ 011278   Immigration Inspector
日本国

# T R A V E L E R ' S
# S·P·A·I·N
# C O M P A N I O N

ADMITTED
20 OCT. 1988
Status:   4-1-16
Duration   180 day
Port:   HANEDA
Signature

THE UNITED STATES
OF AMERICA
NONIMMIGRANT VISA
ISSUED AT
SED   Air Port

U.S. IMMIGRATION
170 HHW 1710
JUL 20 1998

HONG KONG
(1038)
- 7 JUN 1987
IMMIGRATION
OFFICER

## The 1998–1999 Traveler's Companions

ARGENTINA • AUSTRALIA • BALI • CALIFORNIA • CANADA EAST • CANADA WEST • CANADA • CHINA • COSTA RICA • CUBA • EQUADOR • FLORIDA • HAWAII • HONG KONG • INDIA • INDONESIA • JAPAN • KENYA • MALAYSIA & SINGAPORE • MEDITERRANEAN FRANCE • MEXICO • NEPAL • NEW ENGLAND NEW ZEALAND • PERU • PHILIPPINES • PORTUGAL • RUSSIA • SPAIN • THAILAND • TURKEY • VENEZUELA • VIETNAM, LAOS AND CAMBODIA

### Traveler's SPAIN Companion
First Published 1998
The Globe Pequot Press
6 Business Park Road, P.O. Box 833,
Old Saybrook, CT 06475-0833
http://www.globe.pequot.com

### ISBN: 0 7627 0234 6

By arrangement with Kümmerly+Frey, AG, Switzerland
© 1998 Kümmerly+Frey, AG, Switzerland

Created, edited and produced by
Allan Amsel Publishing, 53 rue Beaudouin,
27700 Les Andelys, France. E-mail: aamsel@aol.com
Editor in Chief: Allan Amsel
Editor: Fiona Nichols
Original design concept: Hon Bing-wah
Picture editor and designer: Michelle Chan

AUTHOR'S ACKNOWLEDGEMENTS
A writer inevitably incurs a large number of debts during the research phase
of any project and this book was no exception. I would, however, like to limit my
thanks to four people who helped more than they probably realized. Pilar Vico, the former
Director of Public Relations in Spain's National Tourist Office in New York, played an
indispensable part in helping photographer Nik Wheeler and myself with our travels in Spain.
She also made many useful suggestions when she read the text. Tom Burns, journalist and
veteran travel writer, counseled us in Madrid and introduced us to his own excellent work,
*Spain: Everything Under The Sun,* on which I have lent heavily for the listings of useful
information for the traveler. Luladey Befekadu spent several hot New York summer days
laboring on those same listings, and last but by no means least, my wife, Helen,
created space and gave encouragement when both were needed.

Printed by Samhwa Printing Co. Ltd., Seoul, Korea

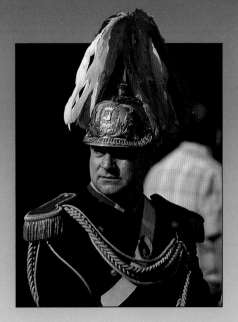

# TRAVELER'S SPAIN COMPANION

by John de St Jorre

Photographed by Nik Wheeler

Kümmerly+Frey

The
Globe
Pequot
Press

Old Saybrook

# Contents

MAPS
Spain                                    8–9
Madrid                                    90
Central Spain                            114
Catalonia and the Levante                126
Andalusia                                178
Northern Spain                       202–203
The Balearic Islands                     238

TOP SPOTS                                 11
Sleep in a Castle, a Palace or
a Monastery                               11
Grace and the Grape: Pilgrimage
Through La Rioja                          12
Flamenco: Spain's "Deep Song"            12
*Tapas* Tasting                          14
Bullfighting                             14
The Running of the Bulls                 16
*Al Andalus* — Spain's Orient Express    18
Triangle of Art (Madrid)                 19
Alhambra                                 19
Monastery-Palace-Mausoleum:
El Escorial                              22
Seville's Rites of Spring                23

YOUR CHOICE                               27
The Great Outdoors                        27
Sporting Spree                            30
The Open Road                             34
Backpacking                               40
Living it up                              40
Family Fun                                42
Cultural Kicks                            44
Shop Till You Drop                        46
Short Breaks                              48
Festive Flings                            50
Spain's National Holidays                 55
Galloping Gourmets                        55
Special Interests                         59

WELCOME TO SPAIN                          61
The Sun-Tanned Hide                       63

OF ROMANS AND MOORS                       65
Before the Romans                         67
The Romans and Their Legacy               67
The Visigoths                             68
The Moors                                 69
The Catholic Monarchs                     70
The Monarchy in Decline                   72
The Spanish Civil War                     74
The Franco Years                          74
Into Today's World                        76

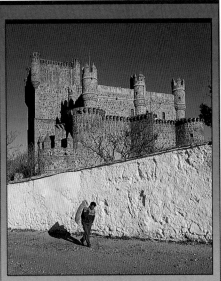

THE CULTURAL LEGACY 79
A Legacy in Full View 81
Spain's Great Buildings 81
  The Moorish Masterpieces • The
  Churches of Northern Spain
The Visual Arts 84
Intellectual Life and Literature 86
Music and Dance 87

MADRID AND CENTRAL SPAIN 89
Madrid 91
Seeing the City 91
  Public Transport
The Major Attractions 92
  Paseo del Arte • Retiro Park •
  Old Madrid • Palacio Real •
  Other West-Side Sights •
  Salamanca District • Tourist
  Information • Nightlife •
  Around Madrid
Toledo 104
  Seeing the City • Ecclesiatical
  Treats • The Jewish Quarter •
  Cristo de la Luz • Toledo's
  Festivals • Useful Information •
  Hotels and Restaurants
Sierra Guadarrama 109
El Escorial 109
  Valle de Los Caidos
Ávila 115
  Hotels and Restaurants

Segovia 116
  Hotels and Restaurants •
  Segovia to Madrid
Longer Excursions 118
Valladolid 118
  Hotels and Restaurants
Salamanca 119
  Hotels and Restaurants
Zamora 120
Extremadura 121
  Cáceres • Trujillo • Monastery
  of Guadalupe • Badajoz and
  Mérida
La Mancha 122
  Cuenca

CATALONIA AND THE LEVANTE 125
The Mediterranean Connexion 127
  Catalonian *Cavas* • Catalans
  at Play
Barcelona 129
  Barri Gotic • Ramblas •
  Ensanche • Sarrià • Getting
  Around • Tourist Information
Around Barcelona 137
  Montserrat • Sitges
Further Afield 139
  Tarragona • Costa Brava •
  Figueres • Girona • Rural
  Catalonia • Andorra
Levante 143
Valencia 143
  Sightseeing • Tourist Information
Murcia 145

ANDALUSIA 147
A Moorish Spirit 149
Seville 150
    Seeing the City • The Giralda •
    The Cathedral • The Alcázar •
    Barrio de Santa Cruz • Other
    Sights • Museums • Wander,
    But Carefully • Seville's
    Festivals • Tourist Information
The El Rocío Pilgrimage: A very
Spanish Affair 160
The Frontier Towns 165
Arcos de La Frontera 165
Jerez 166
    Hotels and Restaurants •
    The Bodegas • Royal Andalusian
    School of Equestrian Art • Los
    Alburejos Ranch
Sanlúcar de Barrameda 171
Cádiz 171
Gibraltar 172
Ronda 172
    Sightseeing • Hotels and
    Restaurants
Costa del Sol 175
    Accommodation: A Surfeit of
    Choice
Tarifa 177
Estepona 177
Marbella 177
Fuengirola 179
Torremolinos 179
Málaga 179

To the East 179
Heading Inland 180
La Alpujarra 180
    Lanjarón
Sierra Nevada 181
Granada 181
    The Alhambra • The Cathedral •
    The Albaicín • Sacromonte
    Caves • The Cave Dwellers of
    Guadix • Tourist Information
Northern Andalusia 190
Córdoba 190
    The Mezquita (Mosque) • The
    Old City • Judería • Museo
    Taurino • Tourist Information

ARAGÓN AND NORTHERN SPAIN 199
Aragón 201
Zaragoza 201
    Sightseeing • Tourist Information
Navarre 203
Pamplona 204
    Festival of San Firmín • Tourist
    Information
Roncesvalles Pass 209
The Pilgrims' Way 209
Rioja 210
Logroño 211
    Tourist Information
Haro 211
Anguiano 211
San Millán de La Cogolla 211
Santo Domingo de La Calzada 212

| | |
|---|---|
| Burgos | 214 |
| Tourist Information • Leaving Burgos | |
| Santo Domingo de Silos | 216 |
| León | 216 |
| Sightseeing • Tourist Information | |
| Santiago de Compostela | 219 |
| An Improbable Legend • The Road to St. James • Sightseeing • Celebration of the Legend • Tourist Information | |
| The Northern Coastline | 225 |
| Galicia | 225 |
| Asturias and Cantabria | 226 |
| Picos de Europa: Spain's "Alps" | |
| Santander | 229 |
| Santillana del Mar and Altamira Caves • Tourist Information | |
| The Basque Country | 231 |
| San Sebastián | 233 |
| Tourist Information | |

| | |
|---|---|
| **THE BALEARIC ISLANDS** | **237** |
| Spain's Mediterranean Islands | 239 |
| Majorca | 240 |
| Palma de Mallorca • Tourist Information • Seeing the Island | |
| Minorca | 244 |
| Cuidadela and Mahon • Minorca's Festivals • Tourist Information | |
| Ibiza | 246 |
| The Old Town • Around the Island • Tourist Information | |
| Formentera | 249 |

| | |
|---|---|
| **TRAVELERS' TIPS** | **251** |
| Getting There | 252 |
| By Air • By Sea • By Train • By Car • Frontier Towns • Visas • Spanish National Tourist Offices | |
| Travel in Spain | 253 |
| Internal Flights • Trains • Car Hire • Buses and Urban Transport | |
| Accommodation | 254 |
| Paradors | |
| Eating and Drinking | 255 |
| Tourist Offices | 256 |
| Dress | 256 |
| Currency | 257 |
| Public Holidays | 257 |
| Post Offices and Telephones | 257 |
| Electricity | 257 |
| Health | 257 |
| Toilets | 258 |
| Weather | 258 |
| Embassies and Consulates | 258 |
| Sports | 258 |
| Golf • Hunting, Shooting and Fishing • Water Sports • Skiing • Soccer | |
| Shopping | 260 |
| Keeping in Touch | 260 |
| Tipping | 261 |
| Spanish: A Sampler | 261 |
| FURTHER READING | 262 |

| | |
|---|---|
| **QUICK REFERENCE A–Z GUIDE** | **263** |
| To Places and Topics of Interest with Listed Accommodations, Restaurants and Useful Telephone Numbers | |

# TOP SPOTS

## Sleep in a Castle, a Palace or a Monastery

*HOW ABOUT SLEEPING IN THE CASTLE WHERE THE EMPEROR CHARLES V STAYED WHILE WAITING TO RETIRE TO A MONASTERY?* Or passing a night in the 12th-century fortress where the court of the King of León used to meet? Or taking your evening cocktail in the cloister of a medieval convent? These are all **paradors**, Spain's famous and unique chain of government-owned hotels — a network of ancient castles, palaces, monasteries and convents that combine spectacular medieval settings with all mod cons.

Most of the paradors are furnished with antiques and the food is uniformly good, especially the lavish buffet-style breakfasts that set you up for the day's travel. Not all the paradors these days are old. But many of the new ones have been built to give the visitor a view of something that is often extremely old: a medieval town, a Roman bridge, or a landscape that you wouldn't see in the same way from other hotels. Good examples are the modern paradors affording unparalleled views of Salamanca and Toledo.

Prices range from moderate to expensive but special rates, such as discounts for senior citizens in off-peak periods, can be obtained. There are now 86 paradors strategically sited throughout Spain. Traveling from parador to parador is an ideal way of simultaneously cruising through the Spanish countryside and the nation's history. The parador chain put out a very useful map, called *Paradores de España*, which has photographs and short pen-portraits, including addresses, telephone and fax numbers on one side, and a map of Spain, showing exactly where each parador is located, on the other. This map can be obtained from all Spanish tourist offices, many travel agents, or directly from the paradors' head office, **Central de Reservas de Paradores** ( 435-9700, Calle Velázquez, Nº 25, Madrid.

---

OPPOSITE: Palace Hotel, one of Madrid's refurbished *belle époque* hotels. ABOVE: Hotel de San Marcos, a monastery turned parador in León.

# Grace and the Grape: Pilgrimage Through La Rioja

*IF YOU ENJOY WINE AND HISTORY, YOU CAN CONVENIENTLY COMBINE THE TWO IN THE **RIOJA** DISTRICT OF NORTH-CENTRAL SPAIN.* In one of the happier marriages of geography and history, the **pilgrims' route to Santiago de Compostela** passes through Spain's most renowned wine producing region. The best way to follow **El Camino de Santiago** through Rioja is to take the N-111 from Pamplona to Logroño, Rioja's capital and commercial center, and then travel west on the N-120 towards Burgos. This will provide equal opportunity to see the monasteries, churches, hospices and shrines along the pilgrim's path and, with the occasional side-trip, taste Rioja's delightful wines in the bodegas where they are made.

Places to look out for include: the ancient monastery of **Santa María la Real** in Nájera, resting place of the kings, queens and nobility of Navarre and Castile; **San Millán de la Cogolla** with its twin Benedictine monasteries, **Suso** and **Yuso**; **Haro**, an ancient and unspoilt town

that is the epicenter of the wine trade in Rioja Alta (Upper Rioja) with its famous bodegas such as Paternina, Muga and CUNE; and **Santo Domingo de la Calzada** which was developed in the 11th century as a resting place for weary pilgrims with an inn and a hospital.

**Haro** is a good place to spend the night, if wine is your main interest. There are a dozen different bodegas in and around the town and even the *vino de mesa* (table wine), from the Haro cooperative, is a pleasure to drink. You can stay at **Los Agustinos (** 31-13-08 FAX 30-31-48, at Calle San Agustin, Nº 2, a pleasant, comfortable and moderately-priced hotel in a converted medieval convent; or the inexpensive, family-run pension of **Aragón (** 31-00-04, at Calle La Vega, Nº 9. But if the pilgrim's way captures your imagination, stay in the parador in **Santo Domingo de la Calzada**, a town that, like Santiago de Compostela itself, grew up around the pilgrimage. The parador is on the site of the old pilgrim's hospital and the town is full of reminders of its medieval glory, including a Romanesque-Gothic cathedral, a Cistercian monastery, a convent and old city walls.

# Flamenco: Spain's "Deep Song"

*IF YOU SURF THE AIR WAVES IN SPAIN, YOU WILL HEAR MANY KINDS OF MUSIC — POP, ROCK, REGGAE, RAP AND CLASSICAL AMONG OTHERS.* But flamenco, Spain's special contribution to the world of music, is rare. However, you only need to catch it for a few seconds to feel its power, its depth (true flamenco is called *cante jondo*, "deep song"), its emotion, and its strangeness. Despite flamenco's absence from daily life, it is still Spain's unmistakable musical signature, whether it is heard in a tourist nightclub, at a concert or, occasionally, on the radio or television.

The word, flamenco, which first became identified with the music and the dance in the mid-18th century, poses a mystery. Some people believe it comes from the Spanish word meaning "Flemish" which was used derogatorily of Charles V's rapacious Flemish courtiers whom he brought with him when he ascended the Spanish throne in the early 16th century. Others think it derives from the Arabic for a "fleeing peasant" *(felah mengu)* and referred to the gypsies who, then as now, lived on the edge of society.

Flamenco's origins are as obscure as its name. What is certain is that it is the music of Andalusia where it developed from a mingling of Moorish, gypsy (the gypsies came from India), and Jewish influences. In the 18th century, flamenco became closely identified with the Andalusian gypsies and waxed and waned as a popular art form during the 19th and 20th centuries. But it traveled

well, both to other parts of Spain and through its influence on different musical forms, ranging from classical (Georges Bizet and Joaquín Rodrigo), to jazz (Miles Davis and Gil Evans), and to pop (The Gipsy Kings).

The heart of the music is a passionate, at times almost agonizing, attempt to express the misfortunes of love and life in the ever-present shadow of death. When this happens as perfectly as it can, when the performers lose all sense of self, this is what is known as *duende*, flamenco's moment of truth.

The fiery, swirling, stamping dance associated with flamenco is as much part of the music as the guitar, the voice and the percussive hand-clapping. Flamenco also embraces a collection of styles, songs and rhythms that include the *saeta*, sacred songs that originated with Spain's Jewish community and are sung during Easter's Holy Week in Andalusia, and popular dances like the *fandango* and the *sevillana*.

Spontaneous flamenco performances in a gypsy cave, or an atmospheric bar, are history, but you can still hear and see the real thing on stage in nightclubs in Spain's major cities as recommended in followings. **Madrid**: Café de Chinitas ℂ 548-5135, Calle Torija, N° 7; **Barcelona**: El Cordobés ℂ 317-6653, La Rambla, N° 35; El Patio Andaluz ℂ 209-3378, Aribau,

OPPOSITE: The Monastery of Yuso, La Rioja.
ABOVE TOP: The Rocío Pilgrimage — young girls dance *sevillanas*. ABOVE: Granada *feria*.
RIGHT: Impromptu flamenco in Gijón.

Nº 242; **Seville**: Tablao de Curro Velex ( 21-64-92, Calle Rodo, Nº 7; or Los Gallos ( 21-69-81, Plaza de Santa Cruz, Nº 11; **Granada**: El Curro ( 28-35-37, Lavadero de las Tablas. Check the weekly entertainment guides published in these or other large centers. Flamenco festivals take place during the summer in Andalusia, and Córdoba holds a national flamenco festival every three years: the next one is in 1998. If you want to buy a cassette or a CD of good, genuine, contemporary flamenco, pick up one of the many recordings by **Camarón de la Isla** (singer) and **Paco de Lucía** (guitarist).

## *Tapas* Tasting

TAPAS, *THOSE LITTLE DISHES OF ASSORTED FOOD THAT SIT ON THE TOP OF BARS THROUGHOUT SPAIN, ARE PART OF THE SPANISH WAY OF LIFE.* The origin of the word *tapas*, meaning a cover, dates from the time when innkeepers would place a slice of ham, pie, or omelet on top of the traveler's drink when it was served. They double as tasty snacks to accompany your dry sherry (*fino*), glass of wine (*vaso de vino tinto, rosado* or *blanco*), or draught beer (*un caña*) beer, or serve as a convenient and unusual meal.

For many Spaniards, the local bar is an institution where business is done, friends are met, and the barman becomes a confidant-confessor. And *tapas* are an integral part of that institution. There is in an infinite variety of dishes but some of the more common offerings include: *albondigas* (meat balls in a rich sauce); *boquerones* (fresh anchovies); *croquetas* (meat, fish, potatoes, dipped in bread crumbs and fried); *calamares* (squid); *riñones* (kidneys); *tortilla española* (Spanish omelet: — eggs and potatoes — no onions or pimento in the authentic version); *higado* (small pieces of liver cooked in sherry); *jamón serrano* (cured ham); and *empanadillas* (small pies filled with meat, fish or vegetables).

You can order by the dish (*una ración*) or, if you would like to sample a selection, ask for *un plato combinado*. Bar hopping for *Tapas* is a pleasant, and relatively economical way of spending an evening in somewhere like Madrid, Barcelona, Seville or, indeed, in any large city. Just cruise from bar to bar, sampling the *tapas* and the atmosphere. There is nothing forced, phoney or exorbitant about these places and you will find yourself in good company, Spanish company. Finally, if you become seriously interested in *tapas*, a book on the subject exists — Penelope Casas' *Tapas: The Little Dishes of Spain*.

## Bullfighting

*IS IT A "SPORT," AN "ART," OR A "SLAUGHTER?"* To each, Evelyn Waugh's journalist hero's answer to his boss could apply: "Up to a point, Lord Copper." Casual fans and most foreign visitors regard a bullfight as they might any other form of outdoor entertainment, albeit one with a peculiarly Spanish character. (Bullfights are also popular in southern France, Portugal and in many Latin American countries.) To the aficionado and Spanish newspaper editors, there is no doubt about it. It is the "art of tauromachy" and reporting and commentary is naturally handled in the newspapers' arts and culture sections. For the anti-blood sports fraternity, including Spain's own active league, bullfighting is a blood-thirsty, anachronistic outrage that should be banned forthwith.

Leaving aside the debate for a moment, most visitors to Spain will probably want to see at least one bullfight out of curiosity. That's a good instinct because, apart from anything else, the *corrida* is a quintessential Spanish spectacle. The ring itself with its circle of sand, its wooden barriers, high terraces, lively crowd and moving line of sun and shade is worth seeing. There is also the pageant of the band striking up with the traditional *pasodoble*, the entry of the three teams of toreros in their "suits of lights," and the officials on horseback dressed in doublets, capes, buckled shoes and broad-brimmed hats.

The ritual of the fight rarely changes. The band stops playing, a trumpet sounds

and the bull enters the ring. The animal invariably appears huge, menacing, invincible. Bulls more often weigh in excess of 500 kg (1,100 lb), but they move fast and, if they are good, with the sure-footedness of a dancer. The bull will race around the ring, head held high, and sometimes crash its heavy, angled horns against the barrier in a vain attempt to reach the human prey on the other side.

The fight proceeds in three phases or *tercios*. Members of the *cuadrilla* (team), led by the matador, play the bull with their flowing pink and gold capes to size him up. Then the picadors enter, two large men on horseback wearing low-crowned hats, sequined suits and carrying lances. Their job is to stab the bull in the thick pad of muscle on its neck to weaken it. The bull will charge one of the horsemen, jab its horns into the pads wrapped around the horse's belly and flanks and try to toss both horse and rider.

Until the 1920s horses were not padded and they were often horribly injured and not infrequently killed by the bulls. Today, they are well-padded and blindfolded but

they smell the bull and the fear remains. The picadors, who usually make sure the bull bleeds profusely, are never popular figures with the crowd and are booed noisily if they spend too much time in the ring.

The second act can be one of the most exciting and elegant in the entire bullfight. Banderilleros, assistants to the matador, or sometimes the matador himself, approach the bull at an angle and, running fast, plant banderillas, or wooden-shafted darts with streamers attached, into the back of the bull's neck. This requires great fleetness of foot, split-second timing and daring. The bull is supposed to be on the move which makes the feat more difficult and spectacular. The purpose is to reveal the spirit of the animal and goad it into action.

The third and last act is when the matador faces the bull alone, the *faena*. This is where artistry comes into play. By now the bull's head should be lower than it was but he should have a lot of fight left

ABOVE: The third and last act of the bullfight when the matador faces the bull alone.

in him. The matador begins by putting the animal through a series of moves with the muleta, a short crimson cape draped over a sword. There are a variety of recognized passes, but in recent years many matadors have introduced gimmicks to please the crowd, such as kneeling in front of the bull and tapping it on the nose with the sword. El Cordobés, who carried daring to almost suicidal lengths, was one of the early practitioners. But he was not judged to be a great bullfighter by the experts who frown on such innovations.

The finale is the *suerte suprema*, the moment of truth, the kill. It is not easy, no matter how weak the bull has become. The target area is a five centimeter (three inch) wide space between the bull's shoulder blades. The matador has to keep the bull's head down and still by manipulating the cape, and then launch himself over the horns and thrust the sword home in exactly the right spot. If he misses the sword will buckle and bounce off the bull's bony back. Unfortunately, most matadors miss, often several times. If that happens the matador will use a heavier sword with a cross-piece and jab into in the bull's brain, a more effective way of dispatching him but missing all the artistry and drama of the approved way. However, when a matador does kill his bull with the first blow between the shoulders, and the animal drops like a stone, it is a memorable sight.

The origins of bullfighting go back to the Greeks and Romans, perhaps even further. It has been an important feature of Spanish life since the Middle Ages though fighting from horseback was more popular than on foot for many centuries. El Cid is believed to have fought bulls to celebrate some of his victories and no coronation of a monarch was complete without bullfighting forming part of the festivities. Breeding bulls, a critical aspect of the business, was traditionally a pursuit of the aristocracy and was socially on a par with horse-breeding and hunting.

In the 18th century, under the Bourbons, bullfighting became a popular spectacle. The process of codifying and regulating it began in Andalusia and posters,

advertising forthcoming *corridas*, started to appear. The most famous bullfighter in this period was Pedro Romero, from Ronda, who killed almost 6,000 bulls in his 28 year career without injury.

Bullfighting's greatest era is generally considered to have been in the early part of the 20th century when José Gomez ("Josélito") of Seville and Juan Belmonte were fighting, and in the 1940s and 1950s, when "Manolete" from Córdoba, Antonio Bienvenida, Luis Dominguin and Antonio Ordoñez (Hemingway's favorite) were the stars. "Josélito" and "Manolete" were both killed in the ring, adding to their personal aura and enhancing the drama of the epoch.

Soccer has overtaken bullfighting as Spain's most popular sport, but the *corrida* retains its grip on Spaniards with 40 million spectators — the size of the Spanish population — passing through the turnstiles every year. Breeding bulls in Andalusia and Extremadura is big business and vital for the sport because it is the quality of the bull — its size, speed and bravery — that ultimately determines the quality of the fight. There have been a number of scandals over fixed fights, holding promising young fighters back, and shaving the tips of the bulls' horns, that have afflicted the sport in recent years. However, earlier predictions of bullfighting's demise proved wrong, and the betting is that the *corrida* will be one of the traditions of old Spain that will retain its vitality as the country enters a new era.

## The Running of the Bulls

SPAIN'S NATIONAL SPORT IS NOT TO EVERYONE'S TASTE but by taking in **Pamplona's San Firmín** festival in July (6th to 14th) you present yourself with an interesting choice. If you discover you like bullfights, you can see a good *corrida* every day throughout the festival. If you don't, you can still get an impression of what it is all about, albeit a fleeting one, as the bulls and the runners pound through the narrow

Running of the bulls, Pamplona.

streets. That done, you can put tauromachy behind you and enjoy an authentic Spanish festival in a beautiful city.

The thing that struck me when I was there during the "Sanfirmines", as the locals call it, was the zest and pleasure of the people of Pamplona in their own fiesta. The shadow of Papa Hemingway may lie across the festival for many foreigners who got to know it from reading *The Sun Also Rises*. But there is nothing foreign, touristic or forced about the celebrations that animate the capital of the ancient kingdom of Navarre during the second week of July.

The origin of the festival goes back to the time when Firmín, the first bishop of Pamplona was, according to legend, martyred by being dragged around the town by a bull. Pamplonans seem to love their bishop and bulls in equal measure. Each morning, mass is said for the bishop's immortal soul and then the streets are cordoned off, a rocket explodes and six bulls, weighing about a half a ton apiece, lumber at an astonishing speed through the narrow, cobbled streets scattering the young, the brave and the not-so-young and the not-so-brave (this writer, for one) as they head towards their destiny in the bullring.

But the morning runs and the afternoon fights are only part of the festival. All day long, and for much of the night, there are processions of giant figures depicting historic characters — Catholic kings and queens, Moorish grandees, nobles and knights — marching bands, folk dancing, sporting events, competitions and street parties. Restaurants, bars, cafés and nightclubs seem to forget the concept of "closing time', and a prodigious amount of food and drink is consumed. Pamplona in July is Spain's answer to Rio in February and Munich in October. Try and get there.

# *Al Andalus* — Spain's Orient Express

*IF YOU FEEL LIKE A SPLURGE AND DECIDE THAT A CRUISE ON LAND IS PREFERABLE TO ONE*

*AT SEA, TAKE A RIDE THROUGH ANDALUSIA ON* AL ANDALUS EXPRESS, *SPAIN'S LUXURY TRAIN.* You can join the train by either flying directly to Seville, where it is based, and spending the first night in the Hotel Tryp Colon, or going to Madrid, spending a night in the Ritz Hotel, and then traveling down to Seville on the high-speed AVE train, and returning the same way.

The trip lasts for seven days and six nights and the train takes you to the three great Andalusian cities (Seville, Córdoba and Granada) with side trips (by bus) to Ronda, Marbella and Jerez. Lunches, dinners and a flamenco show are "on shore". You are taken to the main sights: the Mezquita and Jewish Quarter of Córdoba, the Alhambra in Granada, Ronda's Palace of the Marqués de Salvatierra and the oldest bullring in Spain; the Royal Spanish Riding School's equestrian display and sherry bodegas in Jerez; and Seville's royal alcázar, cathedral and Santa Cruz Quarter. Sleeping, breakfasting, pre- and-post-prandial drinking, and dancing (if you fancy it) take place on board.

The train's carriages are 1920s vintage, painstakingly refurbished with mahogany inlaid paneling, art-deco crystal, plenty of brass and velvet-brocaded lounge chairs. There is a bar carriage with live piano music, a lounge car for card games and reading, two *belle époque* restaurant carriages, five comfortable sleepers and two carriages with 20 private shower cabins. The train is fully airconditioned and has television and telephone services on board.

*Al Andalus* operates from early April until the end of October with three trips a month. As you will expect, it is not cheap. Prices range from $2,000 (standard cabin) to $3,000 (suite cabin) for one person, and from $3,750 (standard cabin) to $4,500 (suite cabin) for a couple. For further information in the United States, contact: Marketing Ahead ℂ (1-212) 686-9213, 433 Fifth Avenue, New York, NY 10016. In the United Kingdom, contact: Keytel International ℂ (44-171) 402-8182, 402 Edgeware Road, London W2 1ED, or any Spanish National Tourist Office.

# Triangle of Art (Madrid)

*IN THE WORLD OF ART, MADRID USED TO BE SHORTHAND FOR THE PRADO MUSEUM.* But now two other art museums have been opened that bring a new dimension to picture-viewing in the Spanish capital. These are Baron Thyssen's huge personal collection at the **Palacio Villahermosa** and the exciting collection of modern and contemporary art at the **Reína Sofia**. The great thing about all this is that the three museums are within walking distance of each other in the centre of Madrid. Spaniards are fond of their *paseos*, which means both strolling for pleasure and the place where it is done, so they call

the new configuration, which is roughly triangular in shape, the *Paseo del Arte*.

The **Prado**, notable for its extensive collection of Spanish masters, especially Velázquez, El Greco and Goya, needs no introduction. The second great museum gallery is the **Museo Centro de Arte Reína Sofia** (between the Paseo de Prado and Calle Santa Isabel) which is devoted to modern and contemporary art. The special attractions are works by Picasso, Miró and Dali, with Picasso's famous Civil War painting, "Guernica", stealing the show. After many travels, including one across the road from the Prado's annex, Guernica has finally come to rest and, as a bonus, its bullet-proof screen was removed recently.

The third point of the art triangle is the **Museo Thyssen Bornemisza** (between the Paseo del Prado and Calle San Jerónimo, across the road from the Palace Hotel). Up against stiff international competition, Spain won the right to provide a home for the Baron's astonishing collection of over 700 paintings which are appropriately housed in a former palace. The paintings tell the story of European and North American art. Starting in 13th century the exhibition takes you, in an orderly, well-lit, spacious way from floor to floor until you reach the abstract impressionists and pop artists of the 1950s and 1960s. A wonderful way of rounding off your Madrid galleries tour. You can buy one ticket (Pts.1,050 or about $8.00) that is valid for all three museums.

# Alhambra

*THE LAST MOORISH KINGDOM, IN GRANADA, WAS CONQUERED OVER FIVE HUNDRED YEARS AGO.* Yet the Moorish imprint on Spain — in language, architecture, music, even food — remains. If your time is short and you decide that you cannot "do" all the major Moorish sights, go to the Alhambra in Granada, bearing in mind the words of the poet who wrote: "there is nothing crueler in life than to be blind in Granada."

The best way to approach Granada is from the coast (see YOUR CHOICE, THE OPEN ROAD) and feast on the overall setting from a place called **El Suspiro del Moro** (the Sigh of the Moor) where King Boabdil, the defeated Moorish ruler, is said to have turned to look back on Granada for the last time. What he saw is not that different from what you will see: the red-gold towers, battlements and rooftops of the Alhambra, punctuated by the green of cypress and palm, stand before you, framed by a lush valley below and the snowy canopy on the Sierra Nevada above.

Stay, if you can, in the parador next to the Alhambra. On the site of a palace of the Moorish kings, the **Parador San Francisco** was converted into a Franciscan convent

ABOVE: The Prado Museum, Madrid. OVERLEAF: Moorish Spain: the restored castle of Almodóvar del Rio with the Guadalquivir river below.

by the Catholic monarchs at the end of the 15th century. From there begin your visit and, if possible, allow two days which will also give you time to investigate the rest of the city and take a look at the surrounding countryside. (Your Alhambra entry ticket is valid for two days.)

It is worth buying an illustrated guide-book of the Alhambra, partly to help you around, partly as a lasting souvenir. Also, if you fancy something a little more light-hearted and fanciful, pick up a copy of Washington Irving's *Tales of the Alhambra*, which he wrote after he visited Granada in the earlier part of the 19th century. You will find both readily available in souvenir stores and bookshops close to the Alhambra.

# Monastery-Palace-Mausoleum: El Escorial

*SPAIN IS FULL OF MONASTERIES, PALACES AND MAUSOLEUMS BUT WHERE CAN YOU SEE THEM ALL ROLLED INTO ONE UNIQUE, GIGANTIC*

*EDIFICE?* The answer is in the foothills of the Guadarrama mountains, less than an hour's drive from Madrid. **The Monastery of San Lorenzo of El Escorial**, to give it its full name, was built by King Philip II in the latter part of the 16th century as an all-purpose center for his empire, as a religious retreat and, ultimately, as a sepulcher for himself and his heirs.

Dominating a gently undulating plain, with the snow-capped Guadarrama as a backdrop, El Escorial is a magnificent sight and a poignant reminder of the might, the grandeur and the religious intensity of Spain at the zenith of its power. What you see inside matches the physical impact of the place: the sumptuous rooms in the palace quarters (don't miss the tapestries with their vivid depiction of everyday life), brightened up by the comfort-conscious Bourbons in the 18th century; the king's library with its painted ceilings and 40,000 books and illustrated manuscripts; the museum with paintings by El Greco, Velázquez, Zubarán, Titian and Hieronymus Bosch; and the royal mausoleum with its

marble sarcophagi containing the remains of four centuries of Spanish royalty.

## Seville's Rites of Spring

*THE WORD "FIESTA" — LIKE ITS COUSIN, "SIESTA" — IS SPANISH AND BOTH REMAIN PART OF EVERYDAY LIFE.* Fiestas, large and small, go on all over the country, all-year round. But since choices have to be made, I would recommend a spring visit to Seville, a city where that season, in all its glory, is peaked with two memorable festivals, **Semana Santa** (Holy Week) and the **Feria** (April Fair).

Semana Santa has a special rhythm to it, beginning on Palm Sunday in a somber mood with the re-enactment of Christ's passion and crucifixion, and ending joyously a week later on Easter Sunday. During the week, penitents parade through the streets and fill the churches in white robes with pointed hoods. There are moments of great emotion and religious fervor as swaying floats of Christ and the Virgin, illuminated by candles, converge on the cathedral for the climax of the festival. On Easter Sunday, the streets explode with music and swirling dancers, performing the **Sevillana**, a graceful, pirouetting dance that is related to flamenco.

The **Feria**, or April Fair, is held across the Guadalquivir river in the fair-grounds of **Los Remedios**. It begins ten days after Easter Sunday and lasts for five busy days and five hyper-active nights. The Feria is where Andalusians dress up and show off — on horseback, singing, dancing, or just strolling around the fair-ground or through the streets having a good time. Seville's beautiful old bullring, **La Maestranza**, attracts the star matadors who show what they can do in front of crowds that are as stylish as they are knowledgeable. James Michener, a great Hispanophile who wrote one of his monumental travel books about the country, had this to say: "At any time of the year, Sevilla is a distinguished city. But during Holy Week and the days that follow, it is without peer."

OPPOSITE: Interior and BOTTOM Exterior of El Escorial, King Philip II's magnificent monastery and palace. OVERLEAF: Parque de Maria Luisa, Seville.

*YOUR CHOICE*

This diversity is a bonus any visitor interested in nature in all its shapes and forms. Although competition between the forces of change and those of conservation continues as the country develops its economic infrastructure, Spain has a pretty good record of preserving its natural inheritance. There are five **national parks** — three mountainous areas in the north and two wetland parks in the south. The most interesting are **Covadonga**, the country's first national park, in the Cantabrian mountains of northwest Spain, and the **Coto Doñana** around the Guadalquivir estuary in Andalusia. Bears, wolves, wild boars, otters and chamois roam the Covadonga park safe from hunters and trophy collectors. The Coto Doñana is the largest nature reserve in the country and is home to deer, mongoose, lynx, badger and a huge range of migratory birds that includes, if you a lucky, occasional appearances of the rare imperial eagle, Spain's national emblem.

In addition to the fully-protected national parks there are around 60 reserves where controlled activities, including hunting, are allowed. Further information can be obtained from the government organization responsible for conservation, **ICONA** (Instituto Nacional para la Conservación de la Naturaleza) ( 266-8200, Gran Vía, Nº 35, 28005 Madrid.

One of the great growth activities — amongst Spaniards and foreigners alike —

## The Great Outdoors

It is hard to ignore the open countryside in Spain — there is so much of it. Whether flying, driving or traveling by train, you are constantly reminded that, despite its sophistication, Spain possesses some of the largest, wildest and least spoilt land in Europe. It has everything a nature-lover could want: towering snow-covered mountain ranges, green hills and valleys, tranquil and gushing rivers, wetlands and wildlife, golden beaches, rocky, secretive coves, expansive bays. Spain is a collection of landscapes that can easily be mistaken for Ireland (Galicia), Wales and Scotland (Asturias), Arizona (Almería), and France (Catalonia) for, in truth, the country embraces them all within one national boundary.

OPPOSITE: The Retiro Park, Madrid. ABOVE: Sierra de Grazalema, Andalusia. OVERLEAF: La Calobra and the Torrent de Pareis, Majorca, Balearic Islands.

is hiking. The most popular **trails** are found in the north among the snowy **Picos de Europa** with their almost Alpine atmosphere, and the **Pyrénées**; the **Sierra de Gredos** and **Valle del Jerte** in the center; **Cazorla**, **Sierra de Aracena** and the **Alpujarras** in Andalusia, and parts of the **Balearic Islands**. Don't be put off by a place's popular image. In many people's minds, Mallorca is virtually synonymous with the sun, sea and sin kind of tourism, yet the unspoilt mountainous northwestern side of the island is criss-crossed with trails affording spectacular views of the coastline and the interior of the island. The best way is to contact a travel group specializing in hiking before you travel. There are many in Europe and North America. Two good ones in Britain are: Ramblers Holidays ( (44-1707) 33-11-33, Box 43, Welwyn Garden City, AL8 6PQ; and Exodus ( (44-181) 675-5550, 9 Weir Road, London SW12 0LT.

Waterways are not the first natural feature that come to mind when you think of Spain but they exist and lend themselves to leisure activities. You can rent a boat and **cruise** on the **River Ebro** in Tarragona province; float around the **Albufera** wetlands, just south of Valencia, which doubles as a bird sanctuary and the birthplace of Spain's national dish, the *paella*; and **canoeing** in dams and small rivers across the country.

**Bird watching** enthusiasts can head for **Albufera** if they are in the east; almost anywhere in **Extremadura**, where the black storks come from Africa and build their nests in the cork trees, if they are in western Spain; **Mallorca's bird sanctuary** (another wetland called S'Albufera), if they are in the Balearics; and if they are in the south head for the **Coto Doñana National Park** which is the most extensive area for concentrated birdlife, being the habitat of six world-protected species, including the imperial eagle, and the winter retreat of thousands of migratory aquatic birds.

OPPOSITE: Ski lift in the Sierra Nevada, Granada, the southernmost and sunniest ski resort in Europe.

# Sporting Spree

The sporting scene in Spain is as varied as its landscape, both for the active participant and the spectator. The development of sporting facilities has gone hand-in-hand with the growing fame of Spanish athletes, whether it is the phenomenon of Miguel Indurain, the champion cyclist who won the *Tour de France* five times; Severiano ("Seve") Ballesteros, the golf master; or Arantxa Sanchez, the international tennis star. The impeccable staging of the Olympic Games in Barcelona in 1992 put the seal on Spain's status as a mature sporting country and, if a cap was needed, it came with the successful holding of the World Alpine Ski Championship in the Sierra Nevada in 1996 where, despite Alberto Tomba's initial doubts (he upset the Spaniards by comparing their southern ski resort to Africa), the snow fell by the ton, the organizers got their act together, and he finally won the elusive world championship gold medal.

### Skiing

"Sunny Spain" is not a country you usually associate with skiing and most travel agents do not bother to list it in connection with the sport. This is fine with two million Spanish skiers who are happy to keep their 27 ski stations in the **Pyrénées**, **Andorra**, **Cantabria**, central **Spain** (60 km from Madrid), and the **Sierra Nevada** to themselves. More foreigners are already in-the-know, especially as a result of the 1996 World Alpine Skiing Championships on the slopes of the Sierra Nevada. The Spanish ski resorts are still relatively uncrowded but you have to keep an eye on weather reports to make sure snow conditions are good, especially in the Sierra Nevada. The great bonus in that southern resort is that you can literally ski in the morning and then, just over two hours later, play golf, tennis or swim along the Costa del Sol. (The only other place you can do that in the Mediterranean is in the Lebanon.) You can even combine skiing and golf in a holiday

that provides instruction in both sports. This is organized by the **Sierra Nevada Club** ( (952) 47-48-58, Estación de Ski Sierra Nevada, 18196 Monachíl, Granada.

## Tennis

The growth of tennis courts, training camps and stadiums for competitions has also been remarkable in the last few years. Municipal tennis courts are available in most holiday resorts and in hotels designed for the tourist trade. Again, the **Costa del Sol** is the best-endowed but you will find tennis facilities all over Spain. There are many places where you can stay in comfort and study the game. A good one, founded by the late former Wimbledon champion, Lew Hoad, is the

Campo de Tenis de Lew Hoad ( (95) 247-4858 FAX (95) 247-4908, on Carretera Mijas, Km. 3.5, Apartado 111, Fuengirola, on the coast of the Costa del Sol.

Package tennis tours can also be arranged through specialist travel agents. Two in Britain are: Roger Taylor Tennis Holidays ( (44-181) 947-9272; and The Travel Club of Upminister ( (44-1708) 22-30-00.

## Hunting, Shooting and Fishing

Spaniards are passionate hunters and fisherman. Hunting is strictly controlled and licenses are required but the ethos of hunting is deeply embedded in the Spanish psyche and there is plenty of opportunity. Game includes wild boar, deer, chamois and red-legged partridge. Hunting holidays are quite popular and are arranged by specialist agencies. One such is **HuntinSpain** ( (923) 38-00-01, Pedro-Llen, La Veguillas, 37454 Salamanca. The **Federación Española de Caza** ( (91) 253-9017, Avenida Reína Victoria, Nº 72, Madrid, is the best source of general information. Similarly, the **Spanish Fishing and Casting Federation** ( (91) 232-8352, Calle Navas de Tolosa, Nº 3, Madrid, can supply details on fishing.

## Golf

This is *the* growth sport in Spain, fueled by prosperity, a new emphasis on "quality" tourism, abundant sunshine, sufficient water, and the increasing renown of Spanish golfers. The country has over 260 golf courses and more are being built all the time. The Costa del Sol, with its virtually guaranteed all-year round sunshine, is the premier golfing region. The smartest on the coast are the **Golf Rio Real** in Marbella and the **Club de Golf Valderrama**, further south in Sotogrande, designed by Robert Trent Jones; this is where the 1997 Ryder Cup (Ballesteros is captaining Europe's team) will be held. The Madrid and Barcelona areas are well-catered for and if you want to combine some golf with the cultural experience of visiting the El Escorial, you can tee-off within sight of the monastery at the La Herreria Golf Club. An excellent source of information on golf, in English, is the monthly magazine, *SunGolf*, which is published in Mijas on the Costa del Sol. Useful, too, is the national federation: **Real Federación Española de Golf** ( (91) 455-2682, Calle Capitán Haya, Nº 9, Madrid. Spain's national tourist offices, travel agents and specialist travel organizations can also provide detailed information. Golfing holidays which include green fees and pre-booked tee-off times are readily available. Three specialists in the United Kingdom are: Golf Holidays International ( (44-1480) 43-33-30; Longshot Golf

*El Prat golf course between Barcelona's international airport and the Mediterrranean.*

Holidays ( (44-1730) 26-86-21; and
Sovereign Golf ( (44-1293) 59-99-11.

**Watersports**
Virtually any kind of sporting activity
associated with water — fresh or saline —
can be pursued in Spain. Facilities for
**sailing**, **windsurfing**, **scuba diving** and
**canoeing** are available in most resorts
along the coast and in the Balearic Islands.
New marinas have been built for the
sailing crowd in many areas and boats
can be rented — or bought and sold —
in most yachting centers. For detailed
information on sailing contact: the
**Federación Española de Vela** ( (91)
233-5305, Calle Juan Vigon, N° 23, Madrid.

**Spectator Sport**
**Soccer** (*futbol*) is Spain's universal sporting
passion, outranking bullfighting and
everything else by a long way. Top league
and international games are heavily
televised but, to catch the true flavor, there
is no substitute to going to a game. Hotel
concierges and travel agents can arrange
tickets and give you details of how and
when to get to the stadium. **Bullfights**
are also televised — they are Spain's
summer equivalent of baseball or
cricket — and **basketball** is becoming
increasingly popular both in the flesh
and on television.

# The Open Road

Spain is a large country, the third most
extensive in western Europe after France
and reunited Germany. And because it is
such a varied country — from the lush,
green hills of Galicia in the northwest,
through the great open tableland of the
center, to the deserts of Almería and the
subtropical coastal plain of Murcia in the
south-east — it invites a close inspection
by road. Now, you can bike it, hike it, even
ride a horse over it, but most people will
be content to jump into their rental cars
and drive into the great open spaces.

However, you simply cannot do it
all at one fell swoop unless you are a
transcontinental rally driver. You have to
be selective and a helpful way to plan is
to think of regions or themes. But before
some suggestions, a word of warning.
Spanish roads have improved dramatically
in recent years and there now is a useful
network of highways (*autopistas* or
*autovías*), designated with an "A" or an
"E" in front of the number. Nevertheless,
in many cases you will have no alternative
but to take the old *carreteras nacionales*
(national roads), marked with an "N".
These roads usually have only two, or
sometimes three, lanes and tend to be
congested with heavy traffic, especially
long-distance trucks. Where you have
a choice, I would recommend using
the *autopistas* (many of the trucks
deliberately avoid them to save on the

tolls), or look for the smaller — and less frequented — roads in the "C" and "D" categories. Spaniards, on the whole, drive well, faster than they did in Franco's time, but not as fast as the Germans or the French.

There are many possible itineraries and there is no right or wrong way of doing things because wherever you travel in Spain you will come across varied scenery and interesting places. But I will suggest **two regional rides** and **a thematic one** that might be helpful and provide a good sampling of the Spanish experience.

A handy way of starting, assuming that you have "done" Madrid, is to take a leisurely tour of the cities and sights that

lie in a rough circle around the capital. Begin by driving to **Toledo** on the N-401, a dismal but mercifully short run of about an hour. It is best to spend the night in Toledo (the parador is the ideal spot with its commanding view over the city) and move on the following day to Ávila. The most scenic way to go is to take the N-402 in a northwesterly direction. This passes through the **Sierra de los Gredos**, a beautiful, unspoilt range of mountains with panoramic views over the *meseta*, where you can lunch in a village restaurant or picnic in the hills.

**Ávila**, Spain's most perfectly preserved medieval walled city, comes next. You

Sierra de Alhama.

then turn eastwards on the N-501, cut across the Madrid–Valladolid highway (A-6) on to the N-110 to **Segovia**, justly famous for its Roman aqueduct, its magnificent Alcázar, Gothic cathedral, and good eating, especially suckling pig and game. After Segovia, you swing south and drive up into the snowy **Sierra Guadarrama**. From there you can return to **Madrid** via **El Escorial**, the extraordinary

palace-monastery-mausoleum of Philip II, and the **Valley of the Fallen**, Franco's bizarre monument to the Civil War dead and to himself, thus completing the circuit of major attractions while breaking it up with plenty of country air and mountain scenery.

Another attractive regional circuit takes you through the jeweled cities of **Andalusia**. Leave Madrid on the new *autopista* (E-25) that links the capital with the south. If you fancy a more comfortable and quicker method of reaching Córdoba or Seville, jump on the high speed AVE train at the revamped Atocha station in Madrid and rent your car in either of those cities. (The train journey from Madrid to Seville is now only two hours.) Either way, begin with **Córdoba** which, being relatively small and manageable is a good way to get the feel of Moorish Spain. Head straight for the **Mezquita**, Córdoba's strange and wonderful mosque-church, then wander around the narrow cobbled streets of the old Jewish quarter (*Judería*). From Córdoba to **Seville**, you can either take the highway or, more interestingly,

follow the C-431 which runs along the north bank of the **Guadalquivir river** and passes through a number of picturesque white-washed Andalusian villages. **Peñaflor**, about halfway, is a good place to stop for lunch.

Seville deserves at least a couple of days then head south towards **Jerez** on the A-4. An elegant town, Jerez offers you the performing horses at the **Royal Andalusian School of Equestrian Art** and a dozen or so bodegas for sherry sampling. After that you should turn east on the N-342 and head towards **Granada**. The place to spend the night is in the mountain-top parador in **Arcos de la Frontera**, a marvelous little town that dominates the surrounding countryside and gives you a feeling of what the frontier between Christian and Moorish Spain must have been like.

**Ronda** is your next destination which you reach by continuing eastwards along the N-342 but turning south at **Algodonales** and driving along a twisting mountain road (C-339) to Ronda which, perched over its famous gorge, should not be missed. After Ronda go down to the **Costa del Sol** on the same road and, if you enjoy contrast, sample the sophistication and glitter of **Marbella** with a stroll around the

OPPOSITE TOP: Interior of Franco's tomb, Valle de los Caidos, near Madrid. BOTTOM: Arcos de la Frontera, Andalusia. ABOVE: The medieval walled city of Ávila. RIGHT: La Mezquita, Cordoba, Andalusia.

**Puerto Banus** marina, which caters to the seriously rich yachting crowd, and with a drink or a meal in the **Marbella Club**.

I would not advise lingering on the Costa del Sol which has been mortally wounded by mass tourism. It has the advantage, however, of positioning you for the **Alpujarra** mountains and **Granada** with a stop at **Málaga**, if you wish. You drive along the coastal road until **Motril** and then head inland to Granada. The Alpujarra mountains, made famous by the long residence of Gerald Brenan, the British writer and hispanophile, with their charming villages, are on the right; an optional diversion, but worth it if you have time. Finally, you reach the outskirts of Granada. Stop for a moment at a place romantically called *El Suspiro del Moro* (you can't miss it because there is a totally unromantic gas station that carries the name). From here, a breathtaking view of the city is laid out before you. Legend has it that this is the place where the vanquished king of Granada turned for the last time to look back at his beloved city, and wept. Give yourself plenty of time in Granada to absorb the Alhambra; that it is what you are meant to do — entrance tickets remain valid for two days.

If you are returning to Madrid by car you can finish your Andalusian journey by heading north on the N-323 through countryside, where the olive tree reigns supreme, to *Jaén*, which boasts a spectacular hilltop castle with a parador alongside it, to rejoin the Seville-Madrid highway. If you have taken the train to Córdoba, then drive back to that city along the N-432, drop your car off, and stretch your legs in the spacious AVE train as it whisks you back to Madrid at 200 kph (120 mph).

If you fancy a thematic tour that takes you to a totally different part of Spain, then follow the ancient pilgrims' way from the French border in the Pyrénées to Santiago de Compostela in Galicia. There were two traditional routes. The "Asturian" began at the western end of the Pyrénées and ran along the Asturian coast before turning south. The other, known as the "*Camino Francés*" (French Road), began at the **Roncesvalles Pass**, high up in the Pyrénées where the Frankish hero, Roland, fell in battle in 778.

Unless you are actually driving from France to Spain, the best place to begin is **Pamplona**, the capital of **Navarre**, and worth a visit in its own right whether or not the bulls are running. You can then drive up to Roncesvalles on the twisting C-135 — and hour's run — if you feel like it. From Pamplona you take the N-111 to **Logroño** on the River Ebro, a relatively rapid transition that takes you from the hills and valleys of Navarre to the vineyards of **Rioja**. The passage through Rioja and its opportunity for drinking Spain's most famous wine at source, have already been described (see TOP SPOTS). A good place to spend a night is the parador in **Santo Domingo de Calzada**, an authentic medieval stopping place for the pilgrims which now offers all the comforts of the late 20th century. This puts you close to **Burgos** (continuing on the N-120) which, with its magnificent Gothic cathedral, river frontage, and Castilian elegance, merits a morning or afternoon of sightseeing.

You should now head due west to **León**, Old Castile's other famous city, but

you may consider taking a detour to the south to the Benedictine monastery of **Santo Domingo de Silos**. Two reasons beckon. First, the monastery has the world's best preserved Romanesque cloister, a ravishingly beautiful architectural masterpiece on two levels. The second is the Gregorian chant for which the Silos monks have become famous. To everyone's surprise, including their own, one of their old recordings, Canto Gregoriano, became a chart-busting hit, selling over six million copies worldwide. The monks perform the chant eight times a day in the monastery church.

From Burgos, resume your pilgrimage on the N-120 across the vast, open expanse of the *meseta* through the small towns of **Osorno**, **Villada** and **Sahagúa** until you reach the Valladolid-León main road (N-601). Turn north and within half an hour you will be in **León**, a major pilgrim resting spot. And here you too should rest, preferably in the 12th-century **Monastery of San Marcos**, which was built expressly for the pilgrims and is now a parador. It is a truly marvelous place to spend a night and perfectly in tune with the nature of your journey. Before you leave León, visit its cathedral,

the finest Gothic religious structure in Spain.

The last lap to **Santiago** is at hand. Take the most direct route to **Lugo** (N-120, again, to **Astorga**, then the N-VI). You are now in green **Galicia** whose patchwork, stone-walled fields look more Irish than Spanish. Lugo, a beautiful old town, is slightly off the pilgrims' path but worth a detour, if only to see the well-preserved third-century Roman walls that still completely encircle the town, complete with defensive towers and gateways. The final stretch is best down on country roads. Leave Lugo on the C-630 to **Sobrado**, south to **Arzua** and then west along the C-547 to Santiago where, if your pocket will stand it, you should lodge in another authentic pilgrims' hospice, the magnificent **Hotel Reyes Católicos**, built by Ferdinand and Isabella at the end of the 15th century. It shares Santiago's central square with the cathedral and is the jewel in the paradors' crown.

OPPOSITE: Alhambra gardens, Granada.
ABOVE: Costa Del Sol, Marbella.

# Backpacking

When Laurie Lee stepped out one midsummer's morning and walked across Spain in the 1930s, he did it on a few pesetas a day, supplementing his meager budget by playing his fiddle on street corners. Well, Spain is no longer the backpacker's dream at bargain prices. But neither is it prohibitive. Inexpensive food, lodging and transportation are all widely available and are likely to remain so for the simple reason that the Spaniards themselves are traveling more than ever within their own country.

The key is to prepare yourself with specialist information before you arrive, plug yourself into the network of cheap hostels, pensions, restaurants and trains and buses (you will find many others doing the same thing), and keep your eyes and ears open to the bargains of the moment. First stop, inside Spain, should always be the local tourist offices which will provide you with vital information on accommodation, buses, trains, and on specialist clubs, associations, and companies that deal with different activities and methods of travel. Not only will you cover your basic travel needs but you will also find out about some interesting diversions that may be special to the area you are in, such as mountain biking, horse trekking, mountaineering, skiing, caving, canoeing, and such esoterica as hang-gliding, paragliding and bungee-jumping.

Don't be shy about asking for deals. Off-season, you will find them everywhere. There are also regular special student travel rates on long distance buses and trains and admission to museums. If you are a student, be sure to take appropriate identification. If you are traveling through rural Spain, off the beaten track, inquire about "agro-tourism", a relatively new development where farmers receive government help to open up their farms to visitors for food and lodging at extremely modest cost. It's a great way to plan a hike.

How much will the basics cost? Bed and breakfast in hostels (*hostales*, designated H), guest houses (*casas de huespedes* — CH), and pensions (*pensiones* — P) will cost between Pts.3,000 ($25) and Pts.5,000 ($40) a night, depending on the bathroom arrangements. You can have a sustaining, often surprisingly good lunch or dinner by choosing the fixed-price daily menu (*menu del día*) which is always three — and sometimes four — courses and includes bread and wine. Prices range between Pts.650 ($5.50) and Pts.1,200 ($10). Add on transportation costs, picnic lunches, snacks, and other incidentals and you can get by on between $40 and $50 a day, perhaps less if you are very frugal.

There are camp and caravan sites all over Spain. For detailed information, contact the **Federación Española de Empresarios de Camping** ( 242-3168, Gran Vía, N° 88, 28013 Madrid. For regular cycling and mountain-biking, the **Federación Española de Ciclismo** ( (91) 242-0434, Calle Ferraz, N° 16, 28008 Madrid, is the central organization. And if you are mountain climbing or trekking through mountainous areas, contact the **Federación Española de Montañismo** ( 445-1382, Calle Alberto Aguilera, N° 3, 28015 Madrid, for information on mountain refuges and other places to stay overnight.

# Living it up

If you have ever come across a group of Spaniards on an aircraft, train or bus, or in a restaurant or bar, you will know — without understanding a word of the language — that Spanish people like to eat, drink, laugh and be merry. Add to that the myriad bars, nightclubs and other places of entertainment that have grown up around the tourist industry in Spain and you have a country made for social pleasures. Spain is a late night place. A typical evening will begin with drinks and *tapas* in a bar around eight, dinner will not be thought of until ten, and clubbing rarely begins before midnight. Living it up is part of the culture. In Madrid, they call the action *"la movida"*; but most cities and all resorts have plenty of nightlife of a varied nature.

The usual sources of tourist information — government offices, travel agents, etc — tend to be feeble on identifying where "the action" is in an unfamiliar place. The best bet is to get hold of the standard weekly or monthly city entertainment guide which most hotels put in your room — ask reception for one if there isn't one — and then see what the concierge or information desk recommend. (A word of caution about hotel advice: a vested or family interest may reside in what is recommended.) But the weekly guides are good since, with censorship a thing of the past, they offer a wide range of entertainment that includes theater, movies, concerts of all kinds of music, flamenco performances, discotheques, ballroom dancing, "escort" and "massage" services for all tastes, restaurants, bars, and cafes.

Here is a brief taste of what is on offer in the major cities and resorts. In **Madrid**, a large choice of luxury hotels greets you. The Ritz is still pre-eminent in terms of location, style, elegance and service. But the Palace, from the same *belle époque* era and immaculately renovated, is an excellent alternative at a more affordable price. If you want to try one of Spain's top restaurants, dine at Zalacaín ( 561-4840, Calle Alvarez de Baena, N° 4, reservations are essential. Or, if you have a craving for anything that comes out of the sea, and at moderate prices, La Trainera ( 576-8035, at Calle Lagasca, is a good choice. Madrid's *movida* embraces everything from flamenco to ballroom dancing to sevillanas to jazz and to heavy metal but, while you are making up your mind, go and have an old-fashioned cocktail in a tall glass, expertly made, in Bar Chicote ( 462-3875, at Gran Vía, N° 12.

**Barcelona** rivals Madrid in its elegant hotels and the variety and quality of its restaurants. The Ritz, again, is a classic but if you prefer something ultra-modern, overlooking the sea and city but away from the traffic, try the lofty Hotel Arts in the Olympic port. And if dining with Barcelona's fashionable set appeals to you, reserve a table at Vía Véneto ( 300-7024, at Carrer Granduxer, N° 10-12, in the charming Sarrià district where excellent Catalan and French food is served. For fish go to Botafumeiro ( 218-4230, Gran de Gracia, N° 81, a Galician establishment, which has a busy and cheerful oyster bar. A good place to begin an evening out is in one of the city's *cava* (local champagne) bars such as La Cava del Palau, at Carrer Verdaguer i Callis, N° 10, in the Gothic Quarter.

In **Seville**, the grandest hotel is the Alfonso XIII which opened its doors in 1929 to the monarch whose name it carries. A smaller but elegant alternative is the conveniently sited Doña María Hotel, which is opposite the Giralda. Seville is not as distinguished gastronomically as Marid and Barcelona, but if you want to enjoy the ambiance of an ancient and beautiful Seville mansion and eat some really good pasta, San Marco is the ticket. For *tapas* bars and after dinner drinks head for the narrow streets, small squares and flower-bedecked balconies of the Santa Cruz district, the old Jewish quarter.

In the south, the Mediterranean may beckon and while most of the Costa del Sol should be avoided, **Marbella** is an exception, offering comfort, style and fun. Swanky places to stay are the Don Carlos or Los Monteros or, if you prefer a ranch-style hotel with a fine tropical garden, try the Marbella Club. For the ultimate in luxury in a country setting, stay among the arabesques, pools and gardens of the Byblos Andaluz near Mijas. This hotel has the added attraction of its own golf course. For eating, drinking and nightclubbing, head for nearby Puerto Banus, Spain's ritziest yachting marina.

When in northern Spain, don't miss **San Sebastián**, the classy seaside resort whose history is inextricably linked with royalty, the wealthy and the famous. Here you can combine a great hotel (the María Cristina) with gourmet eating (try Arzak, Spain's best restaurant, according to many of the experts), an animated nightlife (in

La Parte Vieja, the picturesque old quarter) with the bonus of marvellous beaches.

# Family Fun

Spaniards love children. A truism perhaps but noticeable wherever you go. Never hesitate to take your children into a hotel, restaurant or bar. They will not only be welcomed but, very likely, pampered. Spanish kids stay up late, like their parents, so your children will be in good company if your family is eating out late.

"*Vamos a la playa*" ("Let's go to the beach") is a popular children's summer song in Spain and the sea is clearly the best place to head for if you are traveling with your children. Apart from swimming, building sand castles and chasing each other over piles of moribund, oil-drenched roasting flesh, children now have many other diversions down at the beach. Most resorts have pedal boats, windsurf boards, and small sailboats for rent. There are also **coastal excursions** in cruise boats — some with glass bottoms-and quite often aquatic theme parks with exciting water slides and shoots.

Museums, art galleries and churches always pose a problem for the traveling family. While a certain amount of forced-fed cultural sightseeing is no doubt good for the children, you can sweeten the pill by looking for things that might interest them more. Madrid and Barcelona both have new and fascinating **aquariums** housing a huge number of species, ranging from an angel fish to rays and sharks, that swim in close-up in front — and in certain areas — over you. Madrid's aquarium is in a futuristic pyramid-shaped building in the **Casa de Campo Zoo** and Barcelona's is down in the old renovated port (**Port Vell**). Look out for performing dolphins and seals. Madrid zoo has regular dolphin shows and if you happen to be in Mallorca in the Balearic Islands, there is a place called **Marineland**, just outside Palma, that puts on daily dolphin, seal and parrot shows throughout the summer.

In your cultural sight-seeing, keep an eye open for artifacts commemorating Spain's battling and bloody history. Castles, moats, drawbridges and dungeons usually appeal to children. So does armor. When in **Madrid**, bear in mind the **Royal Armory** in the **Palacio Real** where there are enough mounted knights, lances, swords and crossbows to stage a small battle. There are even children — royal princes — clad in armor, not to mention one monarch's favorite dog similarly attired.

In Barcelona, try the **Museu Maritim** (Martime Museum), just across from Columbus's column near the port. Apart from artifacts showing a wide range of shipbuilding through the centuries, there is a virtual reality show that puts you on a galley during the Battle of Lepanto, tosses you through a Caribbean storm in a Spanish sailing ship, and plunges you down to forty meters under the sea in a submarine.

**Port Aventura**

France has Disneyland but Spain has Port Aventura. Opened in 1995, this $500 million theme park at Salou on the Costa Dorada 10 km (six miles) south of Tarragona, managed to pull in 2.7 million visitors during its first season. With none of the fanfare that greeted Disney — and far fewer of the problems — Spain's answer to Donald Duck and Mickey Mouse has been a huge success.

About the same size as Disneyland Paris, Port Aventura, whose principal shareholder and manager is the British Tussauds Group, is a mixture of "worlds" and "rides". There are five different "lands" all with a special theme: "Mediterranea", where you set off by boat, steam train or by foot for the other places; "China", with its recreation of the imperial palace, "Polynesia", a series of islands linked by bridges and covered with dense vegetation and an "active volcano"; "The Wild West", a recreated cow-punchers' town called "Penitence"; and "Mexico", featuring

OPPOSITE TOP: Port Vell (the old port), Barcelona. BOTTOM Barcelona's aquarium.

elements of Mayan and Colonial Mexico. Each area has restaurants, bars, shops and craft centers selling food, drinks and artifacts of the country. Shows that include dancers from the Polynesian islands, Chinese acrobats and a Western stunt show are presented in airconditioned theaters at regular intervals throughout the day.

The main attractions, however, are the rides. The most popular is also the most terrifying. This is the **Dragon Khan** roller coaster, Europe's largest and scariest, which takes its riders up to a height of 45 m (147 ft) and then, at speeds reaching 110 kph (66 mph) an hour hurls them up and down over a distance of one and a quarter kilometers, turning them completely upside down no less than eight times. There are also water rides where you get very wet, and gentler affairs for young children such as canoeing, mechanical ponies on a special track,

log-riding on a small river, carousels and bumper cars.

Port Aventura is open from the end of March to the end of October. Prices, that include all rides and shows, are Pts.3,900 ($32) for adults, Pts.3,000 ($25) for children aged five to twelve; the same for senior citizens and nothing for children under five years old. There is parking for 6,000 cars, 250 buses and a special area for motorbikes and disabled drivers. The theme park is just off the A-7 coastal highway which connects it with Barcelona and France to the north and Valencia to the south. The address is: Port Aventura ( 77-99-00, Autovia Salou/Vila-seca, Km. 2, PO Box 90, 43480 Vila-seca, Tarrogona.

## Cultural Kicks

In a country with as rich a history and cultural legacy as Spain, it is a little bewildering to know where to begin, how to select. The task, however, has been already been broached with previous recommendations in TOP SPOTS (**Granada's Alhambra**, **Madrid's** three art museums — the "**Triangle of Art**", and El Escorial)

ABOVE: Pablo Picasso's famous painting, Guernica, depicting the effects of the aerial bombardment on this Basque town by Franco's forces during the Civil War. OPPOSITE: Joan Miró's famous sculpture, "Woman and Bird", in the Joan Miró Park, Barcelona.

and, in this section, with the **Pilgrims' Way** to **Santiago de Compostela**.

What else? Let's first take museums. In **Barcelona**, the gallery devoted to the work of Joan Miró, at the **Fundació Joan Miró** on Montjuic hill, and the one devoted to Pablo Picasso at the **Museu Picasso** in the Gothic Quarter, should not be missed. And then, there is Salvador Dali, not everyone's cup of tea, but worth considering, especially if you happen to be on the Costa Brava or traveling to or from France. The **Dali museum** is in **Figueres**, his birthplace and half an hour's drive north of Girona on the A-7 highway. It is a truly wonderful evocation of the man and artist which displays his artistic skills, his bizarre imagination, and his towering ego. Children will probably enjoy this museum as much as adults; mine certainly did.

Spain's greatest monuments are its religious buildings, its military fortifications, and its remarkably well-preserved towns. Do not miss the **Gothic cathedrals** of **León**, **Burgos**, **Seville** and, if you happen to be in the **Balearics**, **Palma de Mallorca**. Well-preserved, functioning monasteries and convents abound but put **Santo Domingo de Silos** (near Burgos), **Santa María de Poblet** (north of Tarragona), and the Franciscan **Real Monasterio de Guadalupe** (Guadalupe, Extremadura) on your list.

Mention Spain, and castles immediately come to mind — a subliminal response triggered perhaps by school history books, or by crooked real estate dealers selling gullible and distant clients "a castle in Spain", which sometimes turned out to be nothing more than a shack. There is no shortage of the real thing and of castles' first cousin, the *alcázar*, or **fortress**, that dominates so many Spanish skylines, the most famous being in **Toledo** and **Segovia**.

As for the towns, **Mérida** in Extremadura remains a Roman marvel that should be visited; **Ávila** in Castile, with its unbroken perimeter of granite walls and towers, is the best impression you will ever see of a medieval fortified city in Europe; and **Lugo** in Galicia, is

another ancient walled city on a smaller scale. In both **Ávila** and **Lugo**, You can walk on top of the walls, a perfect way of seeing the towns inside and the landscapes they command outside.

# Shop Till You Drop

Spain's growing sophistication has expanded its shopping horizons. Well-known foreign stores (like Britain's Marks & Spencer and Sweden's Ikea) have opened branches in recent years and a new wave of Spanish entrepreneurship has resulted in a far greater choice. **Shopping malls** have also arrived and you will find them in all the major cities. **Madrid**, for example, has an extremely

elegant one called the **Serrano ABC**, in an old building in the Salamanca district (it has entrances on Calle Serrano and the Castellano), where all the main Spanish and international stores are located. Spain's largest **department store**, **El Corte Inglés**, has swallowed up its main rival, Galerias Preciados, and expanded its operations accordingly. It has also become more sophisticated; men, waiting for their wives, can go to a *tapas* bar in the men's clothing section if they become bored. **Zara**, a phenomenally successful Spanish **clothing** chain (for men and women), is reasonably priced with a fast turnover of the latest fashions. **Sybilla** purveys expensive and stylish **women's clothes**, and **Sebastién Bachiller** is a good place to buy **shoes**, **handbags** and **luggage**. The **Loewe** group, all over Spain, specializes in high quality **leather goods** in the luxury range.

If you are looking for indigenous Spanish **arts and crafts**, a good place to start is at the government-owned **Artespaña** shops which are located in the major centers. The one in Madrid is in the Salamanca district at Calle Hermosilla, Nº 14. They stock a broad selection of furniture, fabrics, pottery, ceramics, glass and rugs — all reflecting traditional Spanish designs and manufacture.

The best place for traditional artifacts, however, is on the spot where they are made. You will of course come across a great amount of tourist junk in your travels but the genuine articles do exist. Fine (and famous) glass and **crystal** can be bought at source in **La Granja**, near Segovia; good hunting, hiking and riding **boots** can be found in **Salamanca**, **Seville** and **Córdoba** (home of the famous flat, black Spanish hat); handmade **furniture fabric** in **Almería** and **Majorca**; jet jewelry and brightly-colored traditional **bedspreads and rugs** (*tenederias*) in Galicia; the best tiles from **Valencia**, which has a fascinating museum devoted to the craft; **cultured pearls** in **Majorca** and wineskins in **Navarre**.

Bargain hunting in Barcelona ABOVE at antique fair and LEFT for paintings; and leather goods OPPOSITE in Córdoba.

*YOUR CHOICE*

# Short Breaks

The idea here is to try to link two rather different Spanish experiences that can be sampled within a brief period of time — a day or two. Let's start at the center — **Madrid**. The notion of circling the historic towns and sights around the capital has been suggested in THE OPEN ROAD section. But similar ground can be covered in short breaks by simply selecting a place at a time. The two that should have priority are **El Escorial** and **Toledo**; the others — Ávila and **Segovia** — can be handled in a single trip.

Then **Seville**, the natural hub of Andalusia. An excellent excursion is to take the E-25 highway or the train to **Córdoba** (about an hour and a half travel time), pace the Córdoba sightseeing with a leisurely lunch, and return to Seville in the evening. Another pleasant trip is to go south on the A-4, or again by train (less than an hour), to **Jerez** and, if you have a car, drive the 25 kilometers north to **Sanlúcar de Barremeda**, a delightful place to have a fresh fish lunch in a beach restaurant, accompanied by the local *manzanilla*, a delicate sherry-style wine that can be drunk throughout the meal.

Moving to **Barcelona**, two forays from the city have appeal. The first is to the famous mountain-top monastery of **Montserrat** with its spectacular setting and Black Virgin, Catalonia's miracle-working national icon. The second is to go south along the coast to the elegant, slightly faded town of **Sitges**, the ideal spot for a day's outing when you are a bit faded yourself. Sitges is distinguished by a fine palm-fringed esplanade, civilized beaches, and rather grand turn-of-the-century houses. Both Montserrat and Sitges can be reached within an hour of Barcelona.

And now, as Monty Python has it, for something completely different. The **Balearic Islands** are not far from the

Relaxing at La Residencia Hotel, Deià, Mallorca.

Spanish mainland: half an hour by air from Barcelona, an hour from Madrid, or overnight by car ferry from Barcelona, Valencia and Alicante. The three islands — **Majorca**, **Minorca** and **Ibiza** — are all attractive and all different. The best plan is to base yourself in **Palma de Mallorca** and take short breaks to visit Minorca and Ibiza (each 20 minutes away by air, or you go by boat in a more leisurely fashion), and to explore Majorca itself. You won't regret it.

# Festive Flings

A number of Spanish words have passed into the universal language and "fiesta" is one of them. ("Siesta," which is what often happens between and after fiestas, is another.) General Franco, a Victorian in a time warp over social behavior, put a severe crimp on many of Spain's festivals. Since his demise there has been a renaissance in merry-making. Festivals never really stop in Spain. There are literally thousands of them and the calendar is full throughout the year. Most of them celebrate religious events and saints, although theses often have pagan antecedents; battles against the Moors and other invaders; wine and other harvests; and some take the form of lengthy pilgrimages.

A few of the most famous have already been mentioned: **Seville's Semana Santa** and **Feria (April Fair)**; **Pamplona's San Firmín** "the running of the bulls" bash which celebrates the city's bishop-saint who was killed by one of the animals; and the **pilgrimage to Santiago**, which ends in a celebratory mass at the saint's shrine in Santiago's cavernous cathedral. Other major fiestas include: the fiery **Fallas** in **Valencia**; **Madrid's San Isidro**; the wine harvest festival in **Jerez de la Frontera** in September; and the **Rocío Pilgrimage** in **Huelva**, near Seville.

Spanish festivals, large or small, famous or obscure, have two things in common. First, they are authentic Spanish entertainments, mounted neither for the tourist trade nor for commercial gain. Second, everyone is welcome; most of them take place in the streets with processions, bands and floats but they rapidly become participatory events for the general public.

Here is a sampling of fiestas which is not exhaustive but will give you a good idea of what is on offer. Spanish tourist offices will be able to give you a comprehensive list, with exact dates for the current year, as well as more background information.

**Winter**

If you happen to be in Spain over the **Christmas holidays** look out for three events. **Christmas Eve (La Noche Buena)** is a time for family reunions with midnight mass in the cathedral or local church and a large dinner afterwards. Spaniards celebrate **New Year's Eve (La Noche Vieja)** with gusto and pop a grape in their mouths on every stroke of the midnight chimes. The **Epiphany (January 6)** is the feast of the **Three Kings (Los Tres Magos)** which is celebrated on the night of **January 5**. This is a time when three people are decked up as the kings who brought gold, frankincense and myrrh to the manger in Bethlehem. The kings usually ride on horses or donkeys and have an impressive entourage. In some places, like the Balearic Islands, they arrive by boat. This is a great favorite with children who are given presents by the "kings" in a church or town hall.

In **January** come the festivals of **San Antonio (16th)** and **San Sebastián (20th)**, occasions for processions, bonfires, folk music and dancing.

In **February** there are mock battles between Moors and Christians — a common feature of many Spanish festivals — at **Bocairente**, near Valencia, and two married women of **Zamarramala**, close to Segovia, take over as "mayoresses" for the day to the accompaniment of folk dancing in 16th-century costumes. The next phase

OPPOSITE: Parade of the "giants" during the San Firmín festival in Pamplona.

gets under way just before Lent when it is carnival time in many towns and villages. Cádiz has the oldest and probably the best carnival in the country but many other towns have a last fling before the Lenten shutdown. One of the most curious carnivals occurs in **Villanueva de la Vera** (Cáceres Province) in Extremadura. A gigantic wooden figure in a dark suit and black hat is carried through the streets and then beaten, beheaded and buried as part of some ancient, almost certainly pagan, ritual. At the other end of the spectrum is urbane **Sitges,** the fashionable and heavily gay seaside resort south of Barcelona. Sitges celebrates its carnival with an antique car rally.

At the **end of February** and in **early March**, it is **carnival** time, again a favorite with children who dress up and get time off to celebrate in and out of school.

**Valencia**'s famous **Fallas** begin on **March 12** and reach their incandescent climax a week later on the night of **San José**. That is when the elaborate floats, which have been circulating through the streets all week, are burnt in a series of vast bonfires. Firework displays add to the din as night becomes day, bands strike up and virtually the entire population pours out into the streets.

### Spring

**Holy Week in Seville** opens the festive season and is replicated in many towns, on a lesser but still fervent scale, around the country. While the basic format of processions, penitents, Christs and Virgins swaying above the crowds, accompanied by chanting, hymn singing and the thud of drums, does not greatly vary, each town or province imparts its own flavor. **Málaga's Holy Week** is also impressive but, as a rule, the celebrations become more austere and religious as you move northwards, the most stark and realistic being in the towns of

OPPOSITE: Colorful parade past the chapel of the Virgin during the El Rocío pilgrimage.

Old Castile, notably Valladolid and Zamora.

What they all have in common is that many of the penitents — accountants, lawyers, clerks and bus-drivers in real life — submit themselves to flagellation and other mortifications of the flesh. For the onlooker this is probably the fastest way of understanding what life must have been like back in the Middle Ages.

After the agony, the joy. **Seville's Feria (April Fair)** is the grand catharsis. **Jerez's Horse Fair (Feria del Caballo)** in **early May** is a wonderful spectacle, especially if you like fine horses. There are many festivals around the country at this time as Spaniards celebrate the rites of spring that have little to do with Christianity. Madrid's **San Isidro Festival** reaches its zenith around the middle of May with some of the best bullfights on the calendar.

**Whitsun**, or **Pentecost**, brings the unique **Rocío Pilgrimage (Romería de Nuestra Señora del Rocío)**, "Our Lady of the Dew", the slow progress of pilgrims from all over Spain, and beyond, through the lovely countryside of the **Doñana Wildlife Reserve**, west of Seville in Huelva Province. The pilgrimage draws Spaniards from all walks of life and can take as long as two weeks depending on which method of transportation the pilgrim chooses. The slow, serious way to go is by horse or mule-drawn covered wagon with plenty of stops in shady copses to eat, drink, sing and dance and get to know your fellow pilgrims.

**Madrid** celebrates its patron saint, **San Isidro**, in the **second week of May**, also a good time, climatically, to visit the Spanish capital. Drama, music, sporting events and the best bullfights of the season take place during the **Feria de San Isidro**. The feast of **Corpus Christi**, which usually falls at the **end of May**, is next and is celebrated all over Spain with religious processions which move solemnly through streets over carpets of freshly-cut hay, straw or flowers, with the host carried in the center by a senior member

of the clergy and groups of robed monks, nuns and choirboys singing traditional hymns. Seville, again, adds the grace note. Young choirboys called *Seises*, dressed in 16th-century costume, sing and dance in front of the host on the high altar in the Cathedral.

### Summer

In **June**, come two important saints' days: **San Juan** on the **24th** and **San Pedro and San Pablo** on the **29th**. Many towns hold local fiestas to celebrate their adopted saint.

In **July**, **Pamplona**, in Navarre, celebrates its martyred bishop, **San Firmín**, with the running of the bulls during the **second week of the month**, and **Santiago de Compostela**, in Galicia, greets the tens of thousands who have made the long pilgrimage on the **25th, the day of St. James' (Santiago)**. **San Pedro Manrique** (Soria Province) has barefooted firewalkers while **Ciudadela** (Minorca) offers brilliantly accoutered horses that dance to music and resist the attempts of the youth of the town to unseat their riders; Catalonian towns in the Penedés wine area vie with each other building human towers.

**Autumn**

This is the time of the **wine festivals** *(vendimias)* in **Jerez (Andalusia), Valdepeñas (La Mancha), Penedés (Catalonia), Rioja (Old Castile)** and other wine-producing regions. **Zaragoza**, the capital of Aragon, celebrates its local Virgin with the **Fiestas de Virgen del Pilar** (Virgin of the Pillar) on **October 12**, a deeply religious event with the women in traditional dress and elaborate floral displays, followed by lively dancing of the *jota*, Aragón's best-known folk dance; this is also a national holiday.

## Spain's National Holidays

January 1: New Year
January 6: Three Kings (Epiphany)
March–April: Good Friday (variable); Easter Sunday (variable)
May 1: Labor Day
May–June: Corpus Christi (variable)
July 25: St. James
August 15: Assumption
October 12: Columbus Day
November 1: All Saints
December 6: Constitution Day

December 8: Immaculate Conception
December 25: Christmas Day

## Galloping Gourmets

There was a time when Spanish food and drink was associated in the foreign mind with *paella* and plonk, and not much else. No longer. The variety of Spanish cuisine, especially its regional diversity, and the renown of Spanish wines have spread far and wide. You may still eat badly in Spain — that happens everywhere, including France — but you will not be bored and, if you keep your eyes and mind open, you are in for a gastronomic treat.

Before starting a quick regional tour, a few general points. Spaniards love **fish**, in all its manifestations, and eat almost five times more per head than the British. Inland cities and towns do as well as coastal ones; fresh fish is hurried in every day from the ports

OPPOSITE: Andalusian girls dancing *sevillanas* during the May fiesta in Cordoba. ABOVE: Travelling to a sanctuary of the Virgin during an annual pilgrimage near Seville.

and sold in the markets, restaurants and hotels. Fish, particularly shellfish, is no longer cheap but it will be fresh and you will find a huge variety from the Mediterranean and the Atlantic to choose from.

Spain is good at the simple things: lovely fresh bread, baked daily; excellent fruit and vegetables; hot (real) chocolate with *churros* (thin strips of dough, deep-fried and dusted with powdered sugar), a warming breakfast on a cold day; and the best **coffee** (whether it is a *café con leche* — with milk, a *café cortado* — black with a dash of milk, or *café sólo*, just black) in the world. Simplicity also applies when you are eating out. Most restaurants serve excellent hors d'œuvres (*entremeses*), fresh salads, and tasty, sustaining sandwiches. *Tapas*, a Spanish gastronomic invention, can be taken as pre-prandial snacks, or serve as a complete meal. In restaurants, remember to check out the **fixed-price menu** (*menu del día*). (All restaurants, modest or grand, are required by law to provide one.) They consist of three or four courses, with wine and bread included, and are invariably excellent value, especially for travelers on a tight budget.

In **Andalusia**, don't miss *gazpacho*, that refreshing cold soup of tomato, cucumber, onion, garlic and olive oil, *pescado frito*, mixed fish lightly fried, and *ajoblanco*, another cold soup of crushed almonds and garlic served with muscatel grapes. Spain's best *jamón serrano* (Parma-style country cured ham), comes from *Jabugo* in Huelva province, and Andalusia offers a wide variety of pastries and confectionery, derived from its Moorish past.

The Spanish heartland — Old and New Castile — is the home of rich soups (*sopas*) and stews (*estafados*), of roast suckling pig (*cochonillo*), lamb (*cordero*) and other meat, of game and of meat and vegetable pies (*empanadas or empanadillas*). If you like pulses, this is the place: chickpeas (*garbanzos*), lentils (*lentejas*), white beans (*alubias*). They are usually cooked in a meat broth with slices of spicy sausage (*chorizo*). Castile is also the land of bread — Spanish bread rivals French bread for the title of best in the world.

Northwest Spain — **Asturias**, the **Basque country**, and **Galicia** — is noted for its fish, especially tuna (*bonito*), squid (*chipirones*), baby eels (*angulas*) and salt cod (*bacalao*). **Asturias** is well-known for a flavorful fish stew, called *caldereta*, and for an interesting way of cooking hake with apple cider (*merluza a la sidra*). Away from the coast, *fabada*, a tasty stew made from

white beans cooked slowly with pork and piquant sausage, is the Asturian equivalent of the French cassoulet.

**Galician** and **Basque** cuisine are generally thought to be the best in Spain. **Galicia** spells fish in all its myriad forms from oysters, scallops and mussels to sole, turbot and salmon. The region is also famous for its ham hocks and turnip greens (*lacón con grelos*), large savory pies (*empanadas*) and, in the dessert department, its pancakes (*filloas*) and ground almond tart (*tarta de Santiago*).

The **Basques** are also great cooks and are renowned for their imaginative skills with that plain Jane of the sea — cod, specifically salt cod (*bacalao*) — extremely tasty cooked in olive oil with sweet peppers and garlic. Try **bacalao a la vizcaina**, a cod casserole with sweet peppers, cured ham and egg yolk or, if you prefer a spicier version, *bacalao a la bilbaina*. Another tasty fish dish is **marmitako**, a stew of tuna, tomatoes and potatoes. A typical Basque dessert is *canutillos de crema*, puff pastry filled with custard dusted with icing sugar and cinnamon.

**Catalonia** is also gastronomically rich. A specialty is combining fruit with fowl and game, such as baby goose with pears (*oca con peras*), duck with apples and figs (*pato con manzanas e higos*) and hare with chestnuts (*liebre con castañas*). If you fancy a seafood mixed grill try *zarzuela de mariscos* and for something

heartier, *escudella de pagés* (a bean, rice and noodle stew with spicy sausage and vegetables).

Finally, to the **Levante** (**Valencia** and **Murcia**) where home-grown rice, fish, chicken, rabbit, peppers, olive oil and saffron all come together in the large open pan that has given its name to Spain's national dish — *paella*. There are many versions of *paella* (seafood, meat and game, eels, etc) and some interesting spin-offs. *Arroz marinera*, for example, is a delicious and filling fish soup with rice that can be a meal in itself. Paella should be cooked while you wait (between 20 and 40 minutes); beware of promises of anything faster, it won't be the real thing. It is worth waiting for (try to not eat anything before it comes) — a dish of culinary beauty in its broad, blackened pan, and a joy to eat.

Mention wine in Spain and most people will think of sherry and Rioja. But Spanish wines are much more varied than that. From the green hills of Galicia to the sun-drenched vineyards of Andalusia, and from the rolling plains of Extremadura to the stony fields of Majorca, grapes are grown and wine is produced. Look in any supermarket in Spain and you will find a huge range of Spanish red, rosé and white

OPPOSITE TOP: Restaurant mural, Córdoba.
OPPOSITE BOTTOM: A restaurant in Seville.
ABOVE LEFT: *Paella*, Spain's best known dish.
ABOVE RIGHT: *Zarzuela de Peix*, a seafood mixed grill in a Barcelona restaurant.

wines, as well as all sorts of sherries, brandies and local liqueurs.

There are 31 official wine-making areas in the government-controlled system of "*Denominación de Origen*"; each bottle of wine has its place of origin marked on it. You will also be able to check the vintage by the harvest date ("*Cosecha 1992*", for example) and the aging process. "*Vino de Crianza*" means that the wine has been in the barrel and bottle for at least two years, usually a year in each; "*Reserva*" means three years of maturing; and "*Gran Reserva*" indicates at least two years in the barrel and three in the bottle before consumption. Less matured wines will be marked "*Vino de Mesa*" (table wine) but normally their region will be also marked with the phrase, "*Guarantia de Origen*".

While **Andalusia** is famous for traditional sherry, its other sherry-related wines should not be overlooked. *Manzanilla* from **Sanlúcar de Barrameda** and *Montilla-Moriles* from **Córdoba** are lighter than Jerez's wines and have the advantage of being drinkable throughout a meal, especially with fish.

**La Mancha** is Europe's largest wine-growing region. Its best known wine is the light red *clarete* of **Valdepeñas** which is drunk all over Spain; a finer red, with a stronger bouquet and flavor, comes from *Almansa* in the east of the region.

**Catalonia** has several important wine-producing areas. *Alella*, a pleasant light white wine in a tall, slender Hock-style bottle, comes from north of Barcelona; *Penedés*, to the south, produces the *cavas* (Spanish champagne) and some strong, fruity reds of which Torres's Sangre de Toro is the best known; and *Priorato*, in the Tarragona area, also turns out some fine red wine, almost purple in color.

Moving west, *Rioja* is familiar to most people, especially the reds. But don't neglect the whites; *Marqués de Cáceres*, in the more expensive price range, is excellent, and lower down, *El Coto* resembles a French Loire wine — light, fruity and with a wonderful bouquet. Just south of Rioja, along the Duero river, is a relatively new wine-producing zone that produces some of Spain's finest vintages, of which the *Vega de Sicilia* reds are the most famous.

**Aragon** is a developing area with its strong reds (*Cariñena*) and Beaujolais-style lighter reds (*Campo de Borja*);

Navarre is also a wine-producer, similar to Rioja but not as sophisticated; the Basque Country makes a light, slightly bubbly "green" wine called *txacolis*, and Galicia is the home of two fresh white wines (*Albariños* and *Ribeiros*) which are also slightly fizzy.

# Special Interests

In recent years, Spain has found itself under increasing pressure from other tourist-minded countries, similarly endowed with mile upon mile of sun-drenched beaches. One of its responses has been to broaden its appeal to people who have special interests. Religious pilgrimages, historic routes, language courses, cookery classes, hunting holidays, mountain trekking, art and literary tours, music festivals, bird-watching trips — you name it, and you will probably find it.

The finding is best done by first calling your nearest Spanish tourist office and then consulting specialized travel agents. But here are a few suggestions. Salamanca, Spain's oldest university town, holds regular residential courses in the Spanish language and literature and Granada is another center for language teaching. Theme tours are becoming more and more popular. "Roman and Medieval Iberia", "Prehistoric Cave Art and Ancient Cultures", and "Arab, Jewish and Gothic Art" are some of the cultural offerings in recent years. Two specialist travel agents in the United States are: Hartours ( (1-617) 482-0076, 20 Park Plaza, Boston, Massachusetts 02116; Spanish Heritage Tours ( (1-718) 520-1300, 116 Queens Boulevard, Forest Hills, New York 11375. In Britain, Swan Hellenic Art Treasures Tours ( (44-171) 247-0401, 47 Canberra House, London E1 7AA, organizes cultural trips to Spain, as well as to Greece.

Hiking and other more vigorous holidays have been covered in THE GREAT OUTDOORS section, but nature lovers such as bird, butterfly and garden enthusiasts will be able to find organized tours to suit them. Ornitholidays ( (44-1243) 821230, in Britain, for example, is one of several travel agencies that caters to bird-watchers. Address: 1–3 Victoria Drive, Bognor Regis, West Sussex PO21 2PW.

If you like cooking and want to spend time in Andalusia, Janet Mendel ( (956) 248-6210, puts on cooking courses in a country house. An American who has lived in Spain for many years, she has written several books on Spanish cooking and writes a culinary column in the English language monthly magazine, *Lookout*. Her address: Apartado de Correos 150, 29650 Mijas, Málaga.

Spain's monasteries offer an interesting travel variation if you want to absorb at close quarters the country's ecclesiastical architecture and history, if you feel like a religious retreat, or if you simply want to spend time in a relaxed and peaceful environment. Many monasteries have accommodation for guests; some are for men only but a growing number cater for men and women and even children. Accommodation is surprisingly comfortable — central heating, private bathrooms, even elevators — and the food always wholesome and plentiful. The way to book is to call the monastery and ask for the *"hospedería"* (hostel).

OPPOSITE LEFT: Williams and Humboldt sherry bodega, Jerez, Andalusia. RIGHT: Traditional wine bar in Seville.

# Welcome to Spain

THE MOORS originally thought that Spain was an island, and in a sense it was. Cut off from the rest of Europe by the Pyrenees and separated from Africa by the sea, Spain grew up through the centuries as an orphan: introverted, unloved, and different. The process was helped by topography and climate. Spain is not a gentle country. Its core is a great plateau, ribbed with ranges of mountains and slashed by largely unnavigable rivers. In most parts the summers are fiercely hot and the winters bitterly cold. The rain in Spain may fall mainly on the plain, but it tends to do so at irregular intervals and often with great violence.

The Iberian peninsula, which includes Portugal, is shaped like a pentagon and has an average height of 600 m (1,968 ft). Diagonally, the peninsula measures between 700 km (435 miles) and 800 km (497 miles). Spain is 80 percent of that area making it Western Europe's second largest country — France is a little bigger — twice the size of Britain, and slightly larger than California.

## THE SUN-TANNED HIDE

The modern traveler flying over Spain may well agree with the ancient description of it looking like a cow hide, pegged out and drying in the sun. The central part of the animal is the *meseta* ("large table"), an upland area that ranges in height from 600 m (1,968 ft) to 1,000 m (3,280 ft). The *meseta* gives Spain its physical and spiritual character. This vast, tawny, undulating plateau with its brilliant skies and limitless horizons is where the Spanish people and the state developed during the centuries of solitude. It is also where the Spanish imagination derived sustenance, where the epic poets looked for material to glorify El Cid, where Goya went for his scenes of every day life, and where Cervantes found Don Quixote philosophizing and tilting at windmills.

But the *meseta* is also deceptive because it suggests uniformity whereas Spain is one of the most diverse countries in the world. On top of the plateau are many mountain ranges, from the Sierra Nevada with the

highest peak in the country (3,478 m or 11,408 ft) in the south, through the Sierra de Gredos and Sierra de Guadarrama in the center, to the Picos de Europa of the Cantabrian Range in the north-west and the Pyrenean wall in the north.

Somewhat surprisingly for a land with so many mountains and a good deal of rain and snow, Spain has few important rivers. The Ebro in the north that runs into the Mediterranean and the Guadalquivir in the south that flows into the Atlantic are the two largest; but they have never been great

waterways in the style of the Rhine in Germany or the Rhône in France. The other main rivers, the Duero, Tajo (Tagus), and the Guadiana all flow westwards and reach the Atlantic through Portugal. By contrast, Spain's long coastline and good harbors have given it access — and made it vulnerable — to northern Europe and the Atlantic, Africa and the Mediterranean.

Geography and climate have shaped the diversity to such a point that it is hard to believe that the moist green countryside of Galicia with its stone walls, cows, and Swiss-looking chalets has anything in common with the sun-drenched olive groves and white-washed houses of Andalusia, especially since the inhabitants of each place speak a different language. But that is Spain.

OPPOSITE TOP: Spain's northern Costa Verde ("green coast") near Gijón, Asturias; OPPOSITE BOTTOM: the spectacularly situated town of Arcos de la Frontera in Andalusia. ABOVE: the Picos de Europe in northern Spain.

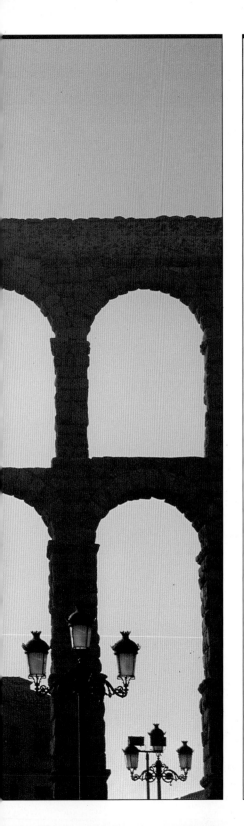

# Of
# Romans
# and Moors

## BEFORE THE ROMANS

While traces of man reach back hundreds of thousands of years to the Neanderthal era, the most significant evidence of early man's presence in Spain was unearthed at the Altamira caves in the north. Here Stone Age hunters lived some 12,000 years BC pursuing stags, wild boars, horses, bison and other game and later rendering them in exquisite paintings on the walls and ceilings of their caves. There are Neolithic cave paintings in eastern Spain (5000 BC to 2000 BC) and Megalithic tombs and other artifacts in the Balearic islands (2000 BC).

The first waves of intruders entered Spain in the Megalithic period with the Ligurians coming from Italy and settling in the northeast, and people known as Iberians crossing the narrow straits from Africa and establishing themselves in the south. Celts, sailing in from Britain and France, settled in northwestern Spain a thousand years before the birth of Christ. There was not a great mingling and the Iberians seemed to have done rather better in the warm, mineral-rich south than the Ligurians and Celts in the north. They are believed to have been the creators of the fabled kingdom of Tartessos in Andalusia ("Tarshish" in the Bible) although no trace of the city has yet been found.

The Phoenicians were attracted by stories of Iberian workmanship in copper, silver and gold. They arrived around 1100 BC and built towns at Gadir (Cádiz), and Malaka (Málaga) and bequeathed the skills of writing and a standardized monetary system. The Phoenicians were followed by their maritime rivals, the Greeks, who established colonies in the seventh and sixth centuries BC at Ampurias (Girona), Dianion (Denia), and Mainake, east of Málaga. The famous stone bust of the Lady of Elche, with her stern gaze and elaborately braided hair and rows of amulets, is a spectacular example of Ibero-Grecian artistic fusion. Strabo, the Greek geographer, reported on some of the contradictions that later became clichés. The peninsula's inhabitants were, he noted, haughty yet hospitable, xenophobic but intrigued by foreigners.

The Greeks introduced the vine and olive to Spain and made a serious attempt at colonization in the attractive coastal lands of the Mediterranean. They also incorporated their new possession into their mythology. One of the labors of Hercules — the golden apples of the Hesperides — was located in Spain, not far from Cádiz which became an important and cosmopolitan city in the Greek period.

Carthaginians and Romans followed the Greeks. Hamilcar Barca led the way up the Mediterranean coast on his way to attack Rome from an unexpected quarter and using a circuitous route. He gave his name to Barcelona and the Carthaginians also founded Cartagena. Hamilcar's son, Hannibal, and son-in-law, Hasdrubal, spent much of their lives in Spain strengthening Carthage's position in the peninsula. The Punic Wars, however, ended Carthage's control when it was forced to surrender its Spanish possessions to Rome in 201 BC.

## THE ROMANS AND THEIR LEGACY

The Romans found out about the character of the peninsula's inhabitants the hard way for it took them almost two centuries to subdue the fiercely independent Celto-Iberians. Rome's best soldiers — Cato, Pompey, Julius Caesar and Augustus — all served in Spain. The province then became a wealthy and important part of the Roman empire and produced the emperors Trajan, Hadrian, Marcus Aurelius and Theodosius, as well as some of the most prominent writers of Rome's "Silver Age" of letters, including the two Sénecas, Lucan, Martial and Quintilian.

During five centuries of Roman rule that lasted until the early fifth century, Spain prospered and the imprint of the period is clear all over the country in Roman amphitheaters, aqueducts, bridges and mosaics. The Romans founded a number of cities such as Hispalis (Seville), Corduba (Córdoba), Tarraco (Tarragona), Augusta Emerita (Mérida), and Caesar Augusta (Zaragoza);

A painting by El Greco commissioned by King Philip II for display in the El Escorial where it still can be seen. El Greco was born in Crete, studied in Italy, and spent the greater part of his life in Toledo.

they also gave Spain things it had never had before: unity, a common language (Latin of course), and law.

The Romans' heritage included an important religious legacy. They left Spain a Christian country, though that was not their original intention. Spain began its Christian life with a number of martyrs, put to death with typical Roman gusto in the centuries before Christianity became the official religion of the Roman Empire. The Romans added another element to Spain's human diversity in the form of a relatively large

Jewish population. It became part of official policy to settle the Jews in far-flung colonies during the Diaspora, an act that later had a significant impact on Spain's economic and cultural development.

As the Roman empire crumbled in the fifth century, Spain became one of the first victims. Vandals, living up to the later meaning of their name, swept down from the north, burning, pillaging, raping and killing as they went. Their momentum took them into Africa, leaving nothing but a wasteland and a name ("Vandalusia" which later lost

The Romans, during a 500-year occupation, made a lasting impact on Spain. A statue in the Roman town of Réalion, just outside Seville, where the Roman emperors Hadrian and Trajan were born.

its "V" to become Andalusia) behind them. Other Germanic tribes, such as the Suebi and Alans, paid plundering visits of varying duration in the north, and the Byzantine Empire, under Justinian, seized part of the south. Relative order was not restored until the Visigoths, ("West Goths") who came from Gaul, established themselves in the sixth century.

## THE VISIGOTHS

A Teutonic and semi-Romanized tribe, the Visigoths were ruled by a military élite who elected their kings. They were never numerous in Spain and for a long time did not intermarry with the local population; and, used to Roman ways, they left much of their predecessors' system intact. The Visigoths established Toledo as the capital of the country and, under King Leovigild in the second half of the sixth century, managed to unite the country by expelling the Byzantines from the south, the Suebi from Galicia, and brought the incorrigibly separatist-minded Basques to heel.

The cult of the warrior caste and the lack of a hereditary system for the throne caused considerable in-fighting within the Visigothic hierarchy, and the three centuries of Visigoth rule in Spain were a turbulent time. The Visigoths also brought with them the schismatic Arian branch of Christianity which did not go down well with the orthodox Hispano-Roman population. This led to more friction but by the end of the sixth century, King Recared, Leovigild's son, had been converted to his subjects' faith, setting a pattern for state and church unity that became a driving, and at times fanatical force during much of Spain's subsequent history. The Visigoths set a trend in that direction too by persecuting the Jews.

The Visigothic period, such a distant and obscure footnote in the story of Spain, may seem scarcely worth recalling. But the Visigoths did re-establish the unity of the country, weld church and state, and leave the occasional — often simple, sometimes surprisingly beautiful — reminder of their 300-year sojourn. Spain still has a few Visigothic churches in the north, plenty of stone

*Of Romans and Moors*

carvings on church walls and friezes, and some fine jewelry on royal artifacts that shimmer and gleam before the 20th-century viewer's eyes, casting a new light on Western Europe's "Dark Ages."

## THE MOORS

The last great invasion came from Africa. In the early eighth century, the Moors established a foothold in the south and within three years had conquered most of the country. (General Franco, coming from the same direction, took about the same time to accomplish the same task 1,200 years later.) The next 800 years were the story of the Moorish dominion and the long, century-by-century struggle of the Christians to drive them out of the peninsula.

The great flowering of the Moors' civilization in all its many ramifications that included agriculture, architecture, medicine, literature, music, design, and the art of making war, can still be seen, heard and sensed wherever you go in modern Spain. The grand monuments such as the Alhambra in Granada and the Mezquita (mosque) in Córdoba need neither introduction nor praise. It is the name of an obscure village, a church tower that began life serving another god, a quavering half-tone overheard as you pass a crowded bar that suddenly remind you how deep was the Moorish impression.

The time of the Moors was also a period when the greatest tolerance and intermingling of Spain's many different peoples took place. Although those eight centuries were also a time of constant if sporadic war, Muslim, Christian and Jew often lived side by side in peace. Moreover, the different people of the northern part of the country — notably the Catalans, Basques, Asturians and Galicians — managed to establish a considerable degree of autonomy and preserve their ancient laws and customs.

The period, especially the earlier part, was remarkable for its lack of fanaticism and the productive interaction of the newcomers with the indigenous inhabitants. Alliances cut across religious lines (El Cid, for example, served Christian and Muslim masters at different times); intermarriage was common even at the princely level; many Christian kings could speak Arabic as well as they could Spanish; Jews were valued members of the community as scientists, teachers, businessmen, and royal ambassadors and advisers.

The influx of more fanatical Moorish factions from North Africa and the launching of the Crusades in the latter part of the Moorish occupation did much to poison the good relations between races and religions. Jews were persecuted again and Christian and Moor fought more bitterly for territorial control. But the picture was never wholly dark. The Moors, reduced to Granada, produced another great outburst of administrative, commercial and artistic energy resulting in the building of the Alhambra. Christians and Moors lived successfully enough under each other's sway to develop distinctive blends of architecture and design that are known to this day as Mozarabic (Christian workmanship under Moorish control) and Mudéjar (Moors, or Moriscos as they were known, developing a distinctive style of craftsmanship under Christian rule).

The Moorish advance in Spain had been halted in an obscure Asturian valley in 718 at a place called Covadonga. The Moors were probably more concerned about their thrust into France at the time, an assault that was decisively checked at Poitiers in 732 by the Frankish king, Charles Martel. However, with Covadonga the Christian *Reconquista* ("Reconquest") began, to end almost eight centuries later with the fall of Granada in 1492.

The story of the Reconquest concerns two parallel developments: the gradual expulsion of the Moors from the peninsula, and the growing unity of the Christian kingdoms. The Christian drive began in the northwest with the kingdoms of Asturias, León, Navarre and Castile forming alliances and eventually merging under the banner of Castile. In the northeast Aragón and Catalonia drew together and began a reconquest of their own in the eastern part of the mainland and the Balearic Islands in the Mediterranean. The final catalyst, however, was the union of these powers in 1474 when King Ferdinand of Aragón married Queen Isabella of Castile.

## THE CATHOLIC MONARCHS

The Catholic Monarchs *(Los Reyes Católicos)*, as they were called, changed Spain in a number of ways that set it on a new course. First, they weakened the existing feudal order and established an absolute monarchy. Second, they increased the power and the militancy of the church through obtaining permission from the Pope to set up the Inquisition. Third, they completed the task of the Reconquest with the capture of Granada in 1492. Fourth, in that same dramatic year, Christopher Columbus made his first landing in the New World under their patronage.

With hindsight, it can be said Ferdinand and Isabella have a lot to answer for. The power of the monarchy, with a few lapses, lasted well into the 19th century, stultifying the growth of a modern state. The Inquisition exerted a terrible arbitrary authority over the lives of Spaniards for several centuries. The end of the Moorish occupation meant greater unity but human, economic and cultural impoverishment. The discovery of the New World brought fabulous wealth to Spain but left in its wake overweening ambition, political decay and economic disaster. (Not to mention the cruelty and destruction inflicted by the Conquistadors and their successors on the people they subjugated across the Atlantic.)

During the next two centuries (1516 to 1700) Spain belonged to the Habsburgs, a foreign dynasty that climbed onto the

Ferdinand and Isabella had decided to expel all those who would not convert to Christianity shortly after the fall of Granada in 1492. The number was around 150,000 and these Sephardic Jews, who moved to North Africa, Greece and Turkey, took their 15th-century Spanish language—Ladino—with them and many of them still speak it.

Charles, who had inherited a large European empire consisting of Austria, the Netherlands and half of Italy, added an even larger American one to it. Hernán Cortés defeated the Aztecs in Mexico and Francisco Pizarro conquered the Incas in Peru under the banner of their king-emperor, and huge amounts of treasure flowed into Seville and other southern ports. Most of it disappeared as rapidly as it had materialized to finance Charles's interminable wars.

This and other abuses resulted in a peasant rebellion in Castile (the Communero Revolt, 1520 to 1521) which shook the establishment but was bloodily crushed as the monarchy tightened its hold on power another notch. While fighting virtually every country in Europe, as well as the Ottoman Turks, Charles launched the Counter-Reformation at home in response to the Protestant surge further north. The Society of Jesus, or Jesuits, were founded by Ignatius of Loyola during Charles's reign. Yet, after 40 years of effort, he had nothing to show for the money spent, the blood spilt, the opportunities missed. So, he did an uncharacteristic thing: he handed everything over to his son, packed his bag and retired in a certain comfort to the monastery of Yuste in Extremadura.

Philip II, his son, was very different — studious, introverted, and pious. He inherited a bankrupt state that was saved only by the gold and silver of Spain's New World possessions. His foreign ventures fared no better than his father's with the one exception of a great naval victory over the Turks at Lepanto in 1571. The Spaniards and their allies were led by Philip's brother, John of Austria, and on one of his ships a Spaniard, who was later to achieve another kind of

Spanish throne by way of the marriage bed. Chauvinistic Spaniards call it the "Golden Age"; dissenters prefer the "Age of Greed" or something equally perjorative. The first of the line was Charles I, a gentleman who spoke no Spanish, had a passion for war and who acquired the title of Holy Roman Emperor. (In Spain he is generally known as Emperor Charles V.) In order to secure his position, he had his mother, Juana, the rightful queen of Spain who was allegedly mad, locked up in a cell where she languished for 40 years before dying.

By the time he took control, Spain had lost its industrious and cultured Jewish population. On the advice of Tomás de Torquemada, the first head of the Inquisition and himself the son of a converted Jew,

Fresco depicting the battle of Higueruela in 1431 where King Juan II defeated the Moors of Granada. This immense tapestry covers one wall of a cloister known as the "Hall of Battles" in El Escorial.

fame, fought hard and was wounded three times, ending the battle with a permanently maimed left hand. His name was Miguel de Cervantes Saavedra, the author of Don Quixote.

Philip lost Spain's Netherlands colonies and saw his great Armada that went to conquer heretical England repulsed more by an unlucky storm than the English guns. At home he focused his attention on stamping out anything that remotely resembled heresy. The Inquisition redoubled its efforts.

For the remaining Jews, roughly twice the number who had been expelled at the end of the 15th century, and the Moors who had decided to accept the apparently generous terms offered them after their defeat, the reality of life under Philip and the Inquisition exceeded their worst fears. In an atmosphere that had a lot in common with Nazi Germany four centuries later, Philip and the Inquisition's network of interrogators, spies, informers and thugs relentlessly pursued anyone suspected being "tainted" by Jewish or Moorish blood. The result was that Spain brutally unraveled what had become a rich and talented mixture of races and, in the process, lost countless skilled, productive people. While all this was happening, Philip was building that huge and unique mausoleum, El Escorial, which reflects his strange cold-eyed, hard-driven personality.

## THE MONARCHY IN DECLINE

The story of the last three Habsburg kings, the imbecilic Philip III, the well-meaning but weak Philip IV and Charles II, another retarded monarch — there was a lot of incest among the Habsburgs who believed in keeping as much as possible in the family — is a story of steady decline. During Philip III's reign Spain's involvement in the Thirty Year's War finished with the loss of more territory, another national bankruptcy and the end of Spain as a great European power.

Internally, Philip III took bad advice and expelled the remaining Moors, over half a million of them, the majority of whom lived in the Valencia region which they had made the most productive part of the country. That self-inflicted blow further undermined the economy and it was during the 17th century that those extraordinarily vibrant and prosperous towns of Castile (Toledo, Segovia, Ávila, León, Burgos and others) became frozen in time.

Charles II had no heir and left Spain and its diminished possessions to Philip of Anjou, a Bourbon and a grandson of Louis XIV. But the succession was disputed, the rival being a Habsburg, the Austrian Archduke Charles. Some of the Spaniards took sides, notably the Catalans who backed the Austrian candidate, but most waited while the European powers fought the "War of Spanish Succession." The English, supporting Charles, won some memorable battles under Marlborough and seized Gibraltar and Minorca but, in the end, it was the French candidate who was installed as Philip V. Thus began over two centuries of Bourbon rule and a new period of experiment, foreign invasion, revolution and more experimenting that took Spain up to the ultimate cataclysm of the Civil War.

Philip, being a French prince, brought French ways and sensibilities and built palaces on a grand scale. The age of Baroque and Rococo had begun. The 18th century was distinguished by the rule of one Bourbon king, Charles III who reigned from 1759–88. He believed in the absolute power of the monarchy as much as any of his Spanish predecessors and his European contemporaries, but he and his progressive ministers also believed in reform. The power of the Inquisition was curbed, the Jesuits were expelled, and the economy was revived. Spain thus shared in the Age of Enlightenment.

Unfortunately, the succeeding Bourbons reverted to type. Charles IV, whose uncle King Louis XVI of France died on the scaffold in 1793, made the mistake of declaring war on Revolutionary France and lost. When Napoleon came to power he engineered Charles's abdication in favor of his son, Ferdinand VII, and then banned him from Spain and handed over the crown to his own brother, Joseph Bonaparte. Spain felt the foot of the invader once again as the French armies marched in and took up occupation.

While the Spanish populace had no love for their feeble monarchs, they regarded

France's uninvited presence as a bitter affront to their patriotism and dignity. On May 2, 1808, a spontaneous uprising occurred. It was brutally repressed by the French — captured in Goya's famous painting of Spanish insurgents being executed by French soldiers — but a struggle, known as the War of Independence, was set in motion.

British forces, led by the future Duke of Wellington, joined in on the Spanish side and six years later the French were finally expelled, plundering and burning Spain's architectural and artistic treasures as they went. During the war, liberal visionaries gathered in Cádiz and drew up a democratic, parliamentary constitution which abolished the power of the monarchy and the church.

It was only a brief moment. When Ferdinand VII returned from exile, he reasserted the absolute power of the monarchy and the influence of the church, including the institution of the Inquisition which had been abolished by the Cádiz constitutionalists. During his reign, which lasted until 1833, Spain lost most of its Latin American colonies since it was powerless to prevent them slipping away.

On Ferdinand's death there was another disputed succession that led to the first of three baffling and inconclusive Carlist Wars. Ferdinand had decreed that his daughter, Isabella, should succeed him but she was challenged by his brother, Don Carlos (hence the term "Carlist"). Isabella, who was still a child, received most of her support from the liberals and anti-clerical groups in the urban areas. The bulk of Carlos's backing came from the conservative elements and the intensely Catholic regions of the north, particularly Navarre and the Basque country.

The liberals won and Isabella eventually became queen, but a second conflict broke out in the late 1840s with the same result. At this period, republican feelings intensified and generals began to force their way to power thus perfecting the art of the coup d'etat. The monarchy continued to survive but with declining power, and the first of several spasms of anti-clericalism resulted in the expropriation of the monasteries and the final collapse of the Inquisition. By the mid-19th century, Spain had become a very confused place.

The second half was not much better. In 1874, the country's First Republic was declared by General Prim, a Catalan, but was soon overwhelmed by an uprising in Andalusia and the third and last Carlist War. An extraordinary succession of dictators, revolts and finally a royalist restoration followed, making Spain look as fragile and immature as any modern banana republic. The century closed with a humiliating foreign defeat in the Spanish–American War of 1898. The peace treaty effectively ended Spain's long imperial career as Cuba

became independent and Puerto Rico and the Philippines were ceded to the United States.

But underneath the political turmoil, more important things were happening. The country was at last industrializing; a great cultural renaissance was under way in Catalonia; modern ideas and ideology were penetrating the Pyrenean defenses with notions such as socialism, communism and anarchism; and a collection of Spanish writers and thinkers, known as the "Generation of '98" began to reassess Spain's position in the modern world.

The royal mausoleum beneath the church in El Escorial where the bodies of Spain's monarchs lie in marble sarcophagi.

Spain wisely opted out of the First World War and managed to pull itself together. The twenties brought prosperity and a military dictator, General Miguel Primo de Rivera, who governed with the approval of King Alfonso XIII until being ousted in 1930. The following year, the left-wing parties won elections and forced the king to abdicate and go into exile, ushering in Spain's Second Republic. Political rivalries, heightened by Europe's widening ideological differences as fascism gained ascendancy in Italy and Germany, became more acute. The Depression, which hit Spain as hard as anywhere, made matters worse. Peasant revolts, industrial strikes, an attempted coup, unilateral declarations of regional autonomy, and the seesawing fortunes of the right and the left at elections scarred the first five years of the republic.

In 1936, the Popular Front, a coalition of left-wing parties, won elections and took power. By this stage Spain looked like a chemistry laboratory for politics. On the left were socialists, communists, Trotskyites, anarcho-syndicalists and more, some supporting the government, others opposing it in different ways and to different degrees, and still others largely ignoring it. On the right, there were monarchists (orthodox supporters of the Bourbons and unorthodox Carlists), conservatives of many hues, ambitious generals, and the new Falange movement, Spain's fascist party. The situation became more anarchic, with political violence becoming commonplace, as the new government struggled unavailingly to maintain control.

On July 18, 1936, the army rebelled and, calling themselves "Nationalists," its generals set out to destroy the government and the Republic. The government initially panicked but eventually gathered itself together, and with the support of militias around the country, a section of the army and police that stayed loyal, and mass mobilization managed to hold its ground.

## THE SPANISH CIVIL WAR

The story of the Spanish Civil War, which ended a little under three years later with over a half-a-million dead, has been chronicled and mulled over in many volumes.

It was a story of its time in that it became the first battlefield in which the ideologies of communism and fascism confronted each other. It quickly attracted outside attention: Italy and Germany supported the Nationalists; the Soviet Union backed the Republicans. Foreigners rushed in to fight on one side or the other, or simply to observe and record for posterity. New techniques of modern warfare were tested in Spain for the first time, the most dramatic being the aerial bombardment of civilians.

But, when all is said and done, it was the *Spanish* Civil War. The two Spains, which had grown out of the single Spain that fought the French invader in Napoleon's time, were so far apart by the 1930s that it seemed almost inevitable that there had to be a bloody catharsis to put them back together again. The great divide between the trinity of king, church and army, backed by a conservative-minded, traditionally Catholic bourgeoisie on one hand, and the coalition of landless peasants, factory workers and ardent regionalists led by anti-clerical intellectuals on the other, split Spain down the middle.

The Republican side, outgunned and weakened by divisions in its ranks, eventually succumbed to General Francisco Franco's better equipped and well-trained forces, which received considerably more support from Italy and Germany than the Soviet Union provided for the Republicans.

In March 1939, Franco's forces marched into a battered and hungry Madrid and the war was over.

## THE FRANCO YEARS

During the next 36 years Franco put his stamp on Spain in a way that differed little from that of a Habsburg or Bourbon monarch. Calling himself "El Caudillo" (the leader), he was merciless, repressive, authoritarian, pious, narrow and unimaginative. The government shot, imprisoned or hounded its Republican opponents in the

OPPOSITE: Valle de los Caídos ("Valley of the Fallen"). Franco's Civil War monument and tomb.

early post-war years. Spain became a police state. Ideas, as well as political opinions, were the target of a smothering censorship. Authority was rigidly centralized in an attempt to squeeze the life out of Spain's regional diversity. Any sign of opposition was crushed with an iron hand. The price was that Spain, pummeled at home and ostracized abroad, turned in on itself once more, hungry, suffering and forgotten.

But Franco differed in some important respects from most of his absolutist predecessors. He was not an ideologue; he never embraced fascism, for example, and kept the Falange movement at a distance. He also knew the limits of Spain's strength. He skillfully avoided joining his old friends, Italy and Germany, when they went to war. When World War II was over, Franco cashed in on the tensions aroused by the Cold War by making an astute deal with the United States that involved renting out military bases in Spain for much-needed dollars. Later, in the 1960s, he allowed a new generation of technocrats their heads in restructuring the Spanish economy.

This new class knew little of the violent past and cared less about the passions that had brought it about. Instead, they concentrated on building factories, improving agriculture, modernizing the infrastructure of roads, railroads, ports and airlines, and encouraging mass tourism. They were helped by the steady flow of foreign currency sent home by over a half a million Spaniards working abroad.

## INTO TODAY'S WORLD

When Franco died in 1975, Spain had at last entered the modern world as far as the economy was concerned. But it lagged behind socially and politically. It was still a pariah in Europe, banned from the European Community and parliament, and from the NATO alliance. It is one of the great ironies of Spanish history that it was, finally, the monarchy that completed Spain's modern transformation. The man who did it was the present

king, Juan Carlos, the grandson of King Alfonso XIII and Franco's appointed heir.

Juan Carlos has guided Spain through the shoals of a difficult transition, transforming it from a repressive military dictatorship into a free-wheeling but relatively disciplined parliamentary democracy with himself presiding as constitutional monarch. It wasn't easy and a critical test came in 1981 when a Civil Guard colonel and his followers tried to launch a coup by seizing the Cortés (parliament) while its members were in session. Some of the army generals were behind the attempt, but after the king stepped in and made it clear that he supported the new order, the plot fizzled out.

Since then Spain has broadened its democracy and granted its regions a large degree

The Olympic Village, Barcelona.

of autonomy and the right to use their own languages. A socialist government has been in power for more than half a decade, extreme right-wing and extreme left-wing parties are legal, if not flourishing, and as you can see from any newspaper kiosk or bookshop, the country is wide open to the world of ideas. Theater, film-making, painting — indeed the arts in general are enjoying a renaissance in the vibrant post-Franco era. "Spain does not change often," said a foreign resident who knows the country well, "but when it does, it changes incredibly fast."

Spain is a fully integrated member of the European Community and of the North Atlantic Treaty Organisation (NATO), whose secretary-general is a Spaniard. Its place in international affairs has been consolidated

by staging the critical first phase of the Israeli-Palestinian peace talks and acting as host to the inaugural meeting of the European and Mediterranean nations. Spain's *annus mirabilis*, 1992, lived up to the great expectations invested in it. Both Expo 92 in Seville and the Olympic Games in Barcelona were well-organised, stylish, and peaceful events that brought hundreds of thousands of visitors and universal praise. This proof of national maturity and international acceptibility occurred during the quincentenary of the fall of Granada and the discovery of America. The hope, shared by 40 million Spaniards, is that the new democratic era, unlike the legacy of the Catholic monarchs, will turn out to be one of lasting rather than illusory glory.

*Of Romans and Moors*

# The
# Cultural
# Legacy

## A LEGACY IN FULL VIEW

One of the great gifts of Spain is that its cultural riches remain highly visible and accessible. Prehistoric artifacts can be seen from a roadside; architectural masterpieces from half a dozen eras look little different from the day they were built; the visitor is overwhelmed with the works of Spanish painters in Madrid's Prado Museum, or made to feel part of the painter's entourage in Salvador Dalí's extraordinary gallery-mausoleum in Figueres; the routine pageantry of the bullfight plunges you into the 18th century; the anguished sound of flamenco's *cante jondo* and the click of the castanets have hardly changed over the centuries; most of Spain's best novelists, poets and playwrights have been widely translated; domestic architecture, especially in the south, has altered little, preserving the Moors' love for patios, balconies, flowers, and fountains; and the makers of pottery and ceramics continue to follow ancient Moorish and Christian designs.

## SPAIN'S GREAT BUILDINGS

Spain is a country of great buildings although these days it tends to be concrete and reinforced steel that captures Spanish architects' imagination as they tumble over each to construct new highways, dams, tunnels and high-rise office and apartment blocks. The Romans really started it all, and there are more Roman architectural remains in Spain than in any other country in the world apart from Italy. There are aqueducts in Segovia, Tarragona and Mérida; bridges in Salamanca, Córdoba, and Alcantará (Cáceres); magnificent city walls in Lugo (Galicia); theaters in Sagunto (Valencia), Mérida, Tarragona and Itálica (Seville). Probably the best place to see the Roman legacy as a whole is Mérida in Badajoz Province, Extremadura. The superb Roman theater there is still used for plays and musical concerts and there is an excellent museum of Roman art (Museo de Arte Romano).

## THE MOORISH MASTERPIECES

The architectural achievements of the Moors in the south ran parallel with those of the Christian kingdoms in the north. The Moorish contribution came in three phases. During the 8th and 11th centuries, the Caliphate of Córdoba produced the unique Mezquita (mosque), the Alcázar (a fortress-palace) and other buildings in a classic Moorish style with double horseshoe-shaped arches, rectangu-

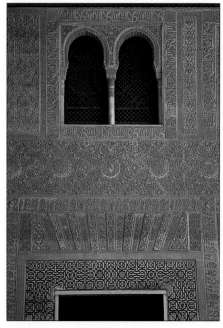

lar patios, and rich geometric and calligraphic ornamentation.

The second period of Moorish architecture began with the arrival of the Almoravids and Almohads in the 11th century. After an initial period of mayhem, they settled down and over the next two centuries built mosques and other structures in a more austere style using brick and glazed tiles (*azulejos*), favoring pointed arches over the traditional horseshoe kind and carved wooden coffered ceilings. Seville, notably

OPPOSITE: Interior of the Alcázar in Seville, a fine example of the Mudéjar style of architecture and design. ABOVE: Detail of the Alhambra Palace, Granada.

the Giralda and the Alcázar, has good examples of this legacy.

The third and greatest expression of Moorish creativity came with the Nasrid dynasty in Granada between the 14th and 15th centuries. Granada was the last of the Moorish kingdoms to survive as the Reconquista swept south. But the Nasrids did not seem to be too worried about their gradual encirclement because the Alhambra was clearly built with comfort, elegance and leisurely pursuits in mind. Or perhaps it was because it was built behind huge stone

Romanesque churches which tended to be small, while Segovia and Zamora have larger churches from the later period. The grandest of all, disguised by a much later, Baroque façade, is the Cathedral in Santiago de Compostela. Ávila's famous city walls also date from this time.

The Arab and European influences produced a unique Spanish style of building and design known as "Mudéjar" which was developed by Moorish architects, craftsmen and builders working under Christian rule after the Reconquest. Using

ramparts that they felt they could leave aside the matter of security. The result is an architectural marvel, miraculously intact, that combines the use of space, light and shade, wood, brick, plaster and tiles, and trees, shrubs and flowers in an unmatched way.

### The Churches of Northern Spain

In northern Christian Spain, the Romanesque style flourished between the 11th and 13th centuries producing somber, stone churches and monasteries with rounded arches, tall square towers and sparse ornamentation. Catalonia and the Pyrenean valleys have many examples of the earlier

brick and tile and preserving geometric patterns and designs, Mudéjar work can be seen all over Spain. But it is particularly striking in the Alcázar in Seville, in the two surviving synagogues in Toledo, and in the towers of the older of the two cathedrals in Zaragoza.

During the 13th century, Spain discovered the joy of Gothic architecture, introduced from France. Taller naves, flying buttresses, pointed or ogival arches instead

---

ABOVE: Altar of the Cathedral in Santiago de Compostela. OPPOSITE: Interior of the church at Roncesvalles in the Pyrenees. Roncesvalles was one of the main entry points for pilgrims journeying to Santiago from France.

of round ones, more elaborate carving and ornament, larger and larger stained glass windows, and a growing sense of confidence — even exuberance — characterized the new style. The Cathedrals of Burgos and León, followed by Toledo, are the best examples. In Catalonia and Majorca, a variation developed with a single, towering nave, and wooden vaulting. The Cathedrals in Barcelona, Girona and Palma are good examples.

The Gothic style became more ornate and unrestrained in the 16th century as Spain entered its "Golden Age." The structural elements of Gothic buildings remained relatively unchanged becoming, if anything, more austere under Philip II. His palace-monastery-mausoleum, El Escorial, reflected this tendency. But when it came to the surfaces of the buildings it was a different matter. Virtually every nook and cranny, every available flat surface became a designer's drawing-board, a craftsman's workbench, an artist's palate. The heavily carved stone surfaces in the interior and on the façades of so many Spanish churches, which you will see as you travel around the country, derive from this period. The style came to be known as "Plateresque" because the carving resembled work done by silversmiths *(plateros)*.

In the 17th and 18th centuries, Baroque arrived and soon took a peculiarly Spanish twist as the Churriguera brothers (Alberto and Joaquín) introduced an even more lavish style of carving and decoration that became known as "Churrigueresque." This was the great era of new and fanciful façades being put on old churches and cathedrals, and of the building of some of Spain's finest squares and city halls. Good examples are the Obradoiro façade on the Cathedral in Santiago de Compostela, the façade of Granada's Cathedral, and the lovely Plaza Mayor in Salamanca.

While the early Bourbons indulged themselves in the Baroque, Charles III, the monarch who nudged Spain into the Age of Enlightenment in the latter part of the 18th century, turned to classical Greece and Rome for inspiration. His Neoclassical legacy can be seen best in Madrid in buildings such as the Prado Museum, the Alcalá Arch, and the Cibeles Fountain. This, in turn, led to another revival with the Neomudéjar architecture of the 19th century which is reflected in many of the country's brick-built churches, railway stations and bullrings.

The end of the 19th century brought Modernism and the genius of Antonio Gaudí whose flowing lines, plant motifs, and use of stone and wrought iron as if they were malleable substances, left an indelible mark on the urban landscape. Barcelona provides a rich panorama of the work of Gaudí and his disciples, from the houses in the center of the city to the Guëll Park, to the Temple of the Holy Family (*El Templo de la Sagrada Familia),* his unfinished masterpiece. In the modern era, Spain has its share of good and bad buildings but they are not what most visitors come to see.

## THE VISUAL ARTS

It is said that the quality of the light in Spain made it inevitable that the country would produce remarkable painters. The light probably did not help the Paleolithic painters of the Altamira Caves in Cantabria, but it seems to have influenced later artists, including sculptors whose work is often enhanced by the clarity of the light and the incisive contrast between sun and shade in Spain.

Painters and sculptors worked hand-in-hand with the church (or the mosque) during the medieval period so a careful look around any major church or monastery in Spain usually reveals interesting carvings as well as paintings. In the Cathedral in Santiago de Compostela, the work of Mateo, the master carver is a special feature; Juan Guas's imprint is on the church of San Juan de los Reyes in Toledo; Gil de Siloé was responsible for much of the fine carving in Burgos Cathedral; and Alonso Cano produced the façade of Granada Cathedral.

---

OPPOSITE: The high altar and retablo of the cathedral-like church of El Escorial. The church was designed by Juan Bautista, a pupil of Michaelangelo.

From the 16th century onwards each century was dominated by a master painter. Domenikos Theotokopoulos — El Greco — who spent much of his life in Toledo, was the first, followed by Diego Velázquez in the 17th century, Francisco de Goya in the nineteenth and Pablo Picasso in the twentieth. The Prado is full of works by the first three and another museum in Madrid displays Picasso's "Guernica," his terrifying depiction of the aerial bombardment of the Basque town of that name in the Civil War.

There are several other painters whose work is worth keeping in mind when traveling in Spain. Zubarán, Murillo and Valdes Leal from the Seville school in the 17th century produced a number of religious and other paintings of merit Jumping to the current century, neither the Joan Miró Museum in Barcelona nor the Salvador Dalí Museum in Figueres should be missed.

## INTELLECTUAL LIFE AND LITERATURE

Literature in Spain began, like much else, with the Romans. The two Sénecas, philosophers and rhetoricians, Lucan, the epic poet, and Martial who was renowned for his epigrams, were born in Spain and spent much of their working lives there. The early Christian period produced little of note but literature had an important place in Moorish Andalusia. Córdoba was the most important center of learning in the Western world in the 12th century and a Jewish philosopher called Maimónides was one of its leading figures whose work influenced subsequent Christian thinkers.

Another Córdoban intellectual was Averroäs, a Muslim philosopher, who was a contemporary of Maimónides and who blended Greek and Muslim learning and produced a body of writing that also had an impact on later scholarship. Muslim Spain was a breeding ground of poets, the best known being Ibn Suhayd and Ibn Hazm.

On the Christian side, Castilian began to develop in literary form with epic and other poetry. The Song of My Cid, appeared in the 12th century and described the heroic deeds of Rodrigo Díaz de Vivar (El Cid) in the previous century. Gonzalo de Berceo wrote religious lyric poetry a hundred years later during a period that was greatly influenced by the king of Castile, Alfonso X (the Wise). This talented monarch made Castilian the language of the court, replacing Latin, and was himself a poet, historian, translator and composer.

Catalan literature was developing at this time. Jaime I of Aragón (the Conqueror) also wrote, composing a number of chronicles, and Ramón Llull from Majorca, a novelist, poet, mystic, philosopher and scientist, was one of the most prominent intellectuals of his day in the Mediterranean world. The 15th century was enlivened by the Marquis de Santillana, an aristocrat, poet and scholar, who is credited with founding literary criticism in Spain, as well leaving to posterity an almost perfect medieval village near Santander in northwestern Spain.

Spain's great century in history — the sixteenth — brought with it new literary figures, the most important being Lope de Vega, a prolific playwright and poet, Tirso de Molina, novelist and playwright, and Miguel de Cervantes Savaadra who needs no introduction. "Don Quixote" is credited with being the first modern novel, a work that was in concept, style and sophistication a long way ahead of its time. It is believed to have influenced Cervantes' contemporary, William Shakespeare, and without doubt countless writers since. It is also a quintessentially Spanish story — it is hard to imagine Don Quixote and Sancho Panzo in any other country — that was at once a perceptive commentary on the frailties of contemporary Spain and a vivid work of the imagination.

After the work of Pedro Calderón de la Barca, a 17th-century writer, Spain seemed to dry up in a literary sense until the 19th century when the Romantic movement brought along the poet, Gustavo Adolfo Becquer, and José de Espronceda, the novelist. The end of the 19th century saw a renaissance of writing in the Catalan and Galician languages and the emergence of the "Generation of '98," a group of Spanish writers, poets, commentators and other intellectuals who were jolted into a reassessment of Spain's place in the modern world after their country's shaming defeat in the Spanish–American War of 1898.

The leader of the group was Miguel de Unamuno, who wrote novels, poetry and philosophical works. Others included Pio Baroja, the novelist, José Ortega y Gasset, the philosopher, and Salvador de Madariaga, critic and essayist. There was also a renaissance in poetry with Antonio Machado and Juan Ramón Jimenez, who later won a Nobel Prize, being the most prominent.

Another generation of poets followed, making its mark in the 1920s and 1930s. The best known and most tragic figure was Federico García Lorca, who also wrote some memorable plays. He was executed in the early days of the Civil War by Nationalist forces in Granada, his home town where he thought he would be safe. His "crime" was that he supported the other side.

## MUSIC AND DANCE

Spain is not as well known for its music, apart from the folk art of flamenco, as it is for its painters and writers. But it has deep musical roots dating from the medieval period when Alfonso X and others produced a body of work, blending the influences of the European north with the Moorish south. The guitar began to emerge as an important instrument in the 16th century and a great deal of religious music was written during the Counter-Reformation.

In the 18th century, the Bourbon kings patronized composers and musicians and the Italians Domenico Scarlatti and Luigi Boccherini spent time at the Spanish court. During the Romantic period in the 19th century, Spain inspired many foreign composers including Ravel, Rimsky Korsakov, Bizet and Rossini as well as producing some of its own, notably Isaac Albéniz, Manuel de la Falla, and Joaquín

Turina. Their music was intensely Spanish and was evocative of the soul-searching that characterized the writers of the same period.

The present century has seen the emphasis in Spanish classical music change to world-class performers, although the composers Frederic Mompou and Joaquín Rodrigo have made their mark, with guitarists Andrés Segovia and Narciso Yepes, and the cellist, composer and conductor Pablo Casals. In opera, Spain has produced several international stars such as Victoria

de los Angeles, José Carreras, Montserrat Caballé and Placido Domingo.

A flamenco show in Seville. Spontaneous flamenco dancing and singing is largely a thing of the past but good performances can be seen in night clubs and theaters in most large Spanish cities.

# Madrid and Central Spain

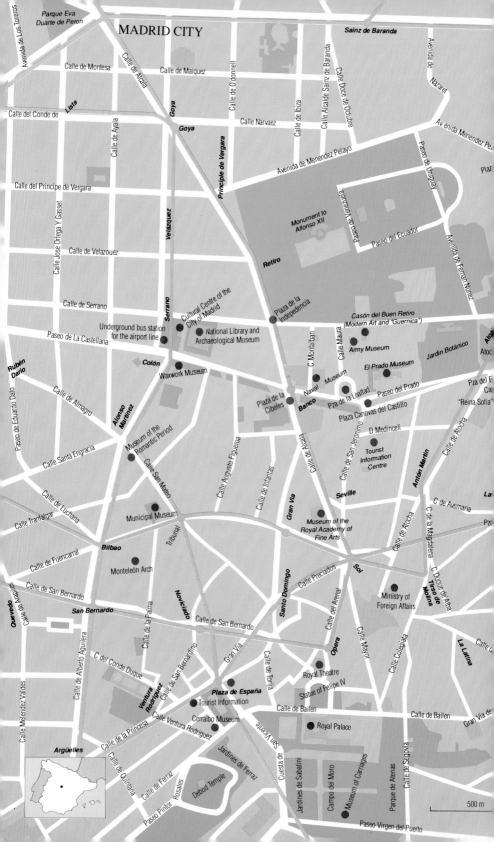

## MADRID

When King Philip II pointed his regal finger at the spot where he wanted Spain's new capital to be built in the mid-16th century, it made administrative sense; but it upset many of his courtiers who had no desire to leave the cosmopolitan delights of Toledo. His choice, however, turned out to be a boon to modern visitors. Madrid is in the center of Spain and there is no better place to launch your Spanish adventure. Apart from its own attractions, the capital is a perfect jumping off point for the rest of the country. And to make it simple, this is where most air-borne visitors enter the country anyway.

Madrid's drawbacks are undeniable but mercifully few. Once placid and leisurely-paced, the city has become bustling, congested and polluted. What hasn't changed is the climate — it can still be hotter than hades in summer and bitterly cold in winter — though late 20th-century airconditioning and central heating make a difference. Madrid does not have the visual impact of some other European capitals. There is still a frumpish, rather tired look about its predominantly 19th-century architecture. There is no easily recognized symbol, no equivalent of the Eifel Tower in Paris, the Houses of Parliament in London, or the Acropolis in Athens.

But Madrid's merits far outweigh its disadvantages and make it worthwhile spending a few days there before heading off in other directions. Most important is the human factor. Capital of a booming, modern and democratic Spain, Madrid is a brighter, more fashionable and more exciting place than it used to be. This is the best place in the country to eat, drink, and be merry. Madrileños, who never had any doubts that they lived in the center of the universe, have few rivals in knowing how to have a good time. They do this publicly — in the streets, the countless *tascas* (taverns) and bars, restaurants, cinemas, theaters, discos, nightclubs, and so on. And they do it late into the night, every day of the week. *La movida*—animation — is the name of the game in Madrid and it transforms the "plain Jane" appearance of the place into something quite different.

Another reason for allotting a few days to Madrid is its treasure trove of fine art. The **Prado Museum** houses one of the world's greatest collection of paintings, and there are other interesting museums dotted around the city. The city also provides a perfect base for day trips to Toledo, Ávila, El Escorial, and Segovia, all places well worth visiting.

When you've put these considerations together, the congestion, noise, and even the climate do not seem so bad. There are ways of circumventing the first, you grow used to

the din especially when you have a glass in your hand, and Madrid's climate has the advantage of being *dry*, regardless of how hot or cold it becomes. High above sea level (600 m or 2,000 ft), there are many lovely sparkling days with golden sunrises and crimson sunsets, days on which Madrid recalls its origins as a fresh-faced village on Castile's broad plateau.

## SEEING THE CITY

The capital, despite its recent growth, is still a relatively compact city, although the countryside can no longer be seen at the end of the streets as one travel writer claimed in the early 1960s. To get your bearings, focus on the **Paseo de la Castellana,** a broad boulevard that sweeps down through the city, bisecting it from north to south, and the **Calle Alcalá,** which cuts across it, west to east. Some

---

ABOVE: The Atocha Railroad Station.

rough compass points are **Estación de Atocha** (Atocha Railroad Station) in the south, the **Palacio Real** (Royal Palace) in the west, **Estadio Bernabéu** (Real Madrid's soccer stadium) in the north, and the **Plaza de Toros** (bullring) in the east.

The northern end of town is where modern, expanding Madrid is happening and where **Barajas Airport** lies. Lower down on the west side is **Old Madrid** (predominantly 17th and 18th centuries) with its winding streets and teeming humanity. On the east, there is the **Retiro Park,** laid out in the 17th century, and the orderly boulevards and the solid houses built for the 19th-century bourgeoisie. A useful point of reference is the **Plaza Cibeles** where the **Calle de Alcalá** crosses the **Castellana.** The traffic swirls around a lovely fountain here and past Madrid's main *correos* (post office), a confectioner's dream of a building that is unmistakable and, as such, an ideal meeting place if you don't know the town.

There are plenty of hotels in this lower segment, on or off the **Castellana,** so this is where you should establish your base. From here you can reach all the sightseeing landmarks in less than half an hour. Madrid has the virtue of a good all-round public transport system. Taxis are plentiful, inexpensive and driven by rational and usually polite people who are not under the illusion that they should have been grand prix drivers.

## PUBLIC TRANSPORT

The **Metro,** or subway system, is excellent: clean, safe, easily understood (lots of maps and clear directions) and frequent trains. You can buy tickets singly (Pts.125 or about $1.00), or in batches of ten (Pts.625 — just over $5.00), at automatic vending machines in the stations. Trains run from 6.00 AM until 1.30 AM every day of the week, including public holidays. The Metro covers the center of Madrid thoroughly and the rolling stock has been modernized, providing a comfort-

able and swift ride beneath the busy streets of the capital.

**Buses** are also available but have more complicated route patterns and are subject to the same delays of all surface transport.

A car is not necessary but if you have one for trips further afield and want to use it, you will find there are few formal parking restrictions. *Madrileños* park anywhere and everywhere, but you will probably be better off leaving the beast at the hotel. In any case, one of the major attractions of Madrid is the

theater of the streets. And the best way to enjoy that is on foot.

## THE MAJOR ATTRACTIONS

### PASEO DEL ARTE

Madrid has three major art museum. While the **Prado Museum** is in a class of its own, the doors have opened in two new art museums, each spectacular in its own way. These are the **Museo Centro de Arte Reína Sofía** and the **Museo Thyssen Bornemisza.** All three are within walking distance of each other in what is known as the "Paseo del Arte" or, more geometrically, the "Art Triangle".

ABOVE: Metro, Gran Vía. OPPOSITE: The Prado Museum.

## The Prado Museum

Let's start on the east side of the **Castellana** with the city's star turn, the Prado Museum. Most museums, palaces and other public buildings are closed on Mondays when everyone makes at least a token effort to recover from the weekend. Early morning and Spanish lunchtime (2 PM to 4 PM) are the best times to visit the Prado to avoid the crowds. The entrance is at the north end, close to the Ritz Hotel, and Neptune's Fountain on the Castellana. Opened in 1819, the museum's vast hoard

of paintings began as an exhibition of the royal collection but has been steadily augmented by purchases ever since.

Here you will not only see the masterpieces of Spain's three greatest painters (Velázquez, Goya and El Greco), but also works from the Flemish school (Breughel, Rubens, Hieronymus Bosch — "El Bosco" to Spaniards — and Memling), and Italian masters (Raphael, Boticelli, Tintoretto, and Titian). This embarrassment of riches is a little overwhelming, and if you have to be selective, concentrate on the Spaniards who, between them cover three centuries, and provide a visual panorama of Spain's eventful history and a not always flattering vision of their royal patrons. Velázquez is

wonderful, but for sheer power, Goya probably leads with his often idealized view of daily life in Madrid in the late 18th century, his dramatic depiction of rebellion against the French invader in the early 19th century, and his tormented "black" paintings that have a room of their own. If you like painting, the museum catalog is well worth buying.

### Museo Centro de Arte Reína Sofía

The **Reína Sofía**, at Paseo del Prado and Calle Santa Isabel, is Madrid's showcase of modern art, notably works by Picasso, Miró and Dali, that also encourages contemporary talent with a programme of exhibitions. Picasso's famous "Guernica", depicting the destruction wrought on the Basque town of that name by aerial bombardment during the Spanish Civil War, is now here, having moved from the **Casón del Buen Retiro** annexe of the Prado. The picture, finally divested of its bullet-proof glass protective screen, is superbly displayed with a fascinating collection of the artist's preliminary sketches and a video-tape documentary explaining the background to the event that inspired the painting.

### Museo Thyssen Bornemisza

Spain won a fierce international contest to become the permanent home of Baron Hans Heinrich Thyssen Bornemisza's remarkable collection of over seven hundred paintings. Appropriately, they are hung in a former palace — Palacio de Villahermosa — now Museo Thyssen Bornemisza, at Paseo del Prado and Calle San Jerónimo, next to the Palace Hotel. It also has a gift shop and cafeteria. The paintings cover the history of European art from the 13th century to the present and are helpfully arranged in chronological order with plenty of space and perfect light. Italian and German Renaissance, 17th century Dutch old masters, 19th century North American works, Impressionism, Cubism and even Pop Art are strongly featured in this marvelous and unique collection. If you want to spend a manageable and enjoyably instructive morning or afternoon looking at pictures in Madrid, the Thyssen collection is the way to go.

## RETIRO PARK

A stroll in the Retiro Park, conveniently at hand, might well be in order at this stage. Sunday is the best day to catch Madrid at ease, but the park is well worth it on any day, and in any season. There are many physical attractions: a lake where you can hire rowboats; a glass and delicate wrought-iron crystal palace for art and other cultural exhibitions, botanical and Japanese gardens, a rich variety of trees and flowering shrubs,

dressed in their Sunday-best; and down a shady avenue, you might see a clutch of jugglers practicing. A particularly pretty spot to rest is behind the **Palacio de Cristal** (Crystal Palace) where there is a pond with a fountain, the home of black and white swans, geese and ducks. All around are stately firs, cedars and graceful willows. Or, if you prefer to watch the slow moving stream of Madrileños, enjoying their Sunday *paseo,* there is no better way than sitting at a café by the lake, with a refreshing drink or a coffee at your side.

and plenty of open air cafés. (There are public toilets but they often seem to be closed, so if you plan to spend some time in the park, "go" before you enter.)

Empty, the park would be simply beautiful; full of Madrileños, it is fun too. Palm and tarot readers, sitting on stools in front of little cloth-covered tables, line the walkway near the lake; small sticks of licorice root ("the best cure for catarrh") are on sale; puppeteers put on shows for children

This area of Madrid has other, if lesser attractions, that include the **Army Museum (Museo del Ejército),** which has El Cid's sword on display; the **Naval Museum (Museo Naval)** with its first map showing the New World and its exquisite models of old sailing ships; the National Museum of Decorative Arts (**Museo de Artes Decorativas**), a showcase of Spanish interior design from the 15th to the 20th centuries; if you like Spanish tiles, don't miss the 18th-century tiled Valencian kitchen on the top floor; and the Archaeological Museum (**Museo Arquelogico**), which is on the right hand side going north up the **Castellana** (entrance from the **Calle Serrano**), and contains Spain's most complete collection of

PRECEEDING PAGES: Lake in the Retiro Park.
ABOVE LEFT: The Archaeological Museum.
ABOVE RIGHT: Knights in armor at the Royal Armory that shares a courtyard with the Palacio Real. OPPOSITE: Palacio de Cristal in the Retiro Park.

archaeological remains, including the famous fifth-century BC bust of the **Lady of Elche,** and a re-creation of the **Altamira Caves** and their prehistoric murals.

## OLD MADRID

Old Madrid is on the west side of the Castellana, and the best way to approach it is by walking up the **Alcalá** which leads you into the **Puerta del Sol,** the traditional center of the city and Spain. All distances are measured from the "Gateway of the Sun" which is, in fact, a bustling arc-shaped plaza where several roads meet. Not far away is the **Plaza Mayor,** a superbly proportioned cobbled square built in the early 17th century and sensibly closed to modern traffic. Its faded ochre walls are best seen in the setting sun, and on the eastern façade there are portraits of Spain's literary luminaries — Cervantes, Lope de Vega and Calderón, among others. You will find similar, though often less lovely, enclosed squares in the center of towns throughout Spain. The Plaza Mayor in Madrid is a place where people meet, eat, drink, and rest before making their next move on the old town.

A jumble of streets, squares, churches, markets, department stores, little shops, restaurants, cafés and bars, old Madrid is eminently walkable. Its rough boundaries are the **Palacio Real (Royal Palace)** in the west, the **Plaza de España** to the north, a few streets beyond the **Puerta del Sol** in the east, and the **Puerta de Toledo** to the south. This is where the Spanish equivalents of London's Cockneys live, work, and play. If the area is more than a little shabby, it is also real. The smarter folk and their habitat are elsewhere. It is most fun after the sun goes down. While you can eat well in plenty of atmospheric restaurants, the *tascas* and cervecerias (beer-halls), where you stand at the bar, drink and munch on *tapas*, the delightful and infinitely varied snacks that are a Spanish specialty, are the main attraction. In the old days, there used to be a lot of spontaneous flamenco singing, hand-clapping, and even dancing. This can still happen, but a more likely sight is a troupe

RIGHT: A panoramic view of Madrid.

of students in medieval doublet and hose, with mandolins and guitars singing folk songs and peddling cassettes of their own music.

## PALACIO REAL

Back on the sightseeing trail, the Palacio Real, is worth a visit. The most pleasant approach is down **Calle Arenal** from the **Puerta del Sol,** past the **Opera,** and into the **Plaza de Oriente,** a graceful, leafy square guarded by statues of Spanish kings with

worn stone faces. While the relatively austere Habsburgs were responsible for the Plaza Mayor, it took their grandiose successors, the Bourbons, to conceive and construct this vast palace in the 18th century. Philip V seemed to have had Versailles in mind when the old palace burned down and he had to replace it. Overlooking the park of the Campo del Moro, the palace has 2,800, repeat 2,800 rooms and a courtyard of gray limestone the size of a football field. Accordingly, a sampling, rather than the complete tour, is advisable. There is plenty to see and it is all incredibly lush: tapestries, lavishly decorated ceilings, silk brocaded curtains, priceless furniture, silverware, massive chandeliers, and a whole roomful

of gold clocks. The last king to live in the palace was Alfonso XIII, who went into exile in 1931. The present monarch, King Juan Carlos, resides in a much more modest palace in Madrid's suburbs, although the Royal Palace is sometimes used for state functions.

At the far end of the courtyard is the **Royal Armory.** Essentially one cavernous room, it is full of men in armor with huge lances, and heavy swords. So many of them are on horseback that you feel you have suddenly burst into a medieval encampment where the king's men are about to tilt at a Moorish army advancing across the plain. Pistols, muskets, swords, shields, lances, and a fascinating selection of cross-bows abound. There are diminutive princes — mere children — and even a dog in armor. All the artifacts, including the cloth banners, and the embroidered and tasseled quilts that cover the horses, are authentic and remarkably well-preserved. Everything is on a large-scale — horses, lances, swords, bows, etc — except the knights themselves who seem strangely frail by modern standards.

## OTHER WEST-SIDE SIGHTS

Other places of interest on this side of the **Castellana** include: the **Ayuntamiento (City Hall)** in the **Plaza de la Villa,** built in the mid-17th century; the **Mercado de San Miguel,** a busy and aromatic fresh produce market; the **Cortés,** or Spanish parliament, where as recently as 1981, a group of disaffected Civil Guards had the deputies diving under their seats in an attempted coup; the **Casa de Lope de Vega,** the restored 16th-century house of the playwright and poet; and the **Convento de las Descalzas Reales,** a richly decorated 17th-century convent that is now brimming with tapestries, paintings, furniture and religious artifacts. The **Plaza de España,** at the north end of the **Gran Vía,** is disappointing apart from its bronze statues of Don Quixote and his stout squire, Sancho Panza. But it is worth going to because the municipal tourist office is in the ground floor of the nearby **Torre de Madrid,** an ugly modern tower that is the tallest building in the city.

In the other direction, south of the Plaza Mayor, there is the famous **Rastro**, or flea market, which flourishes on Sundays and covers a rough triangle bounded by the **Paseo de Toledo,** the **Calle Ribera de Curtidores,** with the **Ronda de Toledo** as its base. There are huge crowds and an awful lot of junk, but it's fun to let yourself flow with the crowd — often you have no alternative—and soak up the scene. You can buy everything from a pince-nez to a pig-skin wallet, from a door knob to a German World War II helmet; you can also stop and play a

lined avenues, solid town houses and apartment buildings, and the comfortable, confident air of the bourgeoisie who have always lived here. In appearance and atmosphere it has much in common with the parts of Paris designed by Baron Haussmann during the same era.

The most exclusive shops are along the **Calle Serrano,** which runs north from the **Puerta de Alcalá,** and is Madrid's equivalent of London's Bond Street or New York's Fifth Avenue. Farther north up, the **Castellana** is the city's most modern section where

game of bingo if the mood takes you. Watch your purse, pockets and camera, and be wary of taking photographs. For reasons best known to themselves but not hard to guess, many of the denizens of the **Rastro** do not welcome the recording of their likeness.

## SALAMANCA DISTRICT

The swanky section of Madrid, where you find the best shops, many of the foreign embassies and consulates, and some of the most popular restaurants, is back across the **Castellana,** north of the Retiro Park. This is the **Salamanca** district. Laid out in a grid pattern in the 19th century, it has broad tree-

the major banks, offices, international hotels, and newest residential buildings are located. Some of the architecture is interesting, and there is sleekness about this part of Madrid which contrasts with the older parts of the city, and reflects Spain's new prosperity, entrepreneurial spirit and glitter.

A few random thoughts before leaving Madrid. Curiously, the city has no classic cathedral, an omission that Spain's other major towns redress in no uncertain fashion. But it has lovely fountains almost wherever you turn; beautifully-lit, they are particularly spectacular and romantic at night.

OPPOSITE: Plaza de Oriente. ABOVE :Puerta de Alcalá — Madrid's equivalent of London's Bond Street or New York's Fifth Avenue.

Finally, Madrid offers the best eating in Spain, followed closely by Barcelona; splurge here and tighten your belt later.

## TOURIST INFORMATION

### Key Telephone Numbers
Provincial Area Code    (1)
From within Spain    (91)
**Tourist Offices:**
Plaza Mayor, N°3. (/FAX 366-4874 or 366-5477. Plaza España, Edificio Torre de Madrid. ( 541-2325.

Duque de Medinaceli, N° 2. ( 429-4995 and 429-4487 FAX 429-0909.
Barajas Airport tourist office ( 305-8656.
Chamartin Railway Station tourist office ( 315-9976.
**Barajas Airport** ( 305-8345/6/7.
**Iberia Airlines** ( 329-5767.
**Chamartin Railway Station** ( 323-2127.
**Atocha Railway Station** ( 328-9020; the AVE (high speed train), ( 534-0505.
**Radio Taxi,** ( 547-8200.

#### HOTELS
*Deluxe* means a night's lodging costs Pts.28,000 and above; *Expensive* Pts.18,000 to Pts.28,000; *moderate:* Pts.8,000 to Pts.18,000; and *inexpensive:* Pts.4,000 to Pts.8,000.

#### Deluxe
**Miguel Angel** ( 442-0022 FAX 442-5320, Calle Miguel Angel, N° 31, is a good international hotel in the newer part of the city off the Castellana.
**Ritz** ( 521-2857 FAX 532-8776, Plaza de la Lealtad, N° 5. Most palatial and elegant of Madrid's older hotels, perfectly situated near the Prado Museum. Nice garden for summer dining. Old world-style extends to obligatory jackets and ties for even the most casual male visitors.
**Villa Magna** ( 576-7500 FAX 575-9504, at the New Paseo de Castellana, N° 22, is a super-luxury hotel.

#### Expensive
**Palace** ( 429-7551 FAX 429-8266, Plaza de las Cortés, N° 7, like the Ritz, is a grand hotel, built in the *belle époque* but more reasonably priced. It is recently renovated and has fine public rooms, ultra-modern bedrooms and sophisticated business facilities.
**Gran Hotel Velázquez** ( 5752-2800 FAX 575-2809, is a good functional hotel in the heart of the Salamanca district.

#### Moderate
**Principe Pío** ( 547-8000 FAX 541-1117, at Cuesta de San Vicente, N° 14, has a good location near the Royal Palace with fine views.
**N.H. Balboa** ( 563-0324 FAX 562-6980, Calle Nuñez de Balboa, N° 112, is another Salamanca hotel with very new, comfortable and excellent service.
**Tryp Gran Vía** ( 522-1121 FAX 521-2424, at Gran Vía, N° 25, is centrally located; old-fashioned but good value.

#### Inexpensive
**Alcázar Regis** ( 247-9317, Gran Vía, N° 61.
**Hostal Delfina** ( 522-2151, Gran Vía, N° 12.
**Europa** ( 521-2900 FAX 521-4696, Calle Carmen, N° 4.
**Mora** ( 420-1569 FAX 420-0564, Paseo del Prado, N° 32.

#### RESTAURANTS
*Expensive* represents meals costing Pts.8,000 and above; *moderate:* Pts.3,000 to Pts.8,000, and *inexpensive:* Pts.1,000 to Pts.3,000.

#### Expensive
**El Bodegón** ( 562-8844, Calle Pinar, N° 15, serves New wave Basque food based on solid reputation in a different setting; try the special menu that provides small portions of many creative dishes.

**Jockey** ( 319-1003, Calle Amador de los Ríos, Nº 6, is one of Madrid's best known and consistently good restaurants with an excellent wine list. It is on the formal side — tie needed.

**La Dorada** ( 570-2004, Calle Orense, Nº 64, serves Andalusian cuisine concentrating on fish. It has pretty decor and is very fashionable and always crowded; the owner has two more restaurants of the same name, one in Seville and the other in Barcelona.

**Zalacaín** ( 561-4840, Calle Alvarez de Baena, Nº4. Widely believed to be Spain's top

**Cabo Mayor** ( 350-8776, on Calle Juan Ramón Jiménez, Nº 37, is an elegant predominantly fish restaurant in the modern part of city; its bread and desserts are homemade.

**Café Gijón** ( 531-0548, at Paseo de Recoletos, has wood paneled walls and Art Nouveau lamps and manages to preserve the turn-of-the-century atmosphere of this famous literary café-restaurant. It's a bit passé as an intellectual watering hole, but is cosy in winter and has tables outside on the Castellana in summer.

restaurant with creative haute cuisine, elegant surroundings and impeccable service. Pricey, but worth a splash or an expense account.

*Moderate*

**Alkalde** ( 576-3359, Calle Juan Jorge, Nº 10, is a rustic-looking Basque restaurant in the Salamanca district and has homely tasty cooking.

**Botín** ( 366-4217, Calle Cuchilleros, Nº 17, is the oldest restaurant in the world according to the Guinness Book of Records (opened in 1725). And is Hemingway's and now American tourists' favorite with its good Castilian food, especially roasts and game, and efficient service.

**La Fuencisla** ( 521-6186, Calle San Mateo, Nº4, is a gourmet's favorite; thoughtful cooking and wide choice of wines.

**La Trainera** ( 576-8035, Calle Lagasca, Nº 60, is a great fish restaurants in unassuming setting. Try the fish soup and then *merluza* (hake) which is lightly steamed then fried; a good wine to accompany this is Fontousal, a light dry white wine from León.

**Viuda de Vacas** ( 366-5847, Calle Cava Alta, Nº 23, is a family-run restaurant near the Rastro (flea-market). It is a great place for weekend lunches, favored by artists, writers

OPPOSITE: Madrid's great "Rastro" (flea market) on a Sunday morning. LEFT: Museo de Jamón. RIGHT: The salon of the Palace Hotel, one of the city's refurbished *belle époque* hotels.

and film stars. It does not take reservations, so come on time — at 2 PM.

*Inexpensive*

There is an enormous range of inexpensive eating places in Madrid, including some popular restaurants, cafés, and *tapas* bars. The **Museo de Jamón** is a well-run and stylish chain, dispensing Spanish "fast-food". They are instantly recognizeable from the scores of hams hanging from the ceilings. A great place for a sandwich or a plate of ham or cheese, with pungent fresh bread, helped

down with a glass of wine or draught beer. Each Museo has a well-stocked delicatessen counter for take-out purchases.

## NIGHTLIFE

As befitting a major European capital, Madrid has a generous share of night spots offering traditional and modern entertainment.

There are over 250 discotheques is the city and if you want to sample a few of the classier ones, try: **Archy** at Calle Marqués de Riscal (corner of Calle Fortuny), a lively place with a restaurant as well; or, **Pacha**, Calle Barcelo, N° 10; or, **Joy**, Calle Arenal.

Flamenco can be found in several places but two of the best places are: **La Peña Flamenca La Carcelera**, Calle Monteleon, N° 10; and **Café de Chinitas** ( 548-5135, at Calle Torija, N° 7.

If you want a classic cocktail to fuel — or re-fuel — the evening, drop into **Bar Chicote** ( 462-3875, Gran Vía, N° 12. Live jazz can be

heard — very inexpensively — nearly every night at the **Café Central** ( 369-4143, Plaza del Angel, N° 10. For classical chamber music, again at low cost, go to the elegant **Salon del Prado** ( 429-3361, Calle Prado, N° 4.

## AROUND MADRID

Around Madrid, all within easy reach by road, are five places no one visiting Spain should miss. These are **Toledo,** and in around the **Sierra Guadarrama** mountains, **El Escorial, Ávila,** and **Segovia**. Let's start with Spain's former capital, Toledo, which is 70 km (44 miles) from Madrid. You head south on the N-401, a rather dreary and congested road, that passes through a series of small industrial towns. But within an hour or so, you will go round a curve and see roughly what El Greco gazed at when he painted this unique town almost four hundred years ago. Stacked up on a hill and dominated by its lofty **Alcázar,** this fortress-city is almost wholly encircled by the River Tagus.

## TOLEDO

Toledo was originally a Roman town and later became the capital of the Visigoths. The Moors captured it in the eighth century and turned it into their northern capital. Under Moorish rule, Toledo established itself as a center of learning and a crossroads of cultures. The city became renowned in the Mediterranean world for its school of translators, its philosophers, alchemists and mathematicians, and its population grew to 200,000, more than three times what it is today. Moorish rule came to an end when King Alfonso VI of Castile and El Cid conquered the city in 1085.

Toledo became the capital of Christian Spain but continued to show tolerance to the country's largest Jewish population and its Moorish residents. During the next three centuries, the city continued to flower, a wonderfully cosmopolitan center where Christian, Jew and Muslim lived in harmony, and where politicians, soldiers, painters, writers, poets, priests and savants gathered.

It was perhaps no accident that Alfonso the Wise, Spain's most erudite monarch, was born in Toledo. All that ended, over four centuries ago, with the expulsion of the Jews and the Moors, the introduction of the Inquisition, and Philip II's decision to make Madrid the new capital of his dominions. Toledo retained some religious importance as the seat of the Spanish primate, but its only short-lived political reappearance was during the Civil War when the Alcázar underwent an epic siege. The town's famous silk and steel industries disappeared to be replaced much later by marzipan and mass tourism. Toledo became a museum city long before museums were invented.

Today, it lives on, and for tourism. This carries with it obvious drawbacks: the rows of shops purveying almost identical goods, the phalanx of tourist buses outside the city gates, the endless stream of visitors, and so on. But the physical unity of the town, and its great wealth of individual attractions make it all worthwhile. Toledo is a splendidly-preserved microcosm of the Spanish experience, and the whole town is a national monument.

## SEEING THE CITY

It's not a bad idea to begin by inspecting it at a distance by driving around the ring road on the outer bank of the Tagus. There is a particularly good view from the **Parador Conde de Orgaz**, a parador on a bluff high above the river. This is also a good place to stay, if you are thinking of spending a night in Toledo. After that the **Alcázar** and its battlements afford the reverse view — a panoramic vista of the unspoilt if bleak Castile-La Mancha countryside.

The present Alcázar (from "castle" in Arabic) was rebuilt after the pounding it received in the Civil War. The site of a fortress since Roman times, it was destroyed and rebuilt on several occasions through the centuries. There is not a lot to see inside: a courtyard, a cloister, some military memorabilia. But for Civil War buffs, the high point will probably be the bullet and shrapnel-riddled headquarters of Colonel José Moscardó, a fifty-eight year old infantry officer who commanded the anti-Republican forces in the early chaotic and bloody stages of the war.

When General Franco and other officers launched their rebellion in Spanish Morocco in July 1936, Colonel Moscardó gathered about twelve hundred soldiers and civil guards, plus five hundred or so civilians who included many women and children, into the Alcázar. The siege lasted ten weeks during which the Alcázar was almost completely demolished by Republican artillery, mines and aerial bombing. The defend-

ers, their numbers reduced by death in battle, disease and starvation, hung on grimly until a column of Franco's Army of Africa relieved them in September. The assault troops, ironically, were Moors, reconquering the city that their ancestors had lost over nine centuries earlier. The most famous incident, according to the winning side's chroniclers, occurred in the first week of the siege when an officer of the attacking forces called Moscardó on the telephone. The ensuing conversation is now displayed in several languages on the walls of Moscardó's office. In short, the Republicans said that if Moscardó did not surrender the Alcázar immediately, they would shoot his sixteen year old son. The boy was put on the telephone and spoke to his father.

"What's happening, son?" Moscardó asked.

OPPOSITE: Student minstrels singing for their supper in a tavern in old Madrid. ABOVE: Synagogue of Santa Maríe le Plenea, Toledo. OVERLEAF: View of Toledo's Alcázar and the city from the terrace of the parador.

"They say they're going to shoot me if you don't surrender."

"Then commend your soul to God, shout "Viva España, Viva Cristo Rey" (God the King), and die like a hero," his father replied. The siege continued and the boy was shot, according to the legend. Anti-Franco accounts, however, say the boy was not killed, although an older brother did die in another war zone; and the incident if not actually apocryphal was over-dramatized and of little significance in the story of the siege. True or untrue, Moscardó went on to

lead a heroic resistance and became famous for his laconic reports during that long hot summer as the Alcázar crashed into ruins around him and his dwindling band of followers. *"Sin novedad en el Alcázar,"* ("All quiet in the Alcázar") the aging colonel would report regardless of what was happening.

Toledo is a city of legends but it is the artifacts that people come to see and there are so many of those that it is hard to be selective. Fortunately, everything is within walking distance, and the narrow, winding streets are a delight to stroll in. In some of them you can actually stand in the middle and touch the buildings on either side simultaneously with outstretched arms.

## ECCLESIATICAL TREATS

The **cathedral** is the focal point and is much more impressive inside than out. Begun in

ABOVE: Calle de los Reyes Católicos, Toledo.

13th century it was finished in the late fifteenth. Essentially Gothic, it has Mudéjar, Mozarabic, Baroque and Rococo flourishes, and the second longest nave in Spain (after the cathedral in Seville.) Under its soaring arches and illuminated through the stained glass of over eight hundred windows, there is a rich assortment of wrought-iron grilles, paintings, sculpture, carved wood and carved stone. For Jan Morris, in her travel book on Spain, the cathedral was "a great hall of triumph, a victory paean for the Christian culture … nothing in Christendom, I suspect, better expresses the militancy of the Church than the *retablo* or reredos of Toledo, which rises in serried magnificence from the high altar to the roof." (*Spain*, p.135. Penguin Books, 1982.)

Another ecclesiastical treat is the **Church of San Juan de los Reyes** and its lovely cloister, built in the 15th century by **Juan Guas** who was also the principal architect for the cathedral. The church was originally intended to be the last resting place of Ferdinand and Isabella, the Catholic Monarchs, but after the conquest of Granada they decided to be buried in that city.

## THE JEWISH QUARTER

Not far from the church is the **Judería**, Toledo's Jewish quarter. Only two of the city's original dozen synagogues survive, and these are **Santa María la Blanca**, and **El Tránsito**, with its **Sephardic** museum, both beautiful and poignant reminders of Spain's Jewish heritage. Also close by is the **Casa del Greco**, a restored 16th-century house. The painter never actually lived there, although he lived in the neighborhood, but the idea was to recreate the kind of dwelling he inhabited during his decades in the city. The house, carefully restored, has a number of El Greco's paintings, including a room devoted to portraits of the Apostles. But the picture that many think is his greatest, *The Burial of the Count of Orgaz*, can be seen in the **Church of Santo Tomé**.

## CRISTO DE LA LUZ

Toledo's Moorish past is exquisitely evoked by the **Church** of **Cristo de la Luz** which is really a mosque and was built in the late 10th century on the site of a Visigothic church. It is very small but has classical horseshoe-shaped arches and airy vaulting, and is one of Spain's oldest and best preserved Moorish structures. There is a legend that when King Alfonso VI and El Cid entered Toledo at the head of their victorious troops, the king's horse stopped dead in its tracks in front of this mosque and refused to move. The king ordered the mosque to be searched and, hidden in the walls, they found a crucifix and an oil lamp dating from the time when the building had been a Visigothic church. The lamp, the story goes, was still burning.

Toledo's two oldest bridges, the 13th-century **Alcantará** bridge and the 14th-century **San Martin** bridge, are worth walking across. They both provide good views and a sense of the physical power of the city in medieval times. There are an abundance of other churches, convents, museums and architectural riches.

## TOLEDO'S FESTIVALS

There are also three festivals of note every year: Corpus Christi, a week of processions, bullfights and concerts during during which the streets are strewn with flowers and herbs; Holy Week with more somber religious processions; and a week-long musical festival in October.

## USEFUL INFORMATION

Some tips for the Toledo visitor. Wear good shoes; there is little room to drive or space to park. Try and stay overnight. Most people arrive with the crowds and leave with them before nightfall, thus only seeing the place awash with humanity. The town takes on a much more natural, relaxed feeling after sunset. Also, Toledo is superbly illuminated at night. There is a large terrace at the **parador** where the nocturnal panorama can be supplemented by a drink or dinner. Finally, a word of warning. All photography, not just with a flash, is banned inside public buildings in Toledo for not clearly understandable reasons. Constant flash photography can harm delicate paintings and mu-rals; ordinary snap-shots, however, present no such threat. But there it is.

## HOTELS AND RESTAURANTS

In Toledo, the **Parador Conde de Orgaz** ( 22-18-50, Calle Cerro del Emperador, is situated outside the town with an unparalleled view of it. The parador is in the expensive category of lodgings, and rooms with a direct view over Toledo cost more than those less scenically endowed. If you prefer to reside inside the town, there are several hotels in the moderate price range that put you comfortably within walking distance of the city's treasures. These include the **Carlos V** ( 22-21-00, Calle Trastemaral; the **Cardenal** ( 22-49-00, Paseo de Recaredo, N° 24; the **Alfonso VI** ( 22-26-00, Calle General Moscardó, N° 2; and the **María Cristina** ( 21-26-50, Calle Marqués de Mendigorria, N° 1. There is a good selection of restaurants, with some of the best in the hotels, notably the **parador,** the **Cardenal** and the **María Cristina** (El Abside Restaurant which specializes in Arab and Jewish dishes). There is also the **Asador Adolfo** ( 22-73-21, Calle La Granada, N° 6, located in a medieval house, and the **Hierbabuena** ( 22-34-63, Calle Cristo de la Luz, N° 9 . Toledo is well-known for its partridge (excellent) and marzipan (not so good).

## SIERRA GUADARRAMA

If Madrid is the heart of Spain, then the Sierra Guadarrama, a range of granitic, pine-covered mountains to the north-west of the city, is its lungs. In an hour or so, you can reach the hills where skiing (at **Navacerrada** and **Cotos**), hiking, fishing, hunting, and crystalline mountain air draw Madrileños and countless others. There are also four major sightseeing attractions in or around this area: **El Escorial**, **Valle de los Caídos** (**Valley of the Fallen**), **Ávila**, and **Segovia**.

## EL ESCORIAL

The **Monastery of San Lorenzo de El Escorial** — it's full title — was Philip II's monument to god, to Spain, to his family, and to himself. It is part palace, part monastery, part pantheon, part museum, and wholly astonishing. Why Philip dedicated such an undertaking to Saint Lawrence (*San Lorenzo*), a relatively obscure religious figure, is not clear. One theory is that it was to celebrate a Spanish victory in France that fell on the saint's feast day. Another is that Philip wanted to give Saint Lawrence his due for allegedly bringing the Holy Grail to Spain. There is also a belief that the rectangular plan of the buildings and courtyards depicts the gridiron upon which the Romans roasted the saint alive.

The derivation of the rest of the name is much more mundane. There was, apparently, a mine in the area, and an escorial is a mine-tailing. In any case, once Philip's orders were issued, his architects and builders did not lose any time. Juan Bautista of Toledo, the first architect, began work in 1563 but died four years later. Construction continued under the direction of his assistant, Juan de Herrera, and was completed in 1584.

Approaching the monastery from Madrid (55 km or 34 miles distant on the C-600 road), you see it from a long way off in the foothills of the Sierra Guadarrama, gray, somber and majestic. It completely dominates the small town of **San Lorenzo de El Escorial** that has grown up in its shadow. Another good view, looking back down on its immense proportions, is from a branch off the road that goes on to **Ávila.** This is where Philip is said to have watched his dream take shape and is known as **La Silla del Rey** (The King's Chair.) El Escorial's impact, like its origins, evokes a variety of conflicting interpretations. The writers of one recent travel guide to Spain had this reaction. "As huge as it is, there's nothing gloomy or menacing about the Escorial. Its clean lines and soft gray granite combine for an effect that is tranquil and airy both inside and out. Everything is remarkably clean, as if dust and age had been banished by royal decree; somehow the Escorial looks as bright and new as the day it was completed." (Cadogan Guides: *Spain*, p. 332.)

The Gothic cathedral in Segovia with the Sierra Guadarrama in the background.

This writer had a very different reaction. The monastery seemed cold, gloomy, and forbidding, depicting the Spanish taste for combining the grandiose and the austere in its most extreme form. Yet there is serenity in the setting, mysticism as well as mystery in the concept, and some lovely surprises inside those fortress-like walls.

You enter on the north side and start with the area Philip considered the least important, the palace quarters. When the House of Bourbon succeeded the Habsburgs on the Spanish throne at the begin-

ning of the 18th century, they were appalled at the bleakness of the place, and spent much time and treasure brightening up the interior. The result was room after room of gorgeous tapestries, marble floors, crystal chandeliers, painted ceilings, gilded window frames and shutters, gold clocks, huge gilt-encrusted mirrors, and sumptuous furniture. The tapestries are not only in excellent condition despite their age, but they also provide a vivid panorama of 18th century life. There are old men playing *boules* or cards, young boys practicing with the matador's cape and a pair of horns on a wicker

ABOVE: Monastery of San Lorenzo de El Escorial built by King Philip II in the 16th century.
OPPOSITE: The king's library in the Escorial.

frame, and bucolic binges in which a reveler, who has had more than he can handle, gets rid of it — all exquisitely woven in rich colors.

The contrast with the Habsburg apartments where Philip lived and finally died in ulcerous agony, is striking, and says a lot about the tastes and state of mind of this Spanish pharaoh. The tapestries cede to plain, white painted walls, the marble floors turn to wooden parquet or gray flagstones, and the animated scenes are replaced by stern religious paintings. Philip's cell-like bedroom, with its four-poster bed, and study are there, and so are the tiny fireplaces that barely took the chill out of the air during the cold, dank winter months. This is where the creator and the lord of the Escorial died in 1598, at the age of 71.

The church is approached across the **Patio de los Reyes**, the monastery's largest courtyard, over which a row of Old Testament kings, carved in stone, glower down. **Juan Bautista**, the architect, was a pupil of Michaelangelo, and the size and the proportions of the Escorial's church genuflect to St. Peter's in Rome. Inside, the centerpiece is the *retablo*, a soaring and richly decorated panoply that is flanked by sculpted figures of the Emperor Charles V (Philip II's father), and Philip himself, accompanied by three of his four wives. (Mary Tudor, the English one, is absent.)

Beneath the church is the royal mausoleum. You descend a spiral staircase and enter a circular chamber. The walls are made of black and pink marble, there is a lot of gilt around, and light is provided by a centrally-hung chandelier. Stacked on shelves around the walls are marble sarcophagi. In all but three lie the remains of nearly every Spanish king who has reigned since the Escorial was built. Queens, princes, and princesses are also accommodated, but there is a traditional waiting period before a royal corpse is interred in the main chamber. On the way to the library and museum, you will pass through the cloister that is also known as the **Hall of the Battles.** Along one wall there is a vast fresco depicting the battle of Higueruela in 1431 where King Juan II defeated the Moors of Granada. The **Library** is a lovely, spacious, well-lit room with

colorful frescoes on the ceiling illustrating the liberal arts and sciences as they were recognized in the 16th century. Philip was a book-worm and bibliophile. There are over 40,000 volumes in his collection and many of the most beautiful illustrated manuscripts are on display. Philip is also still there, in one of his best portraits, gazing down at his books and wearing that familiar black stove-pipe hat.

The **Museum** is really an art gallery and contains paintings by El Greco, Velázquez, Ribera, and Zubarán, by Titian and Tintoretto, and a whole room of stunning canvases by Hieronymus Bosch, including his famous "Creation." (His "Garden of Earthly Delights" is in Philip's bedroom.)

There is one Bosch painting, showing Christ surrounded by a crowd with crafty and knowing expressions on their faces, that effortlessly spans the five centuries since it

was painted, and recalls the satirical film, *The Life of Brian.*

There is more to see, but this should whet the appetite of most travelers. You can take photographs wherever you wish, without a flash. Beware Mondays and public holidays when the Escorial is closed; and plan to spend at least half a day here. As the *Guide Michelin* says of a good restaurant, the Escorial is well worth the detour.

## VALLE DE LOS CAIDOS

Not far from the Escorial, on the road to Guadarrama, there is another monument built by a more modern Spanish leader with similar religious, political and personal motives in mind. This is the **Valle de los Caídos** (the Valley of the Fallen), the brainchild of General Francisco Franco, and built by prisoners from the defeated Republican side in the 1936–39 Civil War. The monument is ostensibly for all those who fell in that bitter struggle, but most Spaniards think of it as Franco's paean to the fascist cause. The dictator is buried here, and whatever you think of the symbolism, it is a spectacular if bizarre edifice in a pretty mountain setting.

To reach it, you go up a long fir tree-lined drive to a monastery (with a hostel for guests), a gigantic granite cross 125 m (410 ft) high, and a basilica buried deep in the rocky hillside. The nave-like tunnel that leads into

## ÁVILA

If you would like to see how most Spanish towns looked in the Middle Ages, take the road to Ávila, a little over an hour's drive on the N-501 from Madrid. The city is totally encircled by crenellated walls and towers of gray granite, and all the modern buildings and factories are outside this stone perimeter. Even today, it's not hard to imagine heavily-armored Castilian knights riding out of the gates with a flourish of trumpets.

the basilica is 260 m (830 ft) long. Lamps high up on the walls, thrust out at an angle, illuminate the tunnel, avenging angels with long swords, large billowing tapestries, and shadowy side chapels. The overall impression is a scene from the *Lord of the Rings*.

The basilica is less mythic and pretentious. Under flagstones, close to the altar, lie the bodies of Franco and José Antonio Primo de Rivera, the founder of the Falange Party, who was murdered by the Republicans early in the war.

The best view, from a distance, is approaching Ávila from Salamanca; a good spot to pause and gaze is at a stone cross, opposite a gas station, just before you reach your destination. From there you can get a sense of the frontier fortress town that Ávila was from Roman times. The medieval walls were built on Roman foundations in the 11th century, after the city was captured from the Moors by Alfonso VI of Castile. There are 88 turrets and nine gates in the walls that stretch for 2.4 km (1.5 miles) around the city. A closer look can be had by simply walking around the perimeter, or by strolling along the top of the walls. The access point is from the garden of the **Parador Raimundo de Borgoña**, inside the town

ABOVE: The medieval walls and battlements of Ávila.

on the northwest side. Ávila is a place of climactic and historic extremes. The highest city in Spain (1,131 m, or 3,710 ft, above sea level), it is broiling hot in summer and ferociously cold in winter. Historically, it is famous for militarism and mysticism: the first associated with its strategic position and its fighting men, and the second with Saint Theresa of Ávila.

There is no mistaking the military nature of the city; even the apse of the cathedral is part of the city walls with the dual function of a place of prayer and a defensive tower. Saint Theresa was a reformist Carmelite nun and a mystic who was born in Ávila in the early 16th century. She came from a wealthy family of Jewish converts but spent much of her life traveling around Spain urging religious orders to return to their vows of poverty and service. She died in 1582, leaving behind her a body of religious writing that earned her the papal title of "Doctor of the Church."

Her memory is now the center of the tourist trade in Ávila, and the local nuns make a rather unpleasant confectionery out of candied egg-yolks (*Yemas de Santa Teresa*) in her honor. Apart from the battlements and the aura of Saint Theresa, there is not much to draw a visitor there. Jan Morris called Ávila "a withered kernel within in a nut," but since it is on the main Madrid-Salamanca road it is conveniently positioned for a brief visit.

## HOTELS AND RESTAURANTS

Ávila has two hotels in the up-market category, the **Palacio de Valderrábanos** ( 21-10-23, Plaza de la Catedral, Nº 9; and the **Parador Raimundo de Borgoña** ( 21-13-40, Calle Marqués de Canales y Chozas, Nº 16. The most renowned restaurant is the **Mesón del Rastro** ( 21-12-18, at the Plaza del Rastro, Nº 1, which serves local specialties such as beans with sausage, game and other fortifying Castilian dishes.

## SEGOVIA

Moving in a northeasterly direction in the circle of easily accessible places from Ma-

drid, Segovia is more mellow and interesting than Ávila, less formal and self-conscious than Toledo. It is in truth a little shabby, but catch its tawny profile in the evening light as the sun sets over the Castilian *meseta,* and it will take your breath — and perhaps your heart — away. Three features distinguish it: the **Roman Aqueduct,** the **cathedral**, and the **Alcázar;** but the whole city, secure and serene on its lofty hilltop, and clothed in a warm limestone, has a physical and human quality that set it apart. It is a favorite spot for

lovers, and for Madrid's literary and film crowd.

The Roman emperor Trajan ordered the building of the **aqueduct** in the second century AD. This monumental piece of plumbing still performs its almost 2,000-year-old function of bringing water into the city from a river several miles away. Its ancient granite columns and arches, laid without mortar, soar over the outskirts of the old city, and the lead-lined water duct that they support are in remarkably good shape. For those who like figures, it has 167 arches, is 728 m (2,388 ft) long, and at

Segovia's heavily-turreted Alcázar.

129 m (423 ft) high is the tallest surviving Roman aqueduct.

The Gothic **cathedral,** the last of its kind to be built in Spain, replaced an early structure which was destroyed in the populist revolt against the monarchy led by Juan Bravo, a Segovian who has a statue honoring him not far from the cathedral. Built by the architect of Salamanca's cathedral, Segovia's has a lighter, more austere feeling. There is a cloister attached that belonged to the original cathedral.

The **Alcázar** rears upward from a rocky promontory on the western edge of the city where two small rivers meet and act as a natural moat. Built as a fortress, and later a royal palace for the monarchs of Castile, it fell out of history — much like Segovia itself — until 1862 when a group of discontented military cadets burnt it down, apparently as a way of making their point that it was time to be transferred to Madrid. It was re-built and festooned with lots of turrets so that it looks more Bavarian than Spanish. However, it is full of the delightful, if predictable artifacts of Castile's golden age: armor, heavy oak furniture, swords, muskets and cannon, tapestries and heraldic banners. There is a dizzying view from the topmost tower, a hard spiraling climb but worth the effort.

## HOTELS AND RESTAURANTS

Segovia, like Toledo, has a parador (**Parador de Segovia** ( 44-37-37, Carretera de Valladolid), a modern building outside the city's walls. If you would like to be in town, **Los Linajes** ( 46-04-75, at Calle Doctor Velasco, Nº 9, is the prettiest location. The hotel is built into the city's northern wall and has a terraced garden. Both hotels are in the upper range of the moderate category. Segovia has a reputation for good food, particularly in winter when the roast suckling pig (*cochinillo*), lamb, beef, and game are at their best. The most famous restaurant is **Mesón de Cándido** ( 42-59-11, Plaza Azoguejo, Nº 5, a picturesque spot that has been attracting the famous — and not so famous — for over half a century. Other good places to eat, at similar middle-range prices to those found in Cándido's, include **Mesón José María** ( 43-44-84, Calle Cronista Lecea, Nº 11; **Mesón Duque** ( 43-05-37, Calle Cervantes, Nº 12; and **Casa Amado** ( 43-20-77, Calle Fernandez Ladreda, Nº 9.

## SEGOVIA TO MADRID

There are two ways back to Madrid by road, and each offers an attraction. Twenty minutes out of Segovia on the N-601 brings you to the village of **San Ildefonso de la Granja** where Philip V, the first Bourbon to ascend the Spanish throne, built a royal palace called **La Granja** (the "Farm.") The name was deceptive. Philip and his successors had an eighteenth sense of scale and style that they indulged freely. Their French ancestors, especially Louis XIV, the "Sun King," seemed to be their principal inspiration. The gardens, on the slopes of the Sierra Guadarrama, are particularly lavish and noted for their fountains.

The other route, along the N-603, takes you close to the **Riofrio Royal Hunting Lodge**, built by Philip V's widow, Isabella de Farnese. This is an Italianate Baroque palace with a hunting museum full of stuffed trophies from the chase: a huntsman's — and a taxidermist's — delight. For gentler nature lovers, there is an elegant park populated by living deer that have no fear of ending up on the hunting lodge's walls.

Continuing the circuit around Madrid, there are some other places of interest. To the east, along the N-11, there is **Alcalá de Henares**, which is the site of Spain's leading university in the 16th century, and the birthplace of **Miguel de Cervantes**, author of Don Quixote. Then there is **Chinchón**, to the southeast along the N-III, a picturesque country town with a pretty main square **(Plaza Mayor)**, and a popular bolt hole for Madrileños at weekends and on holidays.

Due south, on the N-IV, lies **Aranjuez**, a spacious and leisurely-paced town on the banks of the Tagus that was chosen by Philip V to be his Versailles. The palace does not make it, but the gardens are superbly laid out and are well maintained. With its broad plane tree-lined avenues, Aranjuez has a French feel to it. That impression, however, vanishes if you should ever hear the haunting strains of Joaquín Rodrigo's Concierto de Aranjuez; nothing could be more Spanish.

## LONGER EXCURSIONS

A broader sweep from the capital encompasses three quintessentially Spanish regions that most travelers will want to sample however fleetingly. These are the lower part of **Old Castile**, northwest of Madrid; **Extremadura** to the southwest; and **La Mancha** which lies in a southeasterly direction. Moving out beyond Ávila and Segovia, the traveler penetrates the historic core of Spain where the Spanish language, which is still known as *Castellano*, has its roots, and where the kings of Castile began their drive for conquest and unity in the peninsula. There are several interesting towns that give life and character to the Castilian *meseta*, that great interior plateau whose monotony is atoned for by its fecundity and pastoral beauty. The most notable in this outer arc around Madrid are **Valladolid** and **Salamanca**, but there are smaller ones, like **Zamora**, that have appeal. (See NORTHERN SPAIN for the more distant cities of **Burgos** and **León**.)

## VALLADOLID

Twice the capital of Spain in the heyday of empire, Valladolid is where Ferdinand of Aragón and Isabella of Castile — collectively known as the "Catholic Monarchs" — were married, where an impoverished Columbus died and Philip II was born, and where Cervantes wrote the first part of Don Quixote. Today, Valladolid, never a city that could be termed elegant, swims in a smaller pond. It is the capital of the autonomous region of Castile and León, and is an important industrial center. Situated 182 km (109 miles) north of Madrid, Valladolid is linked to the capital by the A-6 freeway and the connecting N-403 road.

Philip II's architect, Juan de Herrera, who designed the Escorial, also started building Valladolid's cathedral but died before it was completed. In fact, the building was never finished although it later received the attentions of Alberto Churriguera in the early 18th century, thus combining the work of a master of austere grandeur with one of Baroque fantasy. Churriguera's plateresque (stone filigree) façades of the cathedral struck Jan Morris "as being, when one has recovered from the riotous shock of them, actually edible." (Jan Morris: *Spain* Penguin Books, 1982, p. 53)

There was something about Valladolid that appeared to uncap the imagination and

fantasies of stone carvers and sculptors, as the **Church of San Pablo** and the **Colegio de San Gregorio** with their ornate decoration demonstrate. The latter also houses the **Museo Nacional de Escultura Policromada** which has the largest collection of polychromed wooden sculpture, mostly of a religious nature, in Spain.

### HOTELS AND RESTAURANTS

Valladolid's best hotels are the **Olid Meliá** ( 35-72-00, Plaza San Miguel, N° 10; **Felipe IV** ( 30-70-00, Calle Gamazo, N° 16 (both expensive); and the older and more moderately priced **Imperial** ( 33-03-00, Calle Peso, N° 4. There are a number of good middle-price range restaurants, the most popular being **La Goya** ( 23-12-59, Calle Puente Colgante, Nº 79; **La Fragua** ( 33-71-02, Paseo Zorrilla, Nº 10; and **Mesón Panero** ( 30-16-73, Calle Marina Escobar, Nº 1.

## SALAMANCA

Salamanca, the ancient university town, is distinguished by its golden sandstone physique and its gentle spirit. The best way to approach it is from the south (N-501

camped beneath it. To complete the cycle, the best night view of Salamanca is from the same side but at a higher elevation. The modern parador **(Parador de Salamanca)**, on a high bluff, provides excellent views of the town with its twin cathedrals in the foreground.

Salamanca's university was founded in the early 13th century. By the middle of that century, it had progressed far enough to rank with Oxford, Bologna and Paris. At its height, in the mid-16th century, it had over 7,000 students, 60 professors and

from Madrid and Ávila) where the countryside edges in close to the town. There is a long Roman bridge, as serviceable as the day it was opened, that crosses the River Tormes and brings the traveler up to the city walls.

But before you cross, preferably in the morning with the early sun warming Salamanca's domes and spires, there is another view closer to hand. The banks of the Tormes, a broad but shallow river, are lined with poplars, larches and silver birches, and the countryside intrudes with flocks of sheep browsing in the lush grass along the water's edge. Later in the day, at the hour of the *paseo*, you may find lovers strolling along the bridge, or gypsies en-

24 constituent colleges. Its greatest teacher, Fray Luis de León, a theologian and poet, was active at this time, but the scourge of the Counter-Reformation undermined its institutions and its liberal spirit, and one of Europe's finest seats of learning went into an irreversible decline.

By the early 19th century, its student body had dropped to little more than 300. A brief resurgence took place in the first decades of the 20th century when the Basque philosopher and novelist, Miguel de

OPPOSITE: The façade of Salamanca's Gothic cathedral which was erected next to the older Romanesque cathedral in the 16th century.
ABOVE: The Plaza Mayor in Salamanca, Spain's ancient university town.

Unamuno, taught there. However, another intellectual blight, in the shape of Franco's narrow-minded outlook on matters of the mind and soul, seriously damaged its recovery. Today, it ranks about seventh in the country's college ratings, although it has become well-known abroad for its excellent courses on Spanish history, language and culture for foreign students.

A good feeling for what Salamanca University represented can be had by walking around the courtyard of the **Patio de las Escuelas**, into the lecture hall where Fray Luis de León uttered his famous "As we were saying yesterday..." greeting to his students after four years in the Inquisition's dungeons, and on into the university library. There are plenty of students to add atmosphere and life to this venerable center of learning, but there are also two other special attractions that Salamanca has to offer.

The first is the phenomenon of two cathedrals built almost on top of each other. The one that imperiously dominates the city is the new cathedral which was erected in the 16th century. Late Gothic, it is impressive, but is upstaged by the smaller, older Romanesque cathedral which is entered from the right side of the nave of the new one. With simple columns, fan vaults, and no central *coro* (choir) to block the view, it has a special charm. There are backlit tombs in an aisle off the nave, a cloister, and side chapels where you can sit and rest your feet against the sarcophagus of a medieval bishop without any sense of disrespect.

### Plaza Mayor

Salamanca's last marvel is the Plaza Mayor, built in the early 18th century, and by general acclaim Spain's greatest public square. Made of a rich, loamy sandstone that has turned into a burnished gold through exposure and age, the square is like a gigantic, superbly proportioned carving. It is completely enclosed by houses four stories high that are further bonded by long stretches of wrought iron balconies and underpinned by a colonnaded arcade. After wandering around this golden city's jumbled streets

and squares that are rarely square, there is no better place to sit with a *copa* or *café con leche* at your side, and watch the Spanish world go by.

## HOTELS AND RESTAURANTS

As a university town where many foreign students come to study Spanish history, culture and language, Salamanca has a large inventory of accommodation, restaurants and bars. Its top hotels are the **Gran Hotel (** 21-35-00, Plaza Poeta Iglesias, N° 5; the **Monterey (** 21-44-00, Calle Azafranal, N° 21; and the **Parador de Salamanca (** 22-87-00, Teso de la Feria, N° 2, which is undistinguished architecturally but has a swimming pool and overlooks the Roman bridge that leads to the city's walls. The **Residencia-Albergue Juvenil Salamanca (** 26-91-41/21-31-93 FAX 21-42-27, Calle Escoto N° 13–15, is the only youth hostel in the city center.

There is a rich selection of *tapas* bars and modestly-priced restaurants in the back streets around Plaza Mayor but if you want a little more style try **El Candil Nuevo (** 21-90-27, Plaza de la Reina, N° 2, which has good snails and delicious grilled kidneys, and **Chez Victor (** 21-90-27, Calle Espoz y Mina, N° 26, which specializes in French dishes. Both are in the moderate price range.

## ZAMORA

If you want to get a fuller flavor of the Castilian countryside, go on to Zamora which is north of Salamanca on the N-630 and less than an hour's drive. At harvesting time in this region it is still possible to see oxen yoked together pulling high-wheeled hay wagons, and peasant women in traditional black with kerchiefs covering their hair, and pitchforks on their shoulders. Hamlets and villages from another era, with crumbling churches, wooden carts, clumps of olive trees, the smell of dung, and the entire population getting ready to thresh newly-harvested grain imprint themselves on even the most transient visitor's memory.

Zamora is not a large or particularly notable town but it is a pleasant place to stop for lunch or a drink. Rising up above the Duero River (the Douro when it crosses into Portugal), it has the quality of an oasis: cool, dimly-lit buildings, shady squares and niches protected by cypresses, firs and pine trees, and the soothing sound of running water. The Romanesque cathedral dates from the 12th century, and has an unusual Byzantine dome and finely carved 16th-century choir stalls that contrast oddly with the plain, untreated pinewood floors. Zamora was in the frontline of both the Christian-Moorish wars and the conflicts between the Christian potentates themselves. Appropriately, El Cid received his knighthood in a church here.

## EXTREMADURA

Extremadura, which means neither "overripe" nor "extremely hard" but "beyond the Douro River," is one of the least visited parts of Spain, and perhaps all the better for it. This is a wild and beautiful if impoverished land, a changing landscape of wheat fields, evergreen oaks, eucalyptus and cork trees, framed by hazy mountain ranges. It is also a land of bull-breeding, of whitewashed villages, of storks untidily nesting on the top of castle turrets and church steeples, and of ancient unspoilt towns.

Extremadura has a long history, but its highpoints are separated by clusters of centuries rather than a smaller measure of time. The Romans were strongly attracted by the region's strategic position, its rivers, notably the Tagus and the Guadiana, and by its silver deposits. Their imprint can be seen in bridges, temples, amphitheaters and other artifacts. The Muslim conquest left fewer traces, but the Christian knights who drove the Moors southward in the Reconquest scattered castles and fortified towns throughout the province.

Another long period elapsed before Extremadura came into historical view again, this time with the exploits of the conquistadors in the New World. Hernán Cortés, the conqueror of Mexico, Francisco Pizarro, vanquisher of the Incas in Peru, Francisco Orellana, explorer of the Amazon, Nuñez de Balboa, and many others came from Extremadura. Most of the conquistadors who survived brought their plunder home and the results can be seen in the towns, palaces, and monasteries upon which they lavished their ill-gotten gains.

With the passing of the era of the conquistadors, the province disappeared again only to be re-awakened during the Napoleonic Wars when some epic battles took place between Wellington's army, supported by its Spanish allies, and the French. Today, Extremadura slumbers on.

There is no escaping the fact that the province is off the beaten track. Its main towns and attractions are too far from Madrid to be handled by daily sorties. You need to set aside two or three days or, better still, make it part of your itinerary if you are driving on to Portugal since Extremadura shares a long border with its Iberian neighbor. Head westwards on the N-V from Madrid to **Trujillo**, through **Mérida**, and finally to **Badajoz** which is close to the border, a distance of just over 400 km (240 miles). **Cáceres**, 47 km (28 miles) west of Trujillo, and the **Monastery of Guadalupe**, about the same distance east of Trujillo, can be handled by side trips.

### CÁCERES

There are a number of special places to look out for. Cáceres is the pivot of Extremadura, and ranks as one of Spain's most exquisite medieval towns. The old city, most of it dating from the 16th century when the tide of money from the Americas reached full flood, is surrounded by walls and has been declared a national monument. Magnificent, if a little stagey, Cáceres has often been chosen for the filming of historical dramas.

### TRUJILLO

Trujillo, the birthplace of the Pizarro family, is littered with palaces and grand houses built by the conqueror of Peru and his family. A bronze statue of the famous man — in armor, on horseback, and with sword drawn — stands in the town's main square.

## MONASTERY OF GUADALUPE

The Monastery of Guadalupe, dedicated to the Virgin whose wooden sculpture was allegedly found near the town of that name in the 13th century, is in the eastern part of Extremadura and a good two hours from Madrid If you are approaching it

Roman province of Lusitania that extended into modern Portugal, Mérida is still a showplace for Roman architecture. There is a particularly fine bridge over the Guadiana, a theater (still used), the remains of a Roman house, mosaics, and an amphitheater. All this adds up to Mérida being able to claim that it has the best preserved Roman remains in Spain. The best place to park and launch your tour is on the esplanade in front of the Roman theater and give yourself at least a couple of hours for the sights.

directly from the capital, take the N-V and turn off onto the C-401 at **Talavera de la Reina.** Legend has it that St. Luke carved the image, and that helped the monastery become a place of pilgrimage in the Middle Ages. The conquistadors took the cult to the Americas, and the Caribbean island of Guadeloupe derives its name from this Extremaduran town.

## BADAJOZ AND MÉRIDA

**Badajoz,** close to the Portuguese border, has been battered so much by marauding armies throughout history that there is not a lot to see. However, an hour's drive to the east is **Mérida.** Once the capital of the

## LA MANCHA

Heading southeasterly from Madrid brings you to La Mancha, the vast dry plain with its boundless horizons that is impossible to separate from the figures of Cervantes' imagination: the hallucinatory Don Quixote, his long-suffering nag, Rocinante, and the loyal Sancho Panza. However, as you move deeper into La Mancha, keeping an eye open for those castles and windmills that watch over the fertile plain, another trinity emerges.

This is the land of wheat, olives and vineyards that have provided the essentials of life in the Mediterranean world —

bread, oil, and wine — from time immemorial.

The wind always seems to be blowing in La Mancha, an impression heightened by the almost total absence of trees. It sweeps in great gusts across the wheatfields and along the bare streets of the whitewashed villages. If you want to *feel* La Mancha, go to **Consuegra**, a typical farming town about an hour and a half's drive from Madrid. Drive or walk up the hill above the town and sit in the company of nine windmills and a ruined castle, and watch the sun go down or the moon come up over this ancient land. The colors of the surrounding plain and the distant hills are gentle on the eye: light shades of green, tawny yellows, a splash of ochre, and rolling fields the color of a lion's hide.

The wind that tugs at the tattered sails of the windmills brings the lowing of cows, the growl of a tractor, cries of children playing, and a cock crowing. Narrow your vision in order to shut out the electricity pylons and the farm silos, and it is not hard to see the profile of the demented knight, his lance pointing toward the heavens, riding slowly across the treeless plain.

While it seems clear that Cervantes spent little time in the area he wrote so vividly about, and the word *"mancha"* in Spanish means a "blot" or a "stain," this landscape has a magnetic quality that is hard to resist.

But when it comes to towns or monuments, there is not much to see. The two largest towns, **Ciudad Real** in the south, and **Albacete** to the east, have little to divert the traveler. **Valdepeñas**, the center of Spain's most prolific wine-growing region, is worth dropping by if you feel like sampling some of the light dry red wine that is typical of this area. La Mancha is also the home of one of Spain's best known cheeses, the firm, tangy *manchego*. Then there is **El Toboso**, the home of Don Quixote's beloved Dulcinea, which has a modest Quixote museum.

## CUENCA

Cuenca, in the northern part of La Mancha, close to the Aragón border, is an old town built on top of cliffs overlooking deep gorges. Its famous "hanging houses," *(casas colgantes)* are a bit of a disappointment: there are not many of them and they cling to, rather than hang over their rocky foundations. Inside, however, there is a delightful modern art museum (**Museo de Arte Abstracto Español**). Cuenca is popular with artists who played a role in establishing the museum in the 1960s. The town also has a number of large houses built by the nobility in the 14th and 15th centuries, a few of which have been turned into cozy inns. The best

place for photographing the town and the hanging houses is on a footbridge that is suspended over the River Huecar, and the best time is in the morning; in the afternoon this side of the town is in the shade. The town is 163 km (98 miles) from Madrid; take the N-III towards Valencia and branch off on the N-400 at Tarancon.

OPPOSITE: The "hanging houses" *(casas colgantes)* of Cuenca. ABOVE: Don Quixote country: windmills at Consuegra in La Mancha.

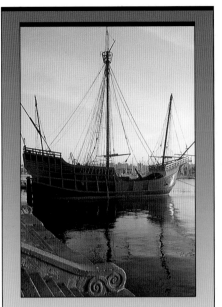

# Catalonia and the Levante

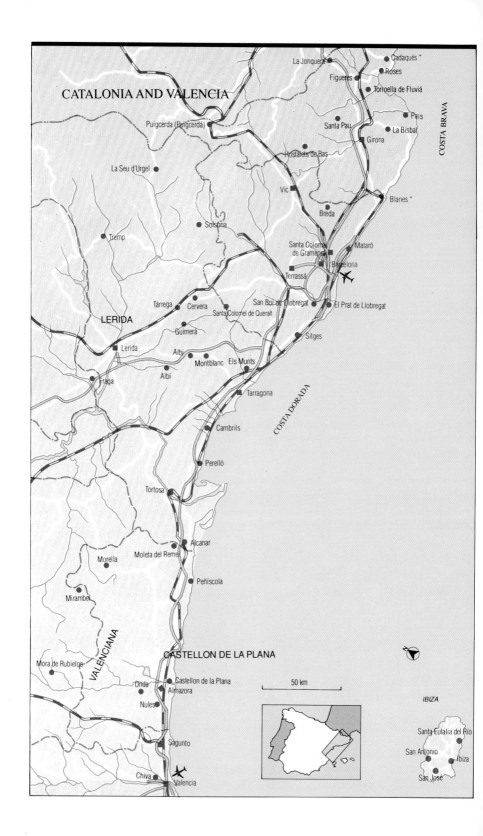

# THE MEDITERRANEAN CONNEXION

No transition displays more vividly the variety of Spain than the northward leap from Andalusia to **Catalonia.** Virtually everything is different — the landscape, the climate, the human temperament, even the language. Catalonia, a triangular wedge of mountains, valleys, plains and coastline in north-eastern Spain, sits astride the main land corridor that connects the country with the rest of Europe. Catalonia is the most European of Spain's ancient kingdoms and Barcelona, its capital, the least Spanish of its cities.

Catalonia reflects the contrasting nature of Spain through its own diversity. It has mountains (the **Pyrenees**), a rugged coast (**Costa Brava**), a gentler shoreline (**Costa Dorada**), pleasant valleys and productive plains, heavy and light industry, the country's largest port (**Barcelona**), and an industrious and creative population. The region also produces some of the best wine in Spain, including the champagne-like *cava.* First settled by the Greeks, Catalonia has always looked to the Mediterranean for its livelihood and its inspiration. The Carthaginians arrived in the third century AD and Barcelona was founded by Hamilcar Barca, Hannibal's father. Then came the Romans who established a thriving province centered on the coastal city of Tarragona. Neither the Visigoths nor the Moors made much of an impression, allowing Catalonia to develop in its own distinctive way. As early as the ninth century AD, the region had established a clear political identity under the Count of Barcelona, Wilfredo el Velloso (Wilfred the Hairy). Catalonia marks its formal existence from the end of the 10th century and celebrated its millennium in 1987.

In the 12th century the Catalan Count Ramón Berenguer IV married Queen Petronilla of Aragón uniting the two states. The union brought brought power and prosperity to the region. Democratic institutions were created, monasteries and cathedrals built, and territory conquered. At its height, the Catalonia-Aragón dominions included the region of Roussillon in France, Valencia and the Balearic Islands in Spain, Sardinia, Sicily, Malta and much of modern Greece.

This was the golden age of Catalonia but the arrival of the Catholic Monarchs, Ferdinand and Isabella, in the last quarter of the 15th century set in motion an uneven but steady decline. Determined to unify Spain under their central authority, they and their successors curbed Catalonia's separatist ambitions and exacerbated internal divisions. The discovery of the New World and the trade monopoly given to Seville isolated Catalonia, cutting it off from the wealth that flowed in from the Americas. The long struggle between Castile and Catalonia, Madrid and Barcelona began.

An attempt at secession in the 17th century and backing the wrong side in the dynastic war of succession in the early 18th century further undermined Catalonia's political aspirations. However, Catalan energy diverted itself into making the region the industrial power-house of Spain, strengthening its capitalists and creating a modern working class. With the declaration of the Second Republic in 1930, Catalonia received a large degree of autonomy which it used to flirt with every imaginable political theory on the left of the spectrum, including anarchism. During the Civil War, Barcelona was the scene of great chaos, unforgettably described by George Orwell in *Homage to Catalonia,* as well as heroic resistance. The city became the last capital of the dying Republic in the final months of the war. After Franco's victory, tens of thousands of Catalans fled across the border to France and the government crushed Catalonia's free-wheeling ways.

The new democratic Spain that emerged after Franco's death in 1975 endorsed a more decentralized form of government. Catalonia duly regained most of its ancient privileges, including its provincial parliament and government, and an almost unfettered use of Catalan, its own language. A word about that *language.* Spoken by about six million people, every one of whom will bridle if he or she hears it called a dialect, Catalan is a Romance language derived from the Romans and much modified by the French connection from the ninth century onwards. It is closely related to Provençal and Langue d'Oc in southern France, looks like a fair mixture of French and Castilian on paper, but sounds like neither when spoken.

Since the death of Franco, under whose iron hand Catalan was banned, the language has flourished and is now recognized as an official tongue. It is taught in schools, used on the radio and television, and has replaced Spanish on streets signs, many official forms and in Catalonian government

be pretty awful when they claimed they were champagne. But, ironically, now that they have come out of the closet and simply say they are made by the "champagne method," they are much improved and are an acceptable substitute for France's real — and invariably expensive — thing.

## CATALANS AT PLAY

The Catalans like to play as well as work and the region has many festivals throughout the year. There are two local specialties that

offices. This makes life a little difficult for the visitor, perhaps already struggling with rudimentary Spanish, but the Catalans feel that the time has come to assert their cultural heritage. To avoid further confusion, while in Catalonia (*Cataluña* in Spanish, *Catalunya* in the local language), the Catalan terms for place names, streets, and so on, will be used. Catalan, or a variation of it, is spoken beyond the region in and around Valencia, and in the Balearic Islands.

## CATALONIAN *CAVAS*

Catalonia produces a number of good wines, notably the reds, whites and *cavas* from the Penedés region. The *cavas* used to

are worth bearing in mind. One is the *sardana,* a dance often performed in traditional costume, described somewhat unflatteringly by Jan Morris in her travel book on Spain as the "faunlike capering of Catalonia." The *sardana* was, like much else in the region, banned in General Franco's time and has a special significance that perhaps only Catalans can appreciate.

The other specialty is the Catalan propensity for building human pyramids. The practitioners are known as *castellers* because they build "castles," and they are particularly active in the small towns of the Penedés wine-growing area west and north of Tarragona during harvest time. The historic center of the "sport" is **Valls** where teams compete against each other to the accompaniment of what the official guide book calls "a rustic wind instrument."

## BARCELONA

Barcelona, the pivot and pride of Catalonia and Spain's second largest metropolis, has a tendency to captivate new visitors or disconcert them. It is not a city of half measures: it bustles, does business with great energy, and plays as hard as it works. For years

buildings, and the development of new beaches, esplanades and marinas.

The Olympic stadium, on a hill overlooking the city, has added a new dimension to sport and public entertainment, and the Olympic village, on the coast, has extended the city northward. Barcelona traditionally turned its back on the Mediterranean; now with many kilometers of new seafront and a renovated port area, sea and city are finally reconciled. To round it off, Barcelona acquired a sparkling and state-of-the-art international airport and a comprehensive

Barcelona had a rather grimy, hangdog look. But in the early 1990s it underwent a dramatic transformation to the point where it was voted the country's leading city by a panel of distinguished Spanish architects and urban planners.

Barcelona's growth during the last hundred years or so has been nurtured by three international events: the Universal Exhibition in 1888, the International Exhibition in 1929 and, most recently, the Olympic Games in 1992. The physical changes wrought by the $9 billion invested to host the Olympics is striking and lasting. The city's old salty face and dreary port have been transformed by cleaning, the removal of old warehouses and obsolete

network of new highways, encircling the city, that enables traffic to flow rapidly in and out. These roads are particularly helpful to the vehicle-borne traveler coming down from France, or arriving at the port, and wanting to get in out of Barcelona with the minimum of time and fuss.

There are plenty of reminders that Barcelona is an ancient metropolis although much of the architectural evidence is either gone or hidden beneath its modern carapace. It is also a city that has always been receptive to new ideas, as well as producing

OPPOSITE: A bird's eye view of Barcelona from Tibidabo. ABOVE: Street scene in the bustling Catalan capital.

many of its own. From its experiments with democratic institutions in the 12th century to libertarianism and anarcho-syndicalism in the 19th and 20th centuries, Barcelona has never been a dull place. Influenced by the European Romantic movement, it experienced a cultural renaissance in the 19th century (the Catalan *Renaixença*). It also nurtured painters such as Pablo Picasso, Joan Miró and Salvador Dalí, musicians like Pablo Casals, and the amazing Antonio Gaudí, the Modernist architect and designer.

Catalan Gothic architecture. It has a pretty cloister with a garden shaded by palm, orange and medlar trees, a fountain and a flock of white geese, said to symbolize Santa Eulalia's virginity. It is worth going up to the top of the cathedral's bell-tower in the newly-installed elevator for a panoramic view of the Gothic Quarter. There is a busy market outside the main entrance on Sundays, and the *sardana*, Catalonia's traditional folk dance, is often performed here.

The **Palau de la Generalitat** in the heart of the Gothic Quarter on the **Plaça de Sant**

The city is best viewed — as Julius Caesar dealt with ancient Gaul — in three parts. First there is the **Barri Gotic** (Gothic Quarter), the medieval section that runs back from the port and is dissected by the **Ramblas** and the **Vía Laietana.** Winding narrow streets, unexpected squares, and a collection of well-preserved buildings dating from the 13th to the 15th centuries, erected over the remains of successive occupations dating back to the Romans, constitute the Gothic heart of the city.

## BARRI GOTÏC

The **cathedral**, begun in the late 13th century, is large and spacious in the manner of

**Jaume** is an almost holy place for Catalan nationalists. Founded by King Jaume I in the 14th century, this is where Catalan parliamentary government began. The actual building dates from the 15th century although it has a number of more modern additions. It is now back in use again after the restoration of Catalan autonomy in 1977 and is the seat of the government. It is only open to the public on Sundays between 10 AM and 2 PM. Across the square is the **Ajuntament** (City Hall) where the "Council of a Hundred" ruled Catalonia from the 14th century until Philip V abolished the region's institutions in 1714. The best façade is not the 19th-century one facing the square but the Gothic façade that overlooks a small street at the side of the building. Inside there is a graceful Gothic gallery, a florid and much photographed late 19th-century staircase, and some elegant reception rooms. The oldest chamber is the atmospheric **Saló de Cent** (Hall of the Hundred), which was begun in the 14th century and, somewhat like the government it symbolizes, added to and subtracted from through the ages up to the present century. It has a wooden beamed ceiling divided by two stone arches and the walls are adorned with the gold and scarlet colors of Catalonia in a heavily brocaded fabric.

Not far north of the Ajuntament is the **Palau de Llonctinent** (Viceroy's Palace) built in the middle of the 16th century in grand style. It houses one of the world's greatest collections of medieval documents built around the archives of the Kingdom of Aragón. Do not miss the small but exquisite **Plaça del Rei** that captures the best of old Barcelona and where the city museum (**Museo d'Historia de la Ciutat**) is located. There is an interesting collection of memorabilia down through the ages commemorating Barcelona's history. But perhaps more intriguing is the **Underground Museum** — the same ticket will get you in — where you can take a walk along the city's Roman and Visigothic streets that have been excavated and see the ruins of a fourth-century Visigothic church.

Crossing the Vía Laietana, there is the **Barrio Santa María del Mar**, another medieval part of the city that clusters around the church of that name. The history of this Catalan Gothic church is inextricably linked with Catalonia's maritime empire. A cool, uncluttered building, it is distinguished by a large central nave, soaring octagonal pillars spaced at unusually wide intervals, and some lovely stained glass windows.

Close by on the **Calle Montcada**, one of the city's most elegant medieval streets, is the **Picasso Museum** in the **Palau Aguila**, a 15th-century nobleman's house. This is an appropriate setting for the great painter who was born in Málaga but lived and worked in Barcelona from 1895 until 1904, his "Blue Period." Picasso's early artistic development is chronicled in the museum

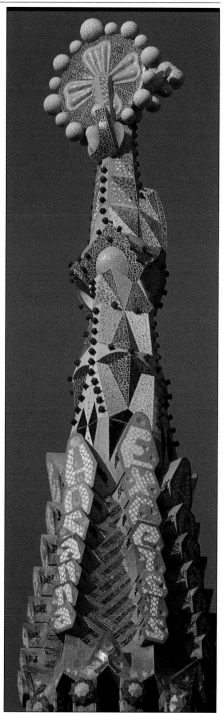

OPPOSITE: The façade of the Gothic cathedral.
ABOVE: One of the spires of Antonio Gaudí's El Templo de la Sagrada Familia (The Church of the Holy Family), his monumental and unfinished church.

but there are also a number of his later paintings on display.

Down in the port area, at the end of the Ramblas, is the **Columbus's Column** where you can take an elevator ride up inside the steel shaft and view the city from the top.

Further down, in the old **Port Vell** dockyard, a new complex of restaurants, bars, shops, cinemas and a fascinating aquarium has been built. The Oceanario, Europe's largest **aquarium**, is alone worth a visit. There are 21 tanks holding nearly 19 million liters (five million gallons) of water that contain 8,000 fish of 300 different species. One tank, 80 meters (87.5 yards) long, is in the shape of a transparent tunnel which you pass through on a slow moving walkway as the sharks, rays and swordfish glide overhead.

## RAMBLAS

The main artery connecting the port with the more modern parts of the city is the famous **Ramblas**, a broad tree-lined avenue with a wide central walkway full of newsstands, flower stalls, cafés, vendors selling canaries, budgerigars and pigeons, performing "artistes" of varying talent, and an endless *paseo* of citizens and visitors drawn by the constantly changing human kaleidoscope.

Going up the Ramblas, away from the port, on the left hand side there is the **Barrio Chino** (the red light district), the **Palacio Güell** (a Gaudí extravaganza built in 1888 for his wealthy patron, the financier Baron Eusebi Güell), the old **Oriente Hotel**, the **Gran Teatre de Liceu** (Spain's most sumptuous opera house, being rebuilt after a disastrous fire), and the marvelously colorful and aromatic covered market, the **Mercado de la Bequería**. On the right, going in the same direction, is the **Plaça Real**, an arcaded square just off the Ramblas that is a bit seedy but turns into an interesting stamp and coin market on Sundays; and a network of small, pungent streets that lead you into the Gothic quarter.

## ENSANCHE

With industrialization, prosperity and a cultural renaissance in the 19th century, Barcelona broke through its medieval walls and expanded with a new section of carefully planned streets and intersections and solid bourgeois housing. This section, which is known as the **Ensanche** in Spanish and **Eixample** in Catalan (the "Broadening" or "Extension") and was the work of **Ildefons Cerdà**, begins when you have reached the top of the Ramblas and arrive at the **Plaça de Catalunya.** The district is reminiscent of the boulevards of Paris or the Salamanca neighborhood in Madrid but with two notable differences. Each intersection in the gridiron pattern of streets has "rounded" corners that give a greater feeling of space; and scattered through the district are a number of the colorful, convoluted creations of Gaudí and other Modernist architects.

The Eixample is where the big department stores, many hotels, restaurants and classy boutiques are located; but it also still the home of many of the city's more affluent residents.

The swankiest avenue is the **Passeig de Gracia** which runs from the Plaça de Catalunya up to the **Avinguda Diagonal** and has a number of Modernist buildings by Gaudí and his contemporaries, notably **Domènech i Montaner** (who also built the lush Art Nouveau **Palau de la Musica Catalana** which is just off the Vía Laietana and is worth seeing), and **Puig i Cadafalch.** The most dramatic Gaudí building is **La Pedrera**, at the top end of the Passeig de Gracia, which was built in 1910 and was the architect's last secular work. An amazing concoction of flowing concrete, wrought iron balustrades, and fanciful chimneys, it represents the Modernist movement at its most flamboyant.

The Eixample's greatest Gaudí monument, however, is the **Templo de la Sagrada Familia** (the Church of the Holy Family) which towers over the busy, tree-lined streets and avenues of the district and is located just across the Diagonal. Unique, strange and unfinished, this modern paean to Christianity in gray reinforced concrete has to be seen to be believed. And it should be seen by anyone visiting Barcelona.

La Pedrera, Gaudí's most ambitious secular builting.

It was begun in 1882 by another architect but Gaudí, at the age of 31, took over in 1891 and continued working on it until his death in a streetcar accident in 1926. During the next decade the façade was finished but the outbreak of the Civil War in 1936 stopped work and nothing much was done until 1954. Gaudí left no plans but work has resumed again using his models, although not without controversy because, as the purists who oppose any further additions point out, Gaudí usually changed his mind as he went along.

The clusters of slender honeycombed towers and spires soar to 108 m (350 ft). Visitors can take an elevator to the top of one of the towers and walk over a gently curved connecting bridge that provides a fine view of the whole building. The church is also a Gaudí museum where you can see a slide show of his other work, models for the building of the Sagrada Familia, and how it will look when it is eventually finished. And down in the crypt, the master lies at peace under the unfinished temple that consumed almost half his life.

ABOVE LEFT: Gaudí's Park Güell. RIGHT: The unmistakable figure of Don Quixote.

## SARRIÀ

The last main section of Barcelona is known as Sarrià which is situated beyond the Diagonal. Largely built in the nineteenth and the early twentieth centuries on a gently sloping incline, this is an area of narrow streets, solid houses, and pretty gardens. Sarrià was originally known for its skilled craftsmen, especially master-builders, but later became a residential district. It is now part of the city and while many of the houses

remain as residences quite a few of them have been converted into offices, restaurants, art galleries and shops. But the human scale of the area and its feeling of neighborhood contrast pleasantly with other more crowded sections of Barcelona of which it is now ineluctably part.

Gaudí leaves his imprint on this district too with the **Park Güell** that lies further up the hillside beyond the **Travesera de Dalt**. The park is a Gaudí fantasy although its original design was meant to be English, hence the spelling of "Park." The entrance is flanked by two pavilions with sweeping roofs covered in mosaics and colored tiles, a grand stairway, and a dragon heading in the direction of the **Sala Hipostila** (Hall of a Hundred Columns). The park is constructed on several levels with terrace walls supported by columns shaped like spreading palms. Nothing is predictable, nothing is dull. Even a park bench has Gaudí's hand upon it with its serpentine shape and covering of bright ceramic tile. It may not be your taste but it certainly is not boring.

Beyond the park is **Tibidabo**, Barcelona's highest hill where a lung-full of clean air and a grand vista of the city and the Mediterranean can be had without dipping your hand into your pocket or purse. There are two other parks, much closer to the sea, that deserve a mention. The first is the **Parc de la Ciutadella**, at the north end of the port, which was the site of a fortress built by the conquering Philip V in 1714 to keep the rebellious Catalans in order. When Barcelona was firmly under the control of its own government again in the 19th century the citadel was razed and a park put in its place. It was here that the city's first international show, the Universal Exposition, was held in 1888.

**Montjuïc** is a hill to the south of the port which it overlooks. The site of the Barcelona's second global fiesta, the 1929 International Exposition, Montjuïc has an extensive park and gardens, the Miró museum (**Fondació Miró**) which alone makes a visit worthwhile, and the stadium for the 1992 Olympic Games.

A cable car connects Montjuic with the Barcelona port and the new beaches at Barceloneta.

## GETTING AROUND

Getting around the city is not too difficult although the dense traffic is a problem. Taxis are cheap and plentiful and should be used; but so should the excellent subway system (Metro) that is similar to the one in Madrid. Buy a good map — you will recognize the three areas described above from the shape of the street patterns and their density — and use your feet in the Gothic Quarter. Barcelona is a gourmet's town and has its own equivalent of Madrid's animated nightlife (*la moguda* in Catalan) though the city closes down much earlier than the Spanish capital. Catalans, unlike Castilians,

always seem to remember that they have to get up and work in the morning.

## TOURIST INFORMATION

**Provincial Area Code**   (3)
From within Spain   (93)
**Tourist Offices**:
El Prat Airport, Terminal A (international), ( 478-4704.
El Prat Airport, Terminal B (national and EU arrivals) ( 478-0565.
Gran Vía de les Corts Catalanes, N° 658, ( 301-7443 and 317-2246, FAX 412-2570.
Carrer de Tarragona N° 149-157, ( 423-1800, FAX 423-2649.
**Iberia Airlines** ( 412-5667.
**RENFE** (Spanish Railways), ( 490-0202.
**Compania Trasmediterranea** (car ferry service to the Balearic Islands) ( 443-2532.
**Radio Taxis** ( 357-7755 and 358-1111.

### HOTELS

*Deluxe* means a night's lodging costs Pts.28,000 and above; *Expensive* Pts.18,000 to Pts.28,000; *moderate*: Pts.8,000 to Pts.18,000; and *inexpensive*: Pts.4,000 to Pts.8,000.

*Deluxe*
**Arts** ( 221-1660 FAX 221-1070, Carrer de la Marina N° 19–21, is located in one of the new skyscraper towers in the Olympic village which is now a fully-fledged seaside town only 10 minutes by taxi from the Ramblas.
**Claris** ( 487-6262 FAX 215-7970, Pau Claris, N° 150, is a modern luxury hotel in a 19th-century palace with a swimming pool and solarium on the roof. It is close to the Passeig de Gracia and the Diagonal.
**Ritz** ( 318-5200 FAX 318-0148, Gran Vía, N° 668, is a classic old hotel as the name suggests; it recreates *belle époque* atmosphere in style and is close to the Gothic Quarter.

*Expensive*
**Avenida Palace** ( 301-9600 FAX 318-1234, Gran Vía, N° 605, is centrally located and lavishly comfortable.
**Colon** ( 301-1404 FAX 317-2915, Avenguda Catedral, N° 7, is an old-fashioned hotel with comfortable rooms and leisurely service. It is right in the heart of the Gothic quarter, opposite the Cathedral.

**Princess Sofia** ( 330-7111 FAX 330-7621, Plaça Pio XIII, though not in centrally located but is fully equipped with swimming pool, sauna, gymnasium, and a good disco (**Regine's**) in the basement.

**Le Meridien** ( 318-6200 FAX 301-7776, Ramblas, Nº 11, formerly the Ramada Renaissance, is an old hotel superbly renovated with commanding view over the Ramblas, and has a useful underground garage.

*Moderate*

**Balmes** ( 451-1914 FAX 451-0049, Carrer Mal-

listing hotels by category on one side and showing where they are on the other.

**RESTAURANTS**

*Expensive* represents meals costing Pts.8,000 and above; *moderate*: Pts.3,000 to Pts.8,000.

*Expensive*

**Botafumeiro** ( 218-4230, Carrer Mayor de Gracia, Nº 81, is a Galician establishment famous for its meat pies, *croquettes* (rissoles) and shellfish. It also has a nice oyster bar.

lorca, Nº 216, is a good, modern hotel within walking distance of the Ramblas and the Gothic Quarter. It serves excellent buffet-style breakfast daily.

**Regina** ( 301-3232 FAX 318-2326, Carrer Bergara, Nº 2–4, is a pleasant and functional hotel just off the Ramblas.

**Wilson** ( 209-8911 FAX 200-8370, is on Avenguda Diagonal, 568.

Barcelona, like Madrid, has a mass of inexpensively priced hotels, hostels and boarding houses. The Barcelona tourist authorities put out an extremely useful map,

**Reno** ( 200-9129 Carrer Tuset, Nº 27, is another Sarrià restaurant that takes pains with its traditional Spanish dishes.

**Vía Veneto** ( 200-7024, Carrer Guaduxer, Nº 10–12, is an elegant and stylish place in the Sarrià district. It serves Catalan and French food and is popular with Barcelona's fashionable crowd.

*Moderate*

**Chicoa** ( 453-1123, Carrer Aribau, Nº 73, is a serious Catalan restaurant specializing in fish dishes (*bacalao* — salt cod, is a specialty). Excellent value. (See photograph).

**Egipte** ( 317-3480, located on Carrer Jerusalem, Nº 3, serves good basic food in Bohemian setting and is a favorite haunt of

ABOVE: Chicoa Restaurant, one of Barcelona's many gourmet restaurants. OPPOSITE: Los Caracoles Restaurant in the old section of the city.

the theater crowd. A second **Egipte** has opened on the Ramblas but this is the one to go to.

**Els Quatre Gats** ( 302-4140, Carrer Montsio, N° 3, in the Gothic Quarter, offers simple but good eating at reasonable prices.

**Los Caracoles** ( 302-3185, Carrer Escudellers, N° 14, offers Catalan cusine in the Gothic Quarter, the atmosphere is good though can be somewhat touristic. (see photograph below).

**Salamanca** ( 221-5033, Carrer Almiral Cervera, N° 34, near the sea in the Bar-

celoneta, serves good *tapas* at the bar and sea-food and grills in the restaurant.

Barcelona is second only to Madrid in its gastronomic delights, although some would say it surpasses the captial in many ways. The ingredients, from the Mediterranean and Catalonia, are superb and most restaurants do something interesting with them. Barcelona is also famous for its pastries and it is a tradition to eat them, English-style, mid-afternoon accompanied by coffee, hot chocolate or tea. The local Penedès (especially the whites), Priorato (especially the reds) and the *cavas* (Spanish champagne) are all highly drinkable, so there is no need to reach beyond the region when it comes to ordering wine.

### Nightlife

Barcelona, as you would expect, has a broad range of night entertainment. Apart from the usual array of *tapas* bars, cafés, and cocktail lounges, the city offers the phenomenon of champagne bars, trading on the *cava* wines that are produced in Catalonia. Try **La Cava del Palau** ( 310-0938, Carrer Verdaguer i Callis, N° 10 opposite the Palau de la Musica in the Gothic quarter. For discotheques, sample: **Nick Havanna** ( 215-6591, Carrer Rossello, N° 208, which styles itself as "the ultmate bar"; **Satanassa** ( 451-0052,

Carrer Aribau, N° 27; **Trauma** ( 487-9447, Consell de Cent, N° 288; **El Otro** ( 323-6759, Carrer Valencia, N° 166; and, for the gay crowd, **Metro Disco** ( 323-5227, Carrer Sepulveda, N° 185.

---

### AROUND BARCELONA

From Barcelona, the traveler can follow the Mediterranean coast in either direction, north or south, or head inland to Aragón and the Pyrenees. But before going that far there are two places that merit attention within comfortable range of the city — each about an hour's drive away; these are the monastery of **Montserrat** (52 km or 31 miles to the west on the N-150) and the seaside town of **Sitges** on the C-246 coastal road to the south.

## MONTSERRAT

Rising out of a placid valley, the **Sierra de Montserrat** is an extraordinary geological phenomenon that seems to defy a rational explanation. About 10 km (six miles) long by five kilometers (three miles) wide, and over 1,200 m (3,936 ft) high, the Sierra is a jumble of jagged peaks, solitary towers of rock worn smooth by the elements, huge

boulders, precipitous cliffs, plunging canyons and ravines, and mysterious caves. Montserrat means "sawn mountain" in Catalan and some of the local names given to the range indicate both its appearance and its power over the minds of men. "The spellbound giant," "the friar," "the sentinel," "the death's head," "the camel," "the parrot," and so on.

From time immemorial Montserrat has evoked wonder and symbolism. Legend has it that St. Peter hid an image of the Virgin carved by St. Luke in one of Montserrat's caves, and in another, Parsifal found the Holy Grail, a story that inspired Wagner to use Montserrat as the backdrop for his opera. The mountains seem to have had a special appeal for German writers and poets. Schiller wrote, "Montserrat sucks a man in from the outer to the inner world;" and Goethe's view was that "nowhere but in his own Montserrat will a man find happiness and peace."

Myths and literary imagery apart, Montserrat has had a historic role as a

religious and nationalist icon for Catalans and Catalonia. Hermitages are known to have existed on the mountains before the Moors took control in the eighth century. Not long after the reconquest in 880, the image of a dark-faced Virgin was found and a chapel built on the site. A monastery dedicated to St. Mary, in honor of the Virgin, was built in the 11th century by the Benedictine monks.

The foundation prospered largely due to the fame of the Virgin, who was affectionately called the "La Moreneta" ("the little dark one"), as a worker of miracles. During the Middle Ages Montserrat became a place of pilgrimage, second only in importance to Santiago de Compostela. Its fame spread and the famous — or later to be famous — trekked up the mountain and paid tribute. Ignatius Loyola was one of them, spending a lonely vigil on his knees in front of the Virgin before dedicating his life to God and founding the order of the Jesuits.

Most of Spain's monarchs, regardless of their views on Catalan nationalism, respected the monastic foundation and revered the Virgin. But Napoleon's occupying army showed no such deference. In 1811, as a reprisal for the local Catalan guerrillas using the monastery as a base for operations, the French looted and destroyed it. It was rebuilt in the 19th and 20th centuries and is now the home of a small group of monks and the destination of about a million visitors every year.

The monastery and basilica themselves are almost as bleak as the mountains that surround them. But there are striking remnants of the pre-restored buildings such as a Romanesque door, and one side of the Gothic cloister. The Black Virgin can be seen by walking up a stairway behind the altar, and Montserrat's famous boys' choir performs twice daily. There is a great deal of commercialization around the monastery — it's big tourist business with Catalans and foreigners alike, especially in the summer — but the mountain range is spectacular. If you have time, take a walk up behind the monastery; from the highest peaks the Pyrenees, and sometimes Mallorca, can be seen. It is also a good place for hikers and, of course, climbers. Not to be missed.

## Sitges

For a completely different outing, go to Sitges, a fashionable seaside resort south of Barcelona with an old-world and slightly decadent air. The town came into its own at the turn of the century when Barcelona's literary and artistic glitterati adopted it as their summer playground. The pivot was Santiago Rusiñol, a kind of Catalan Dr. Johnson, who was a well-known writer, painter and conversationalist in his day.

aside for nudists — both straight and gay. Sitges is also known for its **Corpus Christi Festival** when the streets of the old town are carpeted with flowers, for international theater and cinema gatherings, and for a vintage car rally that starts in Barcelona and finishes on the promenade.

### Hotels and Restaurants

**Hotel Terramar** ( 894-0500, Paseo Marítimo, Nº 30, provides acceptable accommodation in the upper price range, and the aptly named **Hotel Romantic** ( 894-0643, Calle

The Modernist architects, notably Puig i Cadafalch and Domênech i Montaner, also came and built grand seaside homes for wealthy Barcelona patrons. In modern times, Sitges has become a popular rendezvous for gays from all over Europe, changing the flavor but preserving the distinctive style of the resort.

The old town is a collection of cool whitewashed houses and narrow streets nestling behind a picturesque Baroque church, with a curious bell tower made entirely of wrought iron, that overlooks the Mediterranean. There is a fine palm tree fringed promenade which is the place to walk slowly, to observe, and to be observed. There are plenty of beaches, with several set

San Isidro, Nº 33. The Romantic is a conversion of three 19th-century houses, has a fine garden patio, and is moderately priced. Good food, especially fish and Catalan dishes, are found at **La Masia** ( 894-1076, Paseo Vilanova, Nº 164; and **Mare Nostrum** ( 894-3393, Paseo de la Ribera, Nº 60.

## FURTHER AFIELD

Widening the arc around Barcelona, there are a number of places to see that include

ABOVE: The fashionable seaside town of Sitges, south of the Catalan capital. OPPOSITE: The Monastery of Montserrat in its mountainous setting west of Barcelona.

**Tarragona** (100 km or 65 miles south on the A-7 freeway), the **Costa Dorada** (see the following page), two splendid monasteries **(Poblet** and **Santes Creus** — see page141), the **Costa Brava** (especially **Cadaqués**), **Figueres**, and **Girona.**

The last three towns are reached by taking the A-7 freeway north toward the French border. Girona is 96 km (58 miles from Barcelona; Figueres is 37 km (22 miles) further on; and Cadaqués — branch off at Figueres on the C-260 — is 31 km (19 miles) from Figueres.

Tarragona's long history, are neat rectangular pieces of stone laid by the Romans, surmounted by masonry added by the English during the War of the Spanish Succession, and finally some pretty horrible 20th-century brickwork.

### Sightseeing

Tarraco, as the city was called by the Romans, was a great port and strategic base during the Punic wars. Many Roman emperors spent time there, including Augustus between campaigns, and Pontius Pilate was

### TARRAGONA

Tarragona has a rather strange atmosphere — introverted, dour and preoccupied — perhaps as a result of its past pre-eminence and later decline. A city of immense importance during the Roman period, visible traces of an earlier Iberian grandeur remain in the huge blocks of limestone that are the foundations of the walls and ramparts of the old town. On top of those, symbolizing

born there. A good sense of the Roman legacy can be had by walking along the **Passeig Arquelogic;** having a look at the **Archaeological Museum** that has a good collection of mosaics; visiting the **praetorium**, built in the first century BC and reconstructed in the Middle Ages; and taking a trip north of the town, just off the main road to Valls, to see a well-preserved **Roman aqueduct** that soars across the countryside for a distance of 123 m (400 ft). Built on a row of sturdy double arches and second only to Segovia's aqueduct in size, you can walk long the channel where Tarraco's water supply used to flow.

Tarragona also has an interesting **cathedral** built between the 12th and the 15th

ABOVE: The old fishing village of Cadaqués on the Costa Brava, a haunt of Salvador Dalí and other unconventional though not as gifted people. OPPOSITE: The Roman aqueduct, north of Tarragona.

centuries showing the transition from the Romanesque to the Gothic styles of architecture. Wedged into the core of the medieval town, its exterior is nothing to write home about but the interior, especially the main altar, the stained glass and a timeless cloister are all well worth seeing. Tarragona has a commanding presence overlooking the Mediterranean and has picked up recently as the center of the increasingly popular **Costa Dorada** (Golden Coast) which is a strip of 200 km (124 miles) of wide, sandy beaches, interlaced with pine-fringed coves, running south from Barcelona to the Ebro Delta. Another boost to Tarragona has come from the growth of the wine industry, the best being Priorato, a delicious, smooth full-bodied red wine that can be happily drunk with — or without — anything.

Tarragona's grandest hotel is the **Imperial Tarraco** ( 23-30-40, Rambla Vella, N° 2; and **Sol Ric** ( 23-20-32, Vía Augusta, N° 227, which specializes in fish dishes, is its most famous restaurant.

### Taragona environs

There are two medieval monasteries in the Tarragona area, the **Monasterio de Santa María de Poblet** and the **Monasterio de Santes Creus**. Although not formally linked they had similar origins and trajectories of influence and decline. Both were founded in the 12th century by Ramón Berenguer IV as Cistercian houses at the zenith of the fortunes of the Catalan–Aragón monarchy. Both monasteries became powerful, rich and corrupt, and both were sacked in the anti-clerical upheavals of the 19th century. The two monasteries have been lovingly restored since and each evokes, in its own way, the vitality and creativity of the Christian monarchy and church in the Middle Ages.

These monasteries share all the elements one expects in such baronial foundations. Impressive entrances, austere chapels, vast dormitories where more than 100 monks bedded down in a single room, quiet cloisters shaded by cypresses and refreshed by fountains, refectories, kitchens, wine cellars, and spacious gardens. Poblet, sometimes called the "Escorial" of Catalonia, contains the tombs of many of the kings of Catalonia–

Aragón. Visit at least one of these monasteries if you can.

On a more profane note, **Port Aventura**, the $500 million theme park at **Salou**, just 10 km (six miles) south of Tarragona, is a great place for kids — of all ages (see FAMILY FUN, page 42).

## COSTA BRAVA

North of Barcelona is the famous Costa Brava (the "wild" or "rugged coast"), a strip of rocky indented coves and sandy beaches

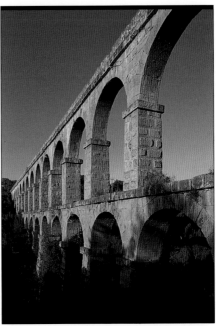

that runs from **Blanes** virtually up to the French border. The first of Spain's big coastal resorts, the Costa Brava is still developing but, unlike the Costa del Sol, the busy season is limited to the summer months, so a visit at other times of the year means less congestion. Also the coast's natural beauty can still be appreciated from the sea by way of local ferry boats that make frequent journeys between the main resorts.

### Cadaqués

There is not much to distinguish one Costa Brava resort from another — the usual sun, sin, sangria and french fries — so go to Cadaqués, at the northern end of the coast on the tip of Cape Creus. A little isolation and a lot of celebrity status have helped to make Cadaqués different. It is difficult to reach by public transport and in summer there is virtually no parking for cars. It has long been a center for Spanish and foreign artists, writers and less serious sojourners. Looming over Cadaqués is the persona of Salvador Dalí who lived for many years in nearby Port Lligat and was happily surrounded by a large entourage of admirers, friends, sycophants and con men. The good news about little Cadaqués is that its natural beauty and charm survive all the hype. Its

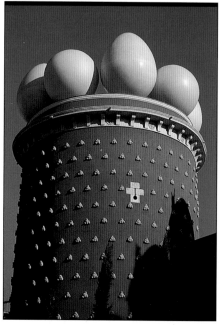

pebbly beaches, cozy bay, whitewashed houses with their red-tiled roofs, and hilly backdrop have not much changed through the years. There are even a few local fishermen who still ply the coastal waters for a living. Out of season it is even better: clean, quiet and uncluttered with just a few foreigners — artists, writers and con men — warming themselves in the winter sunshine at a beachfront café and plotting the next painting, novel, deal or coup.

## FIGUERES

Turning inland, there is Figueres, the birthplace of Dalí and the site of his marvelous museum which is second only to the Prado

in the number of visitors it receives each year. Surrealist painter, collaborator with Luis Buñuel, Spain's greatest film-maker, wry observer of life and flagrant entrepreneur, Dalí was born in the town in 1904 and died there in 1989. His museum is a fitting commentary on his life and his work: inventive, iconoclastic, wacky and above all, entertaining. The building is an old theater that was destroyed in the Civil War and restored later. Festooned with giant eggs and loaves of bread made of plaster, it contains ample evidence of Dalí's painterly qualities as well as of his elliptical view of the world around him. There is a self-portrait of the artist at the age of seventeen; good pencil drawings; the famous oil painting of a loaf of bread so realistic that you feel you can take a bite out of it; many portraits of his wife, Gala; Mae West's lips depicted as a sofa; a bathtub on the ceiling; and his custom-built Cadillac in the central well of the theater where, if you put five pesetas into a slot a light comes on inside revealing a uniformed chauffeur, Dalí and a naked Gala in the back seat festooned with ivy; there is a second's pause and then water pours over the occupants inside the vehicle.

## GIRONA

The central city of this northern part of Catalonia is Girona. An important Roman town, Girona suffered for its strategic position with a surfeit of sieges from the time of Charlemagne's battles with the Moors to Napoleon's invasion of Spain in the early 19th century. Now a modest capital of a wealthy province, Girona is notable for its cathedral and its old quarter.

Introduced by a massive stairway, the cathedral is a Gothic marvel. Built in the 14th and 15th centuries, it has no central *coro* or any supporting columns. Its huge nave, 22.5 m (73 ft) across, is the widest in all Christendom, a striking tribute to the skill and daring of Catalonia's medieval architects. Other Gothic highlights include the silver *retablo* over the main altar and the sepulcher of Bishop Bernard de Pau. The cloister and bell tower date from the earlier Romanesque cathedral, there is a superb 12th-century tapestry depicting the

Creation in the cathedral's museum, and the façade is a later Baroque addition. But it is the feeling of vast vaulted space in the nave that makes the most impact — humanized by a marble sculpture of a knight over a side door, his feet resting comfortably on his dog.

"Fortunately," one guide book puts it, "the old town of Girona has been lovingly neglected." In fact, some restoration has taken place, particularly in **El Call**, the Jewish quarter. The result is an unspoilt hilly medieval town that backs on the Onya River which runs through the heart of Girona. The Jewish quarter is exceptionally well-preserved and was famous in its day for its Jewish mystics and cabalistic studies.

### Hotels and Restaurants

Girona's most central hotel is the **Ultonia** ( 20-38-50, Avenida Jaume 1, N° 22, which is in the expensive category; for eating there is the **Cal Ros** ( 20-10-11, Calle Cort Real, N° 9, and the **Rosaleda** ( 21-36-68, Paseo Dehesa.

### RURAL CATALONIA

Although the region is the most heavily industrialized in Spain, rural Catalonia is extensive, highly productive, and easily accessible. In the north there is the Catalan section of the Pyrenees where the steep-sided valleys running north to south maintain an ecology and way of life little changed by the giant transformation that has occurred elsewhere. There are meadows speckled with cows, villages clustered around sturdy Romanesque churches, streams and birch woods and marvelous mountain air.

### ANDORRA

Further west there is the curiosity of **Andorra**, one of Europe's four miniscule independent principalities. (The others are Luxembourg, Leichtenstein, and San Marino.) Andorra, a historical oversight, is wedged between France and Spain in the Pyrenees. It is ethnically Catalan and has two "co-princes," the President of France and the Bishop of Seu d'Urgell who lives just

across the border in Spain. A tax-free haven, the tiny mountainous principality tends to be overwhelmed by visitors in the summer months, conspicuously consuming the plentiful duty-free goods. But off-season is better and there is some great hiking terrain in the hills beyond the town. Andorra is not easily accessible. It is 220 km (132 miles) from Barcelona (take the N-152 north to **Puigcerda**, the C-1313 to **Seu d'Urgell**, and finally the C-145 to Andorra); and 153 km (92 miles) from **Lleida** on the northbound C-1313.

### LEVANTE

Strongly influenced by Catalonia, although a separate region, is the Levante, or the "East." This is the area centered on **Valencia**, midway down the Mediterranean coast. The Catalans drove the Moors out in the 13th century and re-populated this fabulously fertile part of Spain with their own people. The *huerta*, or cultivated plain, around Valencia is the most densely populated agricultural land in Europe. It produces a spectacular variety of produce and crops including rice, vast groves of oranges, lemons, peaches and apricots, vegetables of every kind, and even mulberry leaves for the voracious silk worm. The local population, who are noted for their industriousness and independent spirit, speak Valenciano, a variation of Catalan, as well as Castilian. Valencia, the principal city, is the country's third largest and a major seaport. This is not mass tourism terrain but if you are driving around the country you may well pass through the Levante and, if you do, a night in Valencia is a pleasant way to break the journey.

### VALENCIA

A prosperous, elegant and confident city, Valencia owes much to the Moors who devised the intricate and still extant irrigation system that is the mainstay of agriculture in

OPPOSITE: Exterior of Dalí's museum in Figueres, where the artist was born and where he died.

the Levante. Water disputes are resolved every Thursday at noon — as they have been for a thousand years — at the **Tribunal de las Aguas** (Water Tribunal) in front of the cathedral.

## SIGHTSEEING

Valencia's best buildings include the Gothic cathedral; the **Palacio de la Generalidad**, where the region's own parliament used to meet; the Baroque **Palacio del Marqués de los Dos Aguas** (water, as you can see, is

pretty important in this part of the world); the **railway station** which is lavishly adorned with ceramic tiles; and a lovely domed **market** with stained glass windows and riot of colorful produce below. Valencia, it should be noted, is the home town of *paella*, Spain's national seafood dish. The city is also renowned for its tiles and it is fitting that Spain's **Museo Nacional de Cerámica** (National Ceramics Museum) is housed in the **Palacio del Marqués de Dos Aguas** where over 5,000 exhibits tell the story of local tile-making in imaginative ways, such as reproducing an all-tiled traditional Valencian kitchen. The city is famous for its festivals, notably **Las Fallas**, a pyromaniac's dream come true. This fiesta is held in the

third week of March every year and celebrates the coming of spring. Rather like the April Fair in Seville, the city is overwhelmed for a week by floats, parades, bullfights, and fireworks. Neighborhoods compete with each other to produce the most impressive papier-mâché figures and tableaux. The climax comes on the last day when everything goes up in smoke and flames to the accompaniment of thunderous detonations, cascades of exploding fireworks, and the sirens of speeding fire engines.

## TOURIST INFORMATION

**Provincial Area Code**   (6)
From within Spain   (96)
**Tourist Offices**:
Plaza Pais Valenciano, 1. ℂ 315-0417.
Calle La Paz, 46. ℂ 332-4096.
**Airport (Manises)** ℂ 370-3408.
**Iberia Airlines** ℂ 325-0500, Calle La Paz, N° 14.
**Railway Station** ℂ 231-0634, Plaza Alfonso el Magnanimo, N° 2.
**Trasmediterranea** (Shipping Company) ℂ 367-6512, Avenida Ingeniero Manuel Soto, N° 15.

### HOTELS

*Expensive* Pts.18,000 to Pts.28,000; *moderate:* Pts.8,000 to Pts.18,000.

*Expensive*
**Astoria Palace** ℂ 325-6737, Plaza Roderigo Botet, N° 15. is on the cavernous side, but central and efficient.
**Dimar** ℂ 334-1807, Gran Vía Marqués del Turia, N° 80, is also in the central area.
**Reína Victoria** ℂ 325-0487, is on Calle Barcas, N° 4.
**Rey Don Jaime Sol** ℂ 360-7300, Avenida Baleares, N° 2, is a modern hotel.

*Moderate*
**Expo Hotel** ℂ 347-0909, Avenida Pio XII, N° 4, is also a modern hotel.
**Feria Sol** ℂ 364-4411, Avenida Feria, N° 2, is close to the Feria de Muestras exhibition center.
**Ingles** ℂ 351-6426, is on Calle Marqués de Dos Aguas, N° 6.
**Lehos** ℂ 334-7800, is on Calle General Urrutia.

**RESTAURANTS**

*Expensive* represents meals costing Pts.8,000 and above; *moderate:* Pts.3,000 to Pts.8,000, and *inexpensive:* Pts.1,000 to Pts.3,000.

**Commodoro** ( 321-3815, is on Calle Transits, N° 3.

**El Condestable** ( 369-9250, on Calle Artes Graficas, N° 15, serves international cuisine.

**El Plat** ( 334-9638, Calle Conde de Altea, N° 41, is a good place for Valencia's best known dish: the *paella*.

**La Hacienda** ( 373-1859, Calle Navarro

United States. Murcia was a favorite location for Italian film-makers during the era of "spaghetti Westerns." The capital, also called Murcia, was founded by the Moors on the banks of the Segura river at the center of a fertile plain. Its principal claim to fame is that it was the home of one of Spain's most renowned polychrome wood sculptors, Francisco Salzillo (1707–1783) and there is a museum of his work in the city. Murcia province is also known for its Holy Week and Spring festivals and particularly good ones can be seen in the provincial capital and

Reverter, N° 12, is an upscale restaurant, favored by businessmen.

**Ma Cuina** ( 341-7799, Gran Vía Germanias, N° 49, has varied menu reflecting what is in season.

All these restaurants fall into the *moderate* category though La Hacienda and Ma Cuina verge on the *expensive* side.

## MURCIA

Between Andalusia and the Levante lies Murcia, one of Spain's "forgotten" provinces. Truly off the beaten track, much of it is arid and sparsely populated with scenery not unlike parts of the southwest of the

in Lorca, which is 62 km (37 miles) southwest of the provincial capital on the N-340. The Murcian coastline is not interesting and perhaps the best way to get a feel of the province is to take the inland road (the N-340) which runs across it from Almeria in the south to Alicante in the north and passes through both Lorca and the capital.

Valencia: Modern art exhibition OPPOSITE and colorful market ABOVE.

# Andalusia

## A MOORISH SPIRIT

In the popular imagination Spain has long been synonymous with Andalusia. The image evoked is a multidimensional kaleidoscope of color, sounds, smells and sensuality. There is the swirl of the gypsy dancer's polka dotted skirt; the spine-tingling wail of the *cante jondo*, the "deep song," that conjures up Andalusia's Moorish past; straight-backed riders with swarthy, arrogant faces under flat black hats; provocative eyes behind restless fans; the strains of the pasodoble fading as the matador raises his sword for the kill; sunlight on a whitewashed wall and a cascade of red geraniums spilling over a balcony; the intoxicating scent of jasmine, and the smell of aging sherry the color of polished teak.

Beneath the romantic flourishes there is a nub of truth. Andalusia has enough of its Moorish heritage left in spirit and stone and to make it distinctively different from the rest of Spain. Flamenco, bullfighting and sherry all originated there. The people have a lightness, sparkle, and fatalism not found elsewhere in the country. When Benjamin Disraeli, a writer and future prime minister of Britain, visited Andalusia in 1830, he observed: "There is a calm voluptuousness about life here that wonderfully accords with my disposition."

The other side of the image was either not seen — or ignored — by the romantics. This was the huge gap between the wealthy landowners and the impoverished peasantry, the lack of industry and infrastructure, an unresponsive church, and an oppressive government. Modern Andalusia is a different place. Poverty and inequality, though still a visible feature of the Andalusian landscape, have been reduced by the impact of dramatic and relatively recent economic changes. Romance, by the same token, has also taken a knock. The land of the Alhambra, Don Juan, Carmen, and spontaneous flamenco dancing has become the land of mass tourism, the family car, and the business lunch.

Today, Andalusia sees itself on the crest of a new wave of development and Spanish-style perestroika. Its leaders are fond of saying that it is on the way to becoming Europe's California. Its detractors, while acknowledging the reality of the economic upsurge, say a down-market Florida is more like it.

Andalusia has a special place in Spanish history. Accessible and attractive, it has invited foreign curiosity from the time of the Phoenicians. The Greeks came later and the Romans settled heavily. But it was the Arab conquest and long sojourn — they came in the eighth century

and were finally driven back into Africa at the end of the 15th century — that gave Andalusia its unique imprint. The Moors were the great civilizers of the Middle Ages turning their beloved Al-Andalus into an earthly paradise with its mosques, palaces, gardens, its irrigated agriculture, centers of arts, crafts and learning. The rest of Europe, including Christian Spain, appeared rough-hewn and philistine by comparison.

Andalusia anchors Spain. As large as Portugal, it straddles the Atlantic Ocean

Parque de María Luisa Seville OPPOSITE, and one of its famous white pigeons ABOVE.

and the Mediterranean Sea and faces Africa. It has one-fifth of the country's population, its highest mountains (the Sierra Nevada), one of its longest rivers (the Guadalquivir), its warmest climate (gentle winters and broiling summers), largest national park (Coto de Doñana), and most developed coastline (Costa del Sol). It is a surprisingly lush and fertile part of Spain, a relief after the interminable and virtually treeless *meseta* of the interior; and it is the cradle of unusually picturesque cities, towns and villages.

## SEVILLE

Seville is Andalusia's capital and the country's fourth largest city, so let us start there. The Andalusian character distills itself in its most pure form in Seville. It is a city of beauty, grace, and spirit. *Sevillanos* are renowned for their wit and spontaneity, for their sense of style, and for their easy-going nature. It has been described as Spain's most Mediterranean city, although it is not actually on it. The city's allure attracted writers (Tirso de Molina, Lope de Vega, and Cervantes who spent some time in Seville's jail where he got a lot work done), and painters (Velázquez, Murillo and Zubarán); it also produced memorable fictional characters such as Carmen, Don Juan, and Rossini's famous Barber. It is unclear how all this came to pass, but there is little doubt that a long and continuous history and a seductive climate had a lot to do with it.

Hercules himself, according to legend, founded Seville on the banks of the Guadalquivir within navigable reach of the sea. Its ancient name was Hispalis and it was the site of Phoenician, Greek and Carthaginian settlements before the Romans made it the capital of Baetica which roughly corresponds to modern Andalusia. Vandals and Visigoths followed, and then in the eighth century the Moors captured the city. Although never the capital of Muslim Spain (Córdoba had that privilege), Seville, or

Isbiliya as it was known, flowered under its Moorish rulers.

Its conquest by Ferdinand III (the "Saint") returned it to Christendom in 1248, and it became the southern capital of the Castilian monarchs. Seville reached its zenith in the 16th century when it profited from the wealth of the New World on whose trade it had a monopoly. (The first man to sight land from Columbus's ship, the story goes, was Rodrigo de Triana, a sailor from Seville.) From those heady decades, the city steadily declined.

The decay continued until the present century when Seville began to prosper again. It hosted the Ibero-American Exposition in 1929 and played the same role for the Universal Exposition in 1992, the quincentenary of Columbus's discovery of America. "Expo 92" had a huge physical impact on Seville. The exhibition site on the Isla de la Cartuja, a largely unused marshy island in the Guadalquivir river, was transformed and linked to the city by several new bridges. New construction included: the expansion of Seville's airport, a new railway station built for the high-speed AVE train that links Seville to Madrid, and a ring road around the city. The Cartuja site is not fully utilised now but retains some of its pavilions, the cable-car and monorail train, and facilities for shows, concerts and exhibitions.

## SEEING THE CITY

Seville has a number of spectacular sights but is infinitely more than the sum of its parts. Its broad avenues, parks and gardens, labyrinthine old quarter, cobbled streets, cool flower-filled patios, and riverine boulevards combine to make it one of Europe's most dazzling cities.

## THE GIRALDA

Seville's emblem, evoking its Moorish past, is the Giralda, the lofty tower that was built as a minaret eight hundred years ago and was preserved by the Christians as they erected a new cathedral beside it. Embedded in Seville's ancient core, the Giralda is what you see when you approach

OPPOSITE: La Giralda.

the city, and it is named after the weather vane that sits on top of it. It provides a magnificent bird's eye view of the Andalusian capital and is well worth the long climb up sloping ramps that take you to where the Moorish muezzins once called the faithful to prayer.

From the summit you can get a sense of the shape of the city and a panorama of the countryside beyond. The first impression, as you look around from a height of 92 m (300 ft), is a colorful jumble of ochre, rust, and umber rooftops, white-washed walls, gray spires, and purple jacaranda trees. If it is the dead part of the afternoon, you may see a line of horse-drawn carriages drawn up under the orange trees at the foot of the Giralda, horses and drivers alike obeying the imperative of the siesta.

On the northern side, there is the **Patio de los Naranjos** which was the mosque's courtyard and is now an orangery, as the name suggests. Beyond is the **Alcázar** and the old Jewish quarter of **Santa Cruz.** Moving around the compass to the northeast, there is the massive density of the **University,** (the second largest building in Spain after the Escorial), which was built in the mid-18th century as the site of the Royal Tobacco Factory where Carmen and the other *cigarreras* rolled — and quite often smoked — their cigars; and beyond that the **Parque María Luisa** (Seville's equivalent of the Retiro Park in Madrid), and the **Plaza de España.**

To the southeast is the **Torre del Oro** (Tower of Gold), built by the Moors and now a maritime museum, and the **Guadalquivir** (the "big river" in Arabic) which still provides a navigable link to the Atlantic Ocean some 45 km (30 miles) away. Due south is **La Maestranza,** Seville's exquisite 18th-century bullring with its Moorish arches and white-washed exterior.

## THE CATHEDRAL

The Cathedral, next to the Giralda, was built in the 15th century on the site of the city's largest mosque. A gigantic Gothic construction, it is the third largest cathedral in the world after St. Peter's in Rome

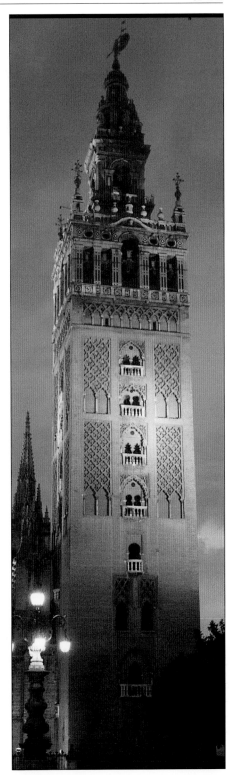

and St. Paul's in London. Its founders are reputed to have said: "Let us raise up so great a church that those who contemplate it should take us for madmen."

They had a point. The place is a cavernous rectangle, at once impressive and oppressive. However, the high altar is superbly offset between a golden screen and an intricately carved *retablo* that is the largest in Spain. At the feast of Corpus Christi, in June, a minuet is danced in front of this altar by a group of young boys dressed up as Renaissance choirboys and called *Seises*. The cathedral also has two richly decorated sacristies (the Sacristy of the Chalices, and the Main Sacristy) in which religious paintings by Zubarán, Murillo, Van Dyck and Luis de Vargas, as well as silverware and vestments, are on display. The cathedral contains the tombs of Ferdinand III, the conqueror of Seville, Alfonso the Wise, Pedro the Cruel, and Christopher Columbus.

Columbus has his own pantheon and his bier is supported by four regal figures representing the kingdoms of Castile, León, Navarre and Aragón. After his death, his remains were destined to make two more journeys across the Atlantic, first from Valladolid to Hispaniola (modern Haiti and the Dominican Republic), then to Cuba and finally back Spain, this time to rest in Seville. Legend has it that some of his remains were left behind in Havana so that, in death as well as life, he straddles two worlds.

## THE ALCÁZAR

Built to accommodate the needs of man rather than to deify the almighty, the Alcázar is an almost necessary antidote to the cold grandeur of the cathedral. The site of royal palaces since the Muslim conquest, most of the buildings are the work of Christian kings, notably Pedro the Cruel who admired the Islamic style and used Moorish workmen to build much of the present complex in the mid-14th century. (He also

La Giralda and the Cathedral. Seville's distinctive landmark that was built as a minaret in the 13th century..

murdered a number of people in it, including his half-brother, thus earning his sobriquet.) Subsequent monarchs and noblemen added pieces to the mosaic and the whole adds up to one of the most intriguing examples of the Christian-Moorish Mudéjar architectural marriage in all of Spain.

There are a number of salons, halls and state rooms to see but the centerpiece is the **Salon de Embajadores** which has hardly changed since the finishing touches were put to it over six hundred years ago. It

has triple horseshoe arches along three sides, a beautiful carved wooden cupola, and doors that were probably the work of Toledo craftsmen. Phrases from the Koran in flowing Arabic script adorn the walls. Pedro was no paragon but his failings did not include religious bigotry or cultural philistinism. There is a tendency to think more kindly of him as you wander past dreamy arabesques, across marble-floored courtyards where a small fountain may spill water into a moss-covered basin, through gardens dense with hibiscus, jacaranda, palms, cypresses, and orange trees where birds sing and the sun's rays are cooled and softened.

## BARRIO DE SANTA CRUZ

From Alcázar, a pleasant walk, a drink, dinner or a flamenco show can be had in the

ABOVE LEFT AND OPPOSITE RIGHT: Outdoor bar and square in Santa Cruz, the old Jewish quarter of Seville. ABOVE RIGHT: The gardens of Alcázar and its interior OPPOSITE LEFT.

**Barrio de Santa Cruz**, the old Jewish quarter of Seville. A good way to enter is from the **Patio de Banderas**, an attractive square close to the Alcázar, and then to follow the narrow streets up to the **Plaza Alfaro**, which is close to the **Jardines de Murillo.** The route is a succession of ancient white-washed houses, flower-bedecked balconies and squares, with restaurants, bars, and cafés on every corner. Gentrification has laid its homogenizing hand on the quarter but there is still plenty of music, laughter and spontaneity in the streets and bars.

## OTHER SIGHTS

There are many other places worth visiting in the city. There are the **Parque de María Luisa**, a lovely park laid out during Seville's renaissance in the 1920s, and the **Plaza de España**, a less-than-lovely arc of neo-Baroque towers, bridges, terraces and staircases, which was the site of the Ibero-American Exposition in 1929. A sense of the domestic architecture of Seville and Andalusia is superbly conveyed in the **Casa de Pilatos** (Pilate's House), so named because it was apparently a copy of Pontius Pilate's palace in Jerusalem. A blend of Mudéjar, Gothic and Renaissance styles, it was built in the early 16th century and contains Roman antiquities, paintings, furniture and some of the best tile-work in the city.

## MUSEUMS

Seville is also rich in museums. There is a fine art museum (**Museo de Bellas Artes**), which is second only to the Prado in Madrid and has a splendid collection of paintings by Bartoleme Esteban Murillo, a native son of Seville, and the Extremaduran painter Francisco de Zubarán, who lived

in the city for many years; an archaeological museum (**Museo Arquelógico**); and an archive of the Americas (**Archivo de Indías**) which documents the discovery of the New World, and Spain's trading relations with it, when Seville was at its commercial peak.

Less than half an hour's drive, on the Huelva road, there is the Roman town of **Itálica**, an open-air museum if you will, near the village of **Santiponce.** On your way there you can see the **Isla de Cartuja**, to the left as you cross the Guadalquivir river, where the Universal Exposition was held in 1992. Itálica was the birthplace of the emperors Trajan and Hadrian, and has the remains of an amphitheater, forum, baths

and several villas. There is a rumpled feeling to the site as if an earthquake had given it a good shaking, and the mosaics, Itálica's best feature, are in Seville's archaeological museum. But the profusion of flowers — oleander, hibiscus, geraniums, and poppies — and the cypress, acacia and fig trees in the formal gardens among the ruins go a long way to redeeming the place.

## WANDER, BUT CAREFULLY

Seville is a lovely city to wander in. It is

relatively compact and one of the few places in the world where to take a horse-drawn carriage is neither an affectation or a rip-off. The superbly maintained carriages drawn by well-fed and well-groomed horses are centrally located, provide a perfect slow-paced, open view of the surroundings, and cost little more than a taxi. The downside is the growing level of street crime. Seville has one of the highest unemployment rates in the country and, like many Spanish cities, has acquired a serious drug problem. Cameras, handbags, purses, and wallets should be carefully guarded, and late night strolling is best confined to populous areas.

## SEVILLE'S FESTIVALS

It is impossible to separate Seville from the great rites of spring: the **Holy Week** penitence and pageantry in the week before Easter, and the joyous, extrovert **April Feria** that follows it. *Semana Santa,* or Holy Week, dates from the 16th century when *cofradías* — charitable brotherhoods or guilds connected to local churches — took to the streets to re-enact the passion and crucifixion of Christ. The ceremonies begin on Palm Sunday with processions of penitents in their white robes and sinister pointed hoods (the Ku Klux Klan in the United States borrowed the design for their own unchristian purposes), and floats bearing images of Christ and the Virgin. The processions, a slow moving river of shuffling sinners and swaying canopies and religious statuary illuminated by candle-

light, converge on the cathedral. There are moments of great fervor such as when the Virgin of La Macarena, the lady whose tears are frozen in glass on her cheeks, leaves her church at midnight on the eve of Good Friday, and when the figure of Christ departs from San Lorenzo Church in the early hours of that day. Imperial Rome is represented by carefully put together legionnaires, and there is no shortage of material for the crowd scenes as the Sevillanos pour into the streets. The festival ends on Easter Sunday with more

processions and floats, but this time on a joyous note with singing, hand-clapping and the sway and swirl of Seville's own graceful dance (the *Sevillana*) engulfing the city.

The April Fair or **Feria** is both younger and older than the rituals of Holy Week. It began as a cattle market fair in the mid-19th century, but its celebration of the coming of spring goes back to pagan times. It used to take place in the center of Seville, but it is now held in fairgrounds of **Los Remedios**, a modern suburb across the Guadalquivir river. It officially lasts five days beginning on a Tuesday ten days after Easter Sunday; but since people hardly seem to go to bed during that time it really adds up to ten days' worth of fiesta. "The most tiring and exhilarating public celebration on the Iberian Peninsula," in the view of one veteran travel writer.

As with Holy Week, the April Fair is a vivid, constantly shifting and unashamedly public theater. During the mornings, people stroll around the fairgrounds admiring the immaculately-turned out horsemen, their bright-eyed señoritas, and the no less gorgeous display of horseflesh and accouterments that parade before them. If Spaniards can ever be said to "strut their stuff," this is the time and the place. There is constant movement as people drop into one caseta after another — these are the gaily decorated stalls that cover the grounds — for a gossip, a drink, a laugh.

A long lunch may be followed by a trip back across the river to **La Maestranza** bull-ring where Spain's leading matadors strut *their* stuff; some of the best *corridas* of the season take place during the April Fair. As the sun goes down the revelers return to the fairgrounds for a night of strolling, drinking, eating, dancing, singing and enjoying themselves. There is no statutory hour for the night's revelry to end. Seville's great Feria, while it is in motion, knows no tomorrow. James Michener, an aficionado of Holy Week and the April Feria, reckoned there was nothing in the world to surpass these festivals, not Mardi Gras in New Orleans, the Palio in Sienna, Bastille Day in Haiti, not even Carnival in

ABOVE: Horse-drawn carriages under orange trees in front of Seville's cathedral. OPPOSITE: The center of Seville.

Rio de Janeiro. "At any time of year Sevilla is a distinguished city," he wrote in *Iberia*, his massive travel book about Spain, "but during Holy Week and the days that follow, it is without peer."

Michener advised setting aside several weeks to cover the spring festivals in and around Seville. Most travelers will not have the luxury of so much time, but if you should miss the Easter period, there is another event on the religious calendar that is rather different yet equally passionate and moving. This is the *Romería del Rocío* (Pilgrimage of

Rocío) that takes place at Pentecost, 60 days after Easter, which means it usually falls in mid-May. Rocío is as rural as Holy Week and the April Feria are urban, and it unfolds in some of the most beautiful countryside in Spain in the Coto de Doñana National Park which lies about 80 km (48 miles) due south of Seville. The best access is from the Seville to the Huelva Road (N-431), branching off about halfway through the villages of Aznalcázar, Pilas, or Hinojos.

## TOURIST INFORMATION

**Provincial Area Code** (5)
From within Spain (95)
**Tourist Office** ( 422-1404, Avenida de la Constitución, N° 21.
**San Pablo Airport** ( 451-0677.
**Iberia Airlines** ( 422-8901, Calle Almirante Lobo.

**Railway Station** ( 423-1918, Calle Zaragoza, N° 29.

### HOTELS
*Expensive* means a night's lodging costs Pts.18,000 to Pts.28,000; *moderate:* Pts.8,000 to Pts.18,000; and *inexpensive:* Pts.4,000 to Pts.8,000.

*Expensive*
**Alfonso XIII** ( 422-2850, Calle San Fernando, N° 2, is the grandest hotel in town; built in 1929 and opened by the king whose name it adopted. His grandson, the present monarch, reopened it after extensive renovation work. The heavy, ornate Sevillian style is a bit gloomy and overpowering but it is unique and luxurious.
**Dona María** ( 422-4990, Calle Don Remondo, N° 19, is a pretty place perfectly sited opposite the Cathedral; great views of the Giralda from roof where there is a sometimes full swimming pool.
**Macarena Sol** ( 437-5700, Calle San Juan de Rivera, N° 2, opposite the basilica of the Macarena, is a bit noisy but has good traditional atmosphere and fine interior patio.
**Inglaterra** ( 422-4970, Plaza Nueva, N° 7, is a nicely situated hotel with gracious public rooms and patio.

*Moderate*
**Fernando III** ( 421-7307, Calle San José, N° 21, is conveniently located close to the colorful Santa Cruz district.
**Monte Carmel** ( 427-9000, Calle Turia, N° 7, is across the river in Remedios, close to where the April Fair takes place.
**Reyes Católicos** ( 421-1200, is on Calle Gravina, N° 57.

*Inexpensive*
**Simon**. ( 422-6660, Calle García de Vinuesa, N° 19, is an centrally located old-fashioned hotel with cool interior patio; service is good.

### RESTAURANTS
*Expensive* represents meals costing Pts.8,000 and above; *moderate:* Pts.3,000 to Pts.8,000, and *inexpensive:* Pts.1,000 to Pts.3,000.

ABOVE: Wine bar in Seville. OPPOSITE: Flamenco dancer and where she performs.

*Expensive*

**La Dorada** ( 445-5100, located on N° 6 of Calle Virgen de Aguasantas of Los Remedios, like its cousins in Madrid and Barcelona, is a great fish restaurant. It is situated across the Guadalquivir where the April Fair unrolls.

**Enrique Becera** ( 421-3049, Calle Gamazo, N° 2, is near the Plaza Nueva and city center and has good selection of Andalusian dishes.

**San Marco** ( 421-2440, Calle Cuña, N° 6, is a lovely old rambling Seville house and

serves haute and nouvelle cuisines. It is more international than Spanish but everything is in exquisite taste.

*Moderate*

**Don Raimondo** ( 422-3355, Calle Argote de Molina, N° 26, is in a cul-de-sac close to the Cathedral. It specializes in Andalusian dishes that have a Moorish influence and has closed patio with large fireplace and much culinary decoration.

**Oriza** ( 427-9585, Calle San Fernando, is a modern bar and restaurant, popular with the literary set, a good place for a light snack or a full-blown meal.

**Rio Grande** ( 427-8371, Calle Betis, is in the Triana district on the river. It is famous

for good fish, especially the assorted fried fish (*pescaditos*) and it has great views over the river to the Tower of Gold and the Giralda.

*Inexpensive*

**La Judería** ( 421-4338, Calle Cano y Cuesto, N° 13, is near the Jardines de Murillo. Simple, honest food are served with the best kind of Spanish service: courteous, efficient and accomplished with a smile.

Seville is full of interesting *tavernas* and *tapas* bars, many are lavishly deco-

rated with the local tile and quite a few serve wine and sherry directly from the barrel.

It is also a good place to see *flamenco*. This invariably takes place in a formal setting these days, and it is best to book the show in advance through your hotel or through buying tickets directly from the restaurant or theater where the performance takes place. The followings are good places for a sampling:

**Los Gallos** ( 421-6981, Plaza de Santa Cruz, N° 11, is in the picturesque Barrio de Santa Cruz.

**Tablao de Curro Velez** ( 421-6492, on the Calle Rodo, N° 7, is the one to go to mix with the locals.

**La Trocha** ( 435-5028, Ronda de Capuchinos, Nº 23, is the liveliest spot with plenty of Sevillana dances.

## THE EL ROCÍO PILGRIMAGE: A VERY SPANISH AFFAIR

Imagine yourself in fields strewn with daisies, buttercups, purple thistles and elderberry flowers. All around are voices, song, laughter; there is the jingle of harness, the snort of a horse with too much dust up

his nose, and the creak of ancient wagon wheels. A quick glance at the caparisoned carts and a shrine of the Virgin in solid silver produces another time warp. There is not a beach, a bikini or a bullfight in sight. Can this be modern Spain, Spain of the European Community, the World Fair, the Olympic Games?

In the southwestern corner of Andalusia, on the edge of the marshland of the **Doñana National Park and Wildlife Reserve**, there is a ghost town called **El Rocío**. A cluster of modern buildings dominated by a brilliantly whitewashed church with a red-tiled roof, El Rocío sits silent and forlorn for most of the year. But then, as spring turns into summer, it becomes the center of the Andalusian universe, a Catholic mecca, as over a million pilgrims converge on it. They come from Madrid, Barcelona, Málaga, and the Canary Islands;

from Ceuta and Melilla, the Spanish enclaves in Morocco; even from Latin America. They come by air, by train, by car; there are mule-drawn carts, oxen dragging heavy drays, elegant surreys, tractor-towed hay wagons, motorbikes, mopeds, horsemen and hikers.

The pilgrims are a sociologist's dream: a rich slice of Spanish society represented by farmers, factory workers, secretaries, lawyers, government officials and clergy. They come because the mysteries of their religion draw them, or because they feel the call of history and culture, or because it is a great excuse for a marathon binge — for dancing, drinking and showing off. Or — and few people seem to think there is any contradiction — all of the above. It is a thoroughly Spanish festival, as important to the people of southern Spain as the pilgrimage to Santiago de Compostela is to their northern compatriots. Every year, Spain doubles its population as the tourists flow in. But very few of those thirty-eight million visitors have heard of El Rocío, much less seen it.

The focus of the pilgrims' attention is a life-sized figure of the Virgin Mary, holding a diminutive Christ and a golden scepter, *Nuestra Señora del Rocío,* Our Lady of the Dew. She has a pale porcelain face and hands, made in the 16th century, and an elaborate gold embroidered dress and celestial crown. Her story is as rich as her appearance, the stuff of legend. The Rocío cult goes back to Moorish times when Christians hid their relics in trees in the marshlands of this area. As the Moorish forces retreated, the relics were recovered and were said to have miraculous properties, the most renowned being the Virgin of Rocío.

In the 13th century, King Alfonso X drove the Moors back and Christianity was once again the official religion of this region. The twist in the Rocío story is that the Virgin liked to be venerated in the wilds, making that desire abundantly clear when a man who found her in a tree tried to take her back to his home town. He rested for a while on the way and awoke to find she had returned to her original sanctuary in the marshes where the Guadalquivir river winds slowly

---

ABOVE: Pilgrims on the road to El El Rocío with a replica of the Virgin in their *simpecado*. OPPOSITE: Parade in front of El Rocío church.

into the sea. This is the spot, the legend has it, where the hamlet of El Rocío stands.

The pilgrimage is organized by lay Catholic brotherhoods called *hermandades*. Each group has a house in Rocío, built with its members' donations, and elects a slate of officials. There is a president, a board of directors, and a man in charge of the *simpecado* (literally "without sin") which is a replica of the statue of the Virgin drawn on a high-wheeled cart by two oxen. Each brotherhood has one of these floats which are heavy, very ornate and lead the slow column of pilgrims along the dusty roads to Rocío, rather in the manner that a regiment of infantry on the move might be preceded by its color guard. The local priest, although not an official of the brotherhood, usually accompanies it. One I met in Rocío was sitting with his group's governing board during a lull in the pilgrimage's activities.

Dressed in a Ralph Lauren polo shirt, he was drinking beer out of a plastic cup and enjoying himself. His role, he said, was to act as the brotherhood's "spiritual counselor."

About one hour's drive from Seville, first on the Huelva highway and then across country, Rocío receives hundreds of thousands of casual visitors as the festival moves towards its climax. But the serious way to go is to join a *hermandad* and travel with its slow moving wagons through the flower-strewn countryside, a 20th-century Spanish version of Chaucer's pilgrims wending their yarn-spinning way to Canterbury. A typical wagon will be divided inside by a wooden platform with the men sleeping on the upper berth and the women and children down below. Washing and toilet facilities are rudimentary and largely alfresco, though some of the more chic pilgrims, looking suspiciously clean, seemed to have managed to take time out to pay homage to modern plumbing on the way.

At dusk the group will choose a place to stop, often in a small copse or shaded area, place the *simpecado* in the center and circle the wagons, horses, oxen and tractors around it. Then the eating, drinking and dancing begin. There is always music: the rattle of castanets, the urgent thrumming of guitars, the beat of a drum, the hard, rhythmic sound of Spanish clapping. And songs. The pilgrims seem to be able to sing all day long, no matter how hot, dry and dusty it becomes. A fire is made, cooking gets under way, the wine skins circulate. Young bloods, wearing high waisted Andalusian trousers, short jackets and low crowned hats, parade up and down on their Arab stallions with their girls side-saddle behind them. In post-Franco Spain, some of the riders are girls themselves. High boots, polka-dotted dresses spread out over the horse's rump and hair swept up and held in place by a large comb and crimped with a carnation or a rose, these young señoritas are as tough as their menfolk. And for an added flourish of independence, a cigarette will often appear followed by a plume of smoke between the horse's ears.

The columns slowly converge on Rocío. At the roadside, two young men offer *copas* of chilled sherry, with the compliments of the maker, to thirsty pilgrims as they trudge by. Two horsemen, reins in one hand and hats in the other, held straight down at their sides, race each other down the road, small puffs of dust spurting from their horses' hooves. Rocío itself, the once-a-year town, has no paved roads and there is a feeling of the American West as the wagons roll down the wide streets, each with its own cloud of dust.

There is also a fairground ambiance with stalls selling food and drink and merchandise (everything from Rocío medallions to Rocío T-shirts, from Moroccan knives to Japanese "ghetto-blaster" radios). The old and new are closely juxtaposed: a young woman, for instance, in a flounced and pleated pink dress and a black flat hat, hitches her glossy-flanked steed to a pay telephone and calls home. In the cool of the

BELOW: El Rocío pilgrims returning home to Jerez.

tact is made. The men carrying the heavy tableau fight off most attackers and steam swirls around the Virgin as she begins her voyage among the faithful.

The scene seems a long way from everyday life in a Western country. As the seething mass of bodies and the swaying but serene Virgin go by, bells clang, church, by way of contrast, a large crowd appears mesmerized by the Virgin, calm and peaceful in her tabernacle and cosseted by tall candles and a forest of pink and white gladioli. "*Viva la Virgen!*" shouts one devotee. There is a scraping sound on the sandy floor as another pilgrim shuffles slowly forward on his knees towards the altar.

By Sunday evening, Seville radio stations report that there are a million and a half people in Rocío and the surrounding area. The midnight mass is televised nationally and most of the leading Madrid newspapers run special reports on the event. The moment to bring the Virgin out of the church and take her around the 80 or so *hermandades* in Rocío has arrived. The honor of carrying her under the silver-roofed canopy goes to the men of Almonte, the oldest brotherhood. The crowd surges forward as the shrine appears at the door of the church and begins its slow perambulation around the town. To touch the Lady of the Dew is to be specially blessed and there are apparently no rules governing how con-

groups of people break into songs of praise, individuals cry out and cross themselves, and rose petals shower down from the rooftops. A man on the edge of the crowd laughs and displays a tooth in his upper jaw that has the Virgin engraved on it. A woman climbs on somebody's shoulders and works her way to the shrine over a sea of backs, heads and necks. She manages to touch one of the silver poles supporting the canopy before being wrenched away. "*Viva! Viva! Viva!*" roars the crowd.

The special power of the Rocío pilgrimage over its devotees seems to derive from its blend of religion, nationalism and rural simplicity. This lovely and surprisingly lush corner of southern Spain has submitted to many conquerors: Phoenicians, Greeks, Romans, the Visigoths and Moors. But the conquest of King Alfonso X and the revival of the Virgin of El Rocío symbolizes the final conquest of the true faith and the

---

ABOVE AND OPPOSITE: Horse-borne pilgrims strutting their stuff at the El Rocío pilgrimage.

Spanish state. It is thus not surprising that Seville radio stations assign reporters to the story on a full-time basis during the pilgrimage, and that Spanish national television covers the climax as if it were the final of the World Cup. The 700th anniversary of the cult was celebrated in 1984. For aficionados, the pilgrimage is confidently expected to roll on for another seven centuries.

Later, a senior official from the Seville tourist office, who was making his first pilgrimage, tried to explain what El Rocío meant to Spaniards: "It's very special but unpromotable, and perhaps just as well," he said. "It's part religion, part adventure, part Paris–Dakar rally. I used to be critical. I thought it was too fanatical. But now that I have actually done it, I've changed my

mind." Meanwhile, Nuestra Señora del Rocío has returned to her marshland sanctuary, and her residence is a ghost town once more.

## THE FRONTIER TOWNS

Heading in a southerly direction from Seville brings the traveler to the "frontier" towns of **Arcos** (91 km or 55 miles south

from Seville turning left onto the C-343 after Venta Neuva) and **Jerez** (90 km or 54 miles from Seville, due south on the N-IV); to the mouth of the Guadalquivir at **Sanlúcar de Barrameda** 17 km or 10 miles west of Jerez on the C-440); to the Atlantic Ocean at **Cádiz** (35 km or 21 miles south of Jerez on the N-IV); and to the Mediterranean at **Gibraltar** (129 km or 77 miles east of Cádiz on the N-340).

## ARCOS DE LA FRONTERA

Off the main Seville to Cádiz road lies the hilltop town of **Arcos de la Frontera**, one of the many beautiful fortress towns that defined the boundary between the Christian south and the Moorish kingdom of Granada. Arcos is on what is now known as the **Ruta de los Pueblos Blancos** (Route of the White Towns) and is without cavil one of the most picturesque of these places. There are marvelous views of Arcos from a distance, inside its rocky defenses, and from its heights. The excellent parador, a restored palace with mod cons and great views at the top of the town, shares a pretty square with the 16th-century church. Further attractions include a ruined castle and

plenty of steeply graded, torturous, cobbled streets that have resisted the assault of the 20th century both physically and in ambiance. It's worth staying a night and the **Parador Casa del Corregidor** ( 70-05-00, Plaza de España, is the place to stay — and to eat.

## JEREZ

**Jerez de la Frontera**, the birthplace, production plant and museum of sherry, is an elegant city that is also known for its equestrian

activities, and as the place where flamenco had its origins. Two great annual festivals celebrate these attractions: the **Feria del Caballo** (the Jerez Horse Fair) that follows Seville's April Feria in early May, and the **Fiesta de la Vendimia**, the wine harvest festival that takes place in September.

The wealth that has derived from Jerez's international wine business over the centuries is evident in the fine aristocratic mansions, the sherry bodegas, many of which are virtual palaces, and the leisurely feel to the clean streets lined with orange trees. The bodega owners have a reputation for being close-knit and over-impressed with their own importance, but the local people are friendly and can be exceptionally obliging. A thoroughly unbureaucratic official at the Post Office, for instance, opened up his window and sold me stamps when I turned up shortly after closing time.

Jerez is a very old town, its roots going back to the Phoenicians. It had already become well-known for its wine under the Romans and Pliny, the Roman historian, made a

point of mentioning it. The Moors also left their imprint with the **Alcázar**, built in the 11th century, the remains of the city's walls, and some baths, all now restored and embellished by gardens and fountains.

Although Islam forbids the drinking of alcohol the art of making sherry survived the Moorish period. Harry Debelius, an American journalist and writer who lives in Spain, had this explanation.

"Even under Arab domination Jerez continued to produce and export wine," he writes in his travel guide on Spain. "José

María Quiros, a chemist from Jerez who has spent a lot of time researching the subject, says the typical stemmed, thin, slightly bulbous sherry glass, the *catavinos*, was invented by the Arabs because, since drinking is prohibited by their religion, they could inhale the aroma, and drink such a small quantity that their sin would be only a small one." (*The Independent Traveller: Spain* by Harry Debelius, William Collins Sons and Company Ltd. London 1988, p.155)

The British connection with Jerez goes back to the Middle Ages and one of the sherry bodegas advertises the fact with a quote from Shakespeare prominently displayed among the slowly maturing casks of the heady stuff. "If I had a thousands sons," says Falstaff in *Henry IV,* "the first human principle I would teach them should be to forswear thin potions and to addict themselves to **sack.**" In a word, sherry.

## HOTELS AND RESTAURANTS

The luxury hotel is the **Jerez** ( 30-06-00, on Avenida Alvaro Domecq, N° 35, which has a nice garden and swimming pool. In the moderate range are the **Ávila** ( 33-48-08, Calle Ávila, N° 3, and the **Mica** ( 34-07-00, Higueras, N° 7. Good, middle-price range

restaurants include **Gaitán** ( 34-58-59, Gaitán, N° 3, and **Tendido 6** ( 34-48-35, Circo, N° 10, a lively spot close to the bullring.

## THE BODEGAS

The bodegas are used to visitors and, whether or not you are a sherry-drinker, it is an aesthetically pleasing and educative experience. Many of the proprietors' names have become household words: Gonzalez Byass (Tio Pepe), Pedro Domecq, Harvey & Sons, Sandeman, Osborne, and so on. While sherry is the lifeblood of the business, a great quantity of brandy is also produced in Jerez.

Long before you reach Jerez by road you see the vineyards. As you approach the town

you smell the sherry, a deep, rich vinous perfume exhaled from the juice that turns into pale straw-colored *finos* (dry, light sherries), golden *amontillados* (also dry but older and with more body and a nuttier flavor than the *finos*), and the teak, mahogany and walnut-colored *olorosos* (medium-to-sweet, aromatic sherries; pure *olorosos* are dry on the palate but they are usually blended with sweet wines to produce medium sweet, cream and brown sherries.)

The sherry bodegas are a fascinating blend of the traditional and the modern.

Sherry "cellars" are above ground, and are light airy structures, often very beautiful and many over a hundred years old. Most of them have large patios shaded by oak, acacia and cypress trees and edged with shrubs and banks of flowers. But in the same complex you will find modern bottling plants, warehouses and computer-driven offices.

Let us take a look at Williams and Humboldt, the makers of Dry Sack sherry. Thomas Spencer, a former London taxi driver who married a girl from Jerez, is our guide. He moved to Jerez 16 years earlier, landed a job with Williams and Humboldt, and is now something of a poet on the subject of sherry. He takes us into the oldest cellar which was built in 1863. The high wooden ceiling is supported by columns made out of simple limestone blocks. There

OPPOSITE LEFT: Hilltop parador at Arcos de la Frontera. OPPOSITE RIGHT and ABOVE: Examining a glass of sherry and its autographed sherry casks in the Humbert & Williams sherry bodega, Jerez.

are no artificial lights, no wiring, nothing except row upon row of casks, or butts, made by hand on the premises. Each butt contains 500 liters (108 gallons) of the precious fluid and weighs half a ton. The floor is clay and is watered in summer to maintain the correct degree of humidity. Sunlight filters in, at a discreet angle, through small windows set high in the walls. "Sherry in the cask," says Spencer, "is a living thing. At night in here, it's very quiet, very peaceful, like a cathedral." Sherry is not a vintage wine. It is neither bottled, nor sold, by the year in which was made. It is aged in wooden butts by the *solera* system to ensure a consistent quality. When sherry is drawn off the most mature batch (the *solera*), it is replaced by younger wine which, in turn is replenished from butts containing still younger wine, and so on. The new wine "refreshes" the old, and the old "fortifies" the new. The normal cycle is five or six years. During that time, unlike other wines, sherry matures with the bung out of the butt so that it can "breathe." White American oak is the best material for the butts because the resin in the wood helps the yeast to bloom and the wine to breathe. The resulting evaporation means a loss of three to four percent, but it helps the wine to consume the yeast in it and leave it clear and dry. The evaporation is known among sherry-makers as "the angels' share," but as Thomas Spencer says in an unpoetic afterthought, it simply sticks on the ceiling.

Carlos Williams, the son of one of the co-founders of the firm, created Dry Sack in 1906 as a medium sherry, blended from *amontillados* and *olorosos*, for the British taste. Falstaff's description of his favorite tipple, "sack," has three possible origins, according to Spencer. The first is that it came from the Spanish verb *sacar*, to draw out, describing the action of taking the sherry from the cask. The second version is that the word derived from the sacks that covered the casks. The third derivation (the most exciting though least likely) is that the term came from the "sacking" of sherry-laden Spanish ships by British predators. Whatever your choice, there seems little doubt that Falstaff, no slouch when it came to drink, had sherry in mind.

## ROYAL ANDALUSIAN SCHOOL OF EQUESTRIAN ART

If you want to work up a thirst for the bodega visit, or, alternatively, sit and be entertained while basking in the golden fluid's afterglow, go to a performance at the **Real Escuela Andaluza del Arte Ecuestre** (the Royal Andalusian School of Equestrian Art). The school is a recent foundation (1973) but has deep roots in Andalusia's riding traditions and its renowned Hispano-Arab horses. These are the horses that the Holy Roman Emperor Maximilian sent to the Spanish Riding School in Vienna when it was founded in 1563.

Dressage and dancing were part of the Andalusian tradition and that is what the visitor sees today. The show is entitled the Dancing Horses of Andalusia and takes place every Thursday at noon. The school is situated in the grounds of a 19th-century mansion and consists of a covered arena, stables for up to 60 horses, and what must be the most elegant tack room in the world that doubles as a museum of equestrian equipment. The spectacle itself is a visual pleasure: the all-white horses contrasting with the rich colors and fabrics of their rider's clothes, the intricate patterns woven by the horsemen around and across the ring; and the 18th-century carriage driven by a woman escorted by top-hatted footmen, and drawn by two powerful black horses. But the over-loud canned music is intrusive and, unless you are a dedicated follower of equestrian art, some of the routines become monotonous after a while.

There is intense competition to enter the school. Some 1,400 applicants apply to enroll every September and only half a dozen are taken. Students remain there for four years, working from 7 AM to 2 PM every day. The average rider is 24 years old and is not from a wealthy family; most are Andalusian although some foreigners are also enrolled.

The man behind it all is Alvaro Domecq Romero. A member of the sherry-making family, rancher and horse-breeder, Domecq founded the school and is now its technical director. But before that he was a *rejoneador*, a bullfighter on horseback, following in his father's stirrups. His official biography recounts that he won his first equestrian trophy at the Seville Fair when he was five years old. He was fighting bulls when he was barely in his teens and throughout his long career fought more than 1,500 corridas in Spain, Portugal, France and Latin America.

There is a saying about Domecq that he knows only two postures — upright on horseback and prone when asleep. Horses are his life and fortunately you can see him in his two most demanding roles. Most Thursdays at noon he is in action at the

and palm trees. The young bulls are tested out in the open by riders armed with lances, but the cows are brought into the ring when they are two years old to see if they should be used to breed fighting bulls. The test begins with young men taking it in turns to play a spirited cow with the cape. When things get too hot, the aspiring matador leaps to safety over the wooden barrier and the cow hits it head-on with a resounding crash.

Then Domecq, on a superb, fleet-footed horse, rides into the ring and begins his joust with the cow. Round and round the ring

school's show, but he also is visible at his ranch where, by arrangement, visitors can watch him testing bulls for breeding purposes.

## LOS ALBUREJOS RANCH

The Los Alburejos ranch is on the right of the Jerez-Algeciras road, just after the turning to Medina-Sidonia. A ruined medieval castle on a hill acts as a marker overlooking lush, heather-sprinkled meadows where the Torrestrella fighting bulls turn grass into muscle.

Behind the house, across a cobbled patio, there is a small bullring with a Toy Town grandstand surrounded by eucalyptus, fig

they go, the cow's horns a few inches away from the horse's flank. Domecq jabs two banderillas (darts) into the thick pad of muscle behind the cow's neck, and changes horses. With masterly control, he turns his mount at sharp angles to see how the cow reacts. He goes through four more horses before the finale. On a fresh mount, he hitches the reins to his belt, grasps a banderilla in each hand, leans down and backwards and, at just the right moment, punches them into the cow's hide. There is a smatter of applause from the visitors and ranch-hands; Domecq raises his dove-gray hat and smiles.

Horsemen performing in the Royal Andalusian School of Equestrian Art, Jerez.

Later, walking back to the stables, someone comments on the high quality of the cow, "I've seen better," he says dryly.

## SANLÚCAR DE BARRAMEDA

While in this area, Sanlúcar de Barrameda, an unspoilt fishing and wine-making town at the mouth of the Guadalquivir, is worth a detour. Its moment in history came in the late 15th century when the explorers Magellan and Columbus left from the port on their

anchor off-shore with others beached on the strand, and the picture is framed by a row of fish restaurant and *tapas* bars. Pilgrims going to and from El Rocío cross the Guadalquivir on primitive ferries that look like small military landing-craft. The bars are atmospheric with their amphorae, fish nets and skeletons, and their delicious seafood snacks. The restaurants are unpretentious and inexpensive, the fish as fresh as the sea itself, and the view, especially at sunset, sublime. Sanlúcar's beach, slightly shabby, uncommercialized and wholesome, typifies

great voyages of discovery. But Sanlúcar is also famous for its **Manzanilla** dry sherry, a delicate creation that is normally served — and enjoyably drunk — throughout a meal. Sanlúcar's large town houses and elegant public buildings reflect the prosperity that the wine-trade brought, but it is the natural beauty of its beachfront that is the town's main attraction.

This consists of a fine sandy beach on the estuary of the Guadalquivir, facing the Doñana National Park and Wildlife Reserve. A garland of fishing boats bobs at

ABOVE: Don Alvaro Domecq Romero tasting the bravery of a brooding cow on the Los Alburejos Ranch near Jerez. OPPOSITE: The historic bullring in Ronda.

Andalusia's Atlantic coast, and contrasts favorably with the modern madness of its Mediterranean shoreline.

## CÁDIZ

Cádiz is a port city built on a rocky promontory that juts out into the Atlantic. It is not on the normal tourist itinerary but it has both history and atmosphere. The origins of Cádiz reach back into mythology with the claim this is where Hercules raised his pillars as he gouged open the Mediterranean Sea so that it could flow into the Atlantic. Less fancifully, there is documented evidence to show that the Phoenicians established a city called Gadir in 1100 BC. Carthaginian, Roman, Moorish and, finally, Christian occupation followed. Cádiz was one of the launching points for the discovery of the New World and the object of Sir Francis Drake's attentions, notably when he sacked it in 1587 boasting he had thereby "singed" King Philip II's beard. In the 18th century it was given the trade monopoly of Spain's New World empire — displacing Seville — and the city prospered. The Franco-Spanish fleet sailed from Cádiz to its doom at Cape Trafalgar in the Napoleonic Wars, and it was here that Spain's first democratic constitution was drafted.

The old town is cocooned in an unpleasant chrysalis of modern suburbs and industrial zones which have to be suffered before the real Cádiz can be seen. No individual building, including the fusty Baroque cathedral, amounts to much on its own, but the tightly woven streets, the faded, salt-bleached colors on stone, brick and paint, and the intensely Spanish feel of the place make it an interesting place to stop for an hour or so.

Cádiz is not renowned for its hotels and cannot make a good claim for an overnight stay. Gastronomy, especially fish, is its strong suite and and it makes sense to time one's visit to include lunch or dinner. **El Faro**, ( 21-10-68, San Felix, Nº 15, and the **Mesón del Duque**, ( 28-10-87, Paseo Marítimo, Nº 12, are both good and moderately priced.

## GIBRALTAR

Gibraltar, the other sentinel at the gates of the Mediterranean, is a culture shock. "The Rock" and its distinctive profile are known to every sea-borne traveler who has passed through the Straits of Gibraltar and to every British child from his or her jingoistic history books. Captured from Spain in the Spanish War of Succession in 1704, Gibraltar has remained a disputed British colony ever since. Its minute yet heterogeneous population prefers British colonialism to Spanish immersion and there the matter rests. Gibraltar offers some splendid views of the Straits and not-so-distant Africa, duty free goods, a colony of Barbary apes whose presence,

according to legend, will ensure the Rock remains British, and the flavor of a somewhat seedy, out-of-date England from the pages of Graham Greene. However, if you are British or an Anglophile and want to absorb a little nostalgia of the old country during your Spanish tour, go to Gibraltar where a valid passport and car insurance will get you across the frontier that doubles as a runway. Once there, you can marvel at the British bobbies wearing blue serge and the traditional domed helmets, the red letter boxes and telephone kiosks, the Union Jack fluttering over a Moorish castle, and enjoy — if you can — a pub lunch consisting of a paralyzed pork pie, (or a stale cheese and tomato sandwich), washed down with a glass of tepid McEwan's ale, and rounded off with a cup of tea and a Walls choc-ice.

## RONDA

The antidote is to plunge back into the hinterland of Andalusia as quickly as you can. There is no better way of doing that than to head north, through a fertile, aromatic countryside where you can occasionally glimpse a wooden plough being pulled by a team of mules, past white-washed villages perched on hilltops, and end up in **Ronda.** Set in its own small range of mountains, Ronda is a spectacular piece of urban sculpture that both attracted and defied the region's successive conquerors. Built on a towering crag that is virtually sheer on three sides, the old Arab town and its more modern companion are separated by a 92 m (300 ft) chasm. It was these natural defenses and the wild surrounding terrain that made Ronda a refuge throughout history for those who were not of a submissive disposition. Iberian warlords held out against the Romans, Christians against Moors, Moors against Christians (Ronda remained Moorish almost to the end of Arab occupation of Andalusia) and Spaniards against the French. When the tides of invasion and conquest had receded, the bandits and highwaymen took over providing both

Moorish gate (OPPOSITE LEFT) of the old town in Ronda (OPPOSITE RIGHT).

genuine hazard and exciting copy for the resolute travelers of the 19th century.

## SIGHTSEEING

The best way to see Ronda is to approach the old town by walking across the **Puente Nuevo** (the New Bridge). This impressive construction was built in the 18th century; the other smaller and much older bridges, the Roman and the Arab, can be seen down the gorge on the left as you cross over. Unfortunately, the assault on the nostrils is

not as pleasant as the impact on the eye. The river, at the bottom of the ravine, stinks. (There are plans, one is told, to clean it up). But the old town is a delicious concoction of shaded squares, solid medieval houses, numerous arabesque arches and filigree façades recalling Ronda's long Moorish occupation, fine wrought iron casement grilles and balconies, and a sense of intimacy, peace and introspection that manages to ignore the steady tramp of the tourist hordes, Ronda's latest conqueror.

The town has a reputation for attracting a variety of artists and personalities. It has a flamenco connection through Vicente Espinel who added the fifth string to the flamenco guitar and was born in Ronda.

Rainer María Rilke, the Austro-German poet, spent some time in the Hotel Reína Victoria, the grand old British-built hotel that has spectacular views of the town and countryside.

Ronda is also renowned for its contribution to the art of tauromachy or, more simply, bullfighting. Its pretty **bullring** was built in 1784 and is the second oldest in Spain, after the one in Seville. It is generally accepted that Ronda is where bullfighting began on foot; before that it was done exclusively from the back of a horse. Few fights are held

in the ring now, but there is an interesting museum beside it and it is a place of pilgrimage for aficionados. Two famous matadors were born in Ronda: Pedro Romero, who is credited with redefining the bullfight early last century, and Antonio Ordoñez, one of the great post-World War II matadors and Ernest Hemingway's hero. Orson Welles, another Ordoñez fan, was a frequent visitor to Ronda; there is a picture of him in the bullfight museum, as well as clothing worn by famous matadors and two stuffed bulls.

## HOTELS AND RESTAURANTS

Ronda can be covered comfortably in a day but its geographic location and its natural

beauty encourage a stop-over. The **Reína Victoria** ( 287-1240, Calle Jerez, Nº 25, is the classic old hotel where the poet Rainer Maróa Rilke stayed. There is a new parador ( 287-7500, Plaza de España, s/n; built on the site of the original town hall and overlooking the gorge. Less expensive but perfectly adequate are the **Polo** ( 287-2447, Calle Mariano Soubirón, Nº 8, and the **Royal** ( 287-1141, Calle Virgen de la Paz, which is near the bullring. The place to eat if you want to feast on the view as well as the food is **Don Miguel** ( 287-1090, Calle Villanueva, Nº 4,

have come the adverse criticism — and the jokes: "Costa Geriatrica," "Costa Mierda," "Costa Fortune," and so on.

The good news is that this coastline was never one of nature's marvels that was wrecked by Mammon. Forty years ago, it was a rather featureless stretch of gray sandy beaches, punctuated by small rocky promontories and bays, and inhabited by desperately poor fishermen. It was the combination of cheap land, great weather, and a low cost of living that made it perfect for northern Europe's sun-starved holiday-

which is perched on the edge of the gorge next to the bridge that links the old and new towns.

## COSTA DEL SOL

The Costa del Sol, the playground of five million tourists every year as well as home for many foreigners, runs from Gibraltar up the coast through Málaga to beyond Motril, a distance of some 300 km (186 miles.) The most densely built-up areas, however, are in the stretch between Estepona and Málaga, and it is here that the explosion of the Spanish leisure industry has earned Andalusia's its comparison to Florida. And with that

makers at a time when air travel became affordable. Today, it is still a rather featureless stretch of gray sandy beaches, punctuated by small rocky promontories and bays — when you can catch a glimpse through the concrete jungle of hotels, apartment buildings, restaurants, cafés and shops. But the Spanish population of the "Sunshine Coast" is a bustling, relatively affluent segment of the Andalusian work force whose knowledge of fishing rarely goes beyond a menu. In this, they are close to the millions of foreigners whom they serve, and it takes only one look at the local teen-age disco scene in

OPPOSITE: A religious procession in the streets of Ronda. ABOVE: The exterior of the Ronda bullring.

a place like Marbella to see Spaniard and foreigner are not far apart socially either.

The only way to see the Costa del Sol properly is to drive along it on the main coastal road. But beware of the hazards. The road is still a *carretera nacional* (national route), not an *autopista* (freeway) which means it is narrow, often winding, and always congested. There is the additional risk of semi-naked pedestrians, weighed down with beach impedimenta, dawdling across it since many of the hotels are on one side of the road and the sea on the other.

parks and adventure playgrounds for children and for the child in the adult. And then there is another kind of playground in the form of resorts that have become prestigious watering holes for an international coterie of the extremely rich.

## ACCOMMODATION: A SURFEIT OF CHOICE

Any travel agent will be able to supply a list of places to stay on the Costa del Sol as long as your arm. However, some general guidelines may be useful.

The coast caters to all tastes. It is perfect for the package tourist on a 10-day spree where the idea is to spend the day on the beach developing a tan that will knock them dead at the office in Manchester, Mannheim, or Malmo, and where the nights can be fruitfully passed eating, drinking, dancing and — assuming the excesses of sun, alcohol, food, and fancy footwork permit — making out. It is also a good place for those who have healthier though equally sybaritic thoughts in mind. There are plenty of opportunities for golf, tennis, riding, sailing, windsurfing and other sports. There are also amusement

**Málaga** is the business capital and the main airport of the coast, but it is not the place to stay or linger in if you are sightseeing, interested in sport, or pursuing the sybaritic pleasures of beach, bar and nightclub.

**Marbella** is the swankiest spot and has a large selection of luxury hotels at luxury prices. The best include: the **Marbella Club** ( 277-1300; the **Don Carlos** ( 283-1140; and the **Los Monteros** ( 277-1700. For golf and tennis, head for the **Del Golf Plaza** ( 281-1750 or the **Golf Hotel Guadalmina** in **San Pedro de Alcántara** ( 278-1400; and for Marbella's casino, try the **Andalucóa Plaza** ( 278-2000. There are plenty of golf courses along the coast (see TRAVELER'S TIPS for more

ABOVE: Seafront resort in the Costa del Sol.
OPPOSITE: New mosque, built with Arab money, outside Marbella on the Costa del Sol.

information), and most of the larger hotels have tennis courts. If you are a tennis enthusiast, a good place to go is **Lew Hoad's Campo de Tenis** ( 247-4858 FAX 247-4908, which is just off the Fuengirola-Mijas road where you can stay, eat and swim as well as have tennis lessons and play the game all day long. If you had to choose a base on the Costa del Sol, **Estepona** is a good candidate. In the luxury category of hotels there are the **Stakis Paraíso** ( 288-3000, just outside the town and the **Atalaya Park,** not far from **Puerto Banus** ( 288-4801, the fancy yachting place, both of which have golf courses, tennis courts, swimming pools and gardens.

## TARIFA

Let us take a sampling of the delights and horrors of the Costa del Sol traveling along the N-340, starting at its southwestern end. The Coast technically begins at Tarifa, the southernmost point of Spain, whose "Hurricane Beach" is probably the best place for windsurfing in the entire country. But it does not become serious until the coastal road begins to run close to the Mediterranean shoreline at **Punta de la Chullera. Sotogrande**, the location of an elaborate resort and leisure complex that includes golf courses, a polo ground and extensive horseback riding facilities, is near by and marks the beginning of the Coast's mid-20th century metamorphosis.

## ESTEPONA

Estepona, once a picturesque fishing village, is now a thoroughly modern town but not quite as overwhelmed as other places further along the coast. A large number of foreign residents live in and around Estepona, and it has an all-year nudist colony in an Andalusian-style village close to the beach just outside the town. The immediate hinterland is always worth keeping an eye on for touches of an older and calmer Spain. Twenty minutes' drive into the hills from Estepona, for instance, brings you to the dazzling white-washed mountain village of **Casares** surmounted by a ruined castle.

## MARBELLA

Continuing along the coast road there are signs of the new Arab conquest, in the shape of an elegant and classically-styled mosque on the outskirts of Marbella. This time, it is the power of the check-book, not the sword, that has returned small parcels of Spain to the Moor. Marbella is the star resort of the Costa del Sol, the place where, as one guide book has it, "the very beautiful and very talented try to rub shoulders with the very rich."

Marbella has 28 km (17 miles) of beaches, acres of luxury hotels, exclusive country-clubs, marinas stuffed with nautical marvels, and fancy restaurants, bars and discotheques. There is a so-called "Golden Mile" of vast mansions on the seafront, many of them belonging to oil-rich Arab princes and their families. **Puerto Banus** has the best marina for watching the rich at play — the floating palaces in the water are complimented by the Rolls Royces, Ferraris, and Mercedes ashore — and a drink at the **Marbella Club**, a comfortable sprawl of buildings set in a tropical garden, will give you the voyeur's satisfaction of watching without having to become more than marginally involved.

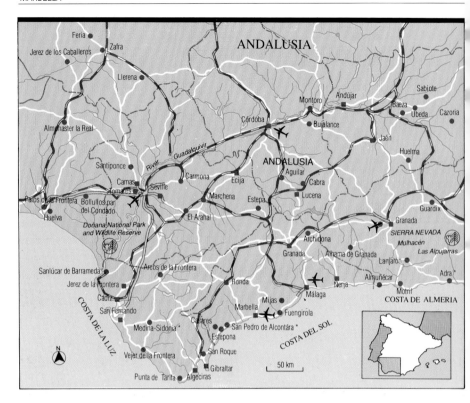

## FUENGIROLA

Next comes Fuengirola, a fairly typical Costa town, that has made a specialty of catering for family-style holidays, as well as handling the legions of singles. There is a small zoo and a *parque acuatico* ("aquapark"), both popular with children. In the hills behind the town the pretty village of **Mijas** sits in the sunshine, once a true Andalusian pueblo but now heavily commercialized by mass tourism. "It is so typical," says the guidebook, *Spain: Everything Under the Sun*, "that half its residents are non-Spanish." However, the curving, hilly streets retain their charm, and there are splendid views of the Mediterranean and the rolling countryside.

## TORREMOLINOS

If Marbella is the Costa del Sol at its most sophisticated, Torremolinos, further along the coastal road just before Málaga, is at its most brash. A peaceful though impoverished fishing village not so long ago, it is the mecca of the package tourist, especially the rowdy Brits, a place of relentless drinking and carousing where all thoughts of tomorrow, including monumental hangovers, are shelved until the homeward aircraft starts its engines. Torremolinos is where the hoary yarns of hotels still being built as the guests poured into the floors that were finished, actually came true. (I passed a noisy night in one in the early 1970s and almost did not live to tell the tale through taking a wrong turn along a unfinished corridor on the seventh floor.)

## MÁLAGA

Málaga, port, capital of a province, and the second largest city in Andalusia, has waxed fat as the service center of the Costa del Sol. Its airport is one of the busiest in Europe and it is a perfect place for the fast track entrepreneur of whom there are many in this part of Spain. But, by no stretch of the imagination is Málaga a lovely city, despite its mellifluous name; it has little to draw the

visitor. There are, however, two striking remains of the city's Moorish past when it was the Kingdom of Granada's outlet on the Mediterranean. These are the largely ruined **Alcazaba** (fortress), built in the 11th century and surrounded by terraced gardens, and the **Gibralfaro Castle,** constructed three hundred years later on the site of a Phoenician fortress. Back in the city, there is a rather ugly 16th-century cathedral that looks lopsided because it has only one tower — the second was planned but never finished — and it is known as **La Manquita**, the "One-Handed One."

## TO THE EAST

The Costa del Sol continues eastwards from Málaga with more of the same, through **Nerja, Motril** and on to **Adra** where the tired and dangerous N-340 cuts inland to **Almeria.**

Throughout the Costa del Sol there is a mushroom-like fecundity of "urbanizations," to use the Spanish term. These range from unimaginative concrete slabs of hotels, shops, restaurants and so on, to contoured clusters of villas, apartments, club-houses and sport facilities, to ambitious attempts to recreate the physical appearance and intimate ambience of the traditional Andalusian *pueblo*, albeit equipped with modern conveniences.

There is no need to search for the first category since it is visible wherever you turn. The more sophisticated developments, often with a specialist purpose in mind, are rarer and vary in quality but they are usually visually pleasant and comfortable to stay in. A good example is the Lew Hoad's **Campo de Tenis, (** 247-4858, FAX 247-4908, set in the hills just off the Fuengirola to Mijas road. Hoad, who won the Wimbledon singles title in 1955 and 1956, died in 1994. The tennis camp, which he founded and ran until his death, caters for tennis players but also provides residents, whether villa owners or renters, with full club facilities including restaurant, bar, swimming pool, as well as tennis coaching and competitions. One of

OPPOSIT: Hotel Byblos, a luxury hotel near Marbella.

the best illustrations of the third category is **Las Lomas Pueblo**, an urban development in the foothills behind Marbella. The brainchild of an another Australian, an architect called Donald Grey, Las Lomas is modeled on a typical Andalusian village complete with tiny squares, fountains, crooked streets, archways, and steps leading up or down into narrow alleyways. The houses, all faithful replicas, have whitewashed, terra-cotta or ochre-colored walls and red-tiled roofs; there is a riot of bougainvillea, jasmine, roses, and hibiscus; birds sing while bees

hum. Everything is for sale and some houses appear to be occupied. Yet, gazing at the empty streets, there is an antiseptic feel to the place, and the word "bijou" comes to mind. However, as a retirement or vacation center, it is a vast improvement on what has been wrought by man along most of the Costa del Sol.

## HEADING INLAND

Heading inland from the Costa del Sol is a refreshing experience for the jaded traveler.

---

ABOVE: Las Lomas Peublo. OPPOSITE: Andalusian man of the soil in the Alpujarra mountains.

First, there is cultivation — orchards, market gardens, wheat and olives — then the countryside begins to undulate and climb to the **La Alpujarra**, and later to the **Sierra Nevada.**

And finally, there are Andalusia's great cities of **Granada** and **Córdoba**, completing the trinity of which Seville is the cornerstone.

## LA ALPUJARRA

The Alpujarra mountains, situated between the Mediterranean and the Sierra Nevada, were until recently one of the remotest corners of Spain. Still off the beaten track, they are nevertheless readily accessible to anyone who has a car and does not mind twisting mountain roads. The N-323 road that links Granada with Motril on the coast provides the best approach; turn east onto the C-332 which will take you through Lanjarón and into the region. This is where many of the Moors, who were expelled from Granada, took refuge and staged the last major Muslim revolt against Christian Spain in the late 16th century.

The chain of white-washed villages, linked by capricious country roads, and the simplicity of life among the friendly inhabitants has drawn foreigners to the **Alpujarra** both as visitors and residents. Gerald Brenan, the British writer who wrote so well about his adopted country, lived in one of the Alpujarra villages for many years in the 1920s and 1930s. And other foreigners — writers, painters, "crafts" people and hippies — have also been attracted.

### LANJARÓN

Tourism, in a modest way, has come too. Lanjarón, at the entrance to the Alpujarra, is a small and pretty spa town where one of Andalusia's most popular mineral waters originates. It has many small hotels and hostels but its flagship hotel is the **Miramar** ( 77-01-61, on Avenida Andalusia, N°10.

There is also a new hotel complex of chalets at **Bubión**, built in the traditional mountain style with pine wood ceilings. Sharing the same valley as Bubión at an altitude of about 1,200 m (4,000 ft) are **Pampaneira** and **Capileira;** and further north is **Trevelez** that claims to be the highest village in Europe and is known for its air-cured hams.

There is no denying that in the **Alpujarra** the air is certainly fresh, the water clean and the pace of life restful, but the region somehow failed to live up the rave reviews in the literature and the ecstasy of the local tourist officials. Perhaps, like the lichen on the rocky hillsides, it takes time to grow on you.

## SIERRA NEVADA

The Sierra Nevada mountains are a surprise for here in the hottest, sunniest region of Spain is an easily accessible mountain range of almost perpetual snow with four months of excellent skiing every year. Only 32 km (20 miles) from Granada and 80 km (50 miles) from the Costa del Sol, the Sierra Nevada has the highest peaks in Spain. **Mulhacen** is 3,478 m (11,408 ft), and **Veleta** reaches 3,392 m (11,126 ft); worn and rounded by countless centuries of snow, ice, wind, rain and sun both peaks can be conquered by a vigorous walk without too much effort in the summer months. At the **Solynieve** ski resort the slopes are between 2,100 m (6,888 ft) and 3,470 m (11,382 ft) above sea level; there are 18 ski lifts and 25 marked ski runs. The mountains are popular among climbers and hikers too, and there are plenty of hotels, restaurants, and discotheques that cater to the *avant* and *après ski* crowds.

## GRANADA

Part of the excitement of traveling in Spain is the approach to an unfamiliar city. Fragments of knowledge from books, articles and traveler's tales, impressions from photographs, and preconceived images rising up from the subconscious coalesce as the distance diminishes. And then the scenery takes over. The approach to Granada, especially through the mountains from the coast, is an adventure in anticipation that absorbs the senses.

The best time of day is early morning or as the sun is setting. After a long climb you reach the inland plateau and catch sight of the snow-covered Sierra Nevada, a cool, ethereal canopy floating above the plain. Emerging from the pines, scrub oaks, wild flowers, and rocky outcrops of the hills, the road sweeps through fields of wheat and barley growing in a rich, red soil. The first glimpse of the city comes from a spot called **El Suspiro del Moro** (the Sigh of the Moor), the place where Boabdil, the vanquished king of Granada, is reputed to have turned

and looked back at his beloved city for the last time and wept. The wind, rippling the grain, is the only sigh these days but the sight that broke the king's heart remains. There is Granada, crowned by the towers, walls, turrets and crenellations of the Alhambra — ancient, sublime, sad Granada. Francisco de Icaza, the Spanish poet, put it well in a much-quoted but still evocative stanza:

*"Dale limosna, mujer, Que no hay en la vida nada / Como la pena de ser / Ciego en Granada."*

"Give him alms, woman, For there is nothing crueler in life than to be blind in Granada."

Granada bears the imprint of the Arab conquest and civilization more emphatically than any other town in Spain partly because the Moors were there longer than anywhere else, and partly because not much of consequence happened before they came and after they left. Unlike its sisters, Seville and Córdoba, it is an upland city, built on hills in the lee of mountains. Granada is 685 m (2,247 ft) above sea level — a little higher than Madrid — a city whose unique character was in good part a result of its defensive topography, its agreeable climate, and its well-watered and fertile soils.

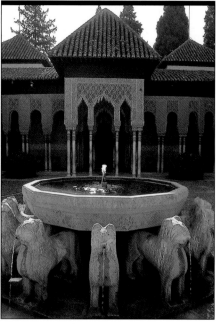

A settlement of no particular note in Iberian, Roman and Visigothic times, Granada had to wait until the Moors arrived from Africa. When Córdoba, the seat of the Caliphate, was in its ascendancy in the 10th century, Granada was a summer resort and leisure center. But in 1236 Córdoba fell to the Christian forces, and the defeated Moors retreated to Granada. Over the next two hundred and fifty years, it became the administrative heart and cultural center of Moorish Spain.

Led by the Nasrid dynasty, founded by Mohammed ibn-Nasr (Mohammed I) at the time of the fall of Córdoba, the kingdom of Granada (or Karnattah as it was called in Arabic) not only survived but expanded and prospered during the 13th, 14th and early part of the 15th centuries extending, at its height, to Gibraltar and Almeria. The Nasrids, technically vassals of the Kings of Castile, managed this more through diplomacy and guile than by force of arms. But it worked, and in the peace and prosperity that they created they turned a small mountain resort into a jewel of a city.

The end came in the late 15th century when the crusading Catholic monarchs, Ferdinand and Isabella, set about reconquering the remaining areas under Moorish control. Fatal divisions within Granada's ruling family made the task much easier and on a cold winter's day in 1492, Boabdil, who had usurped the throne from his father a decade earlier, surrendered the keys of the city to Ferdinand. An agreement that the customs and religion of the Moorish residents should be respected did not survive the advent of the Inquisition and the arrival of Cardinal Cisneros who, according to one chronicler, found the "climate of tolerance intolerable." Persecutions and expulsions finally ended the Moorish presence. The Castilians also began putting their architectural stamp on the city in the shape of the cathedral, churches, convents, monasteries and palaces. Fortunately, most of the Alhambra, though neglected and decaying, survived the ensuing centuries. A new climate of appreciation and renovation of this unique construction came in the 19th century. Granada itself settled into a rather crusty and conservative frame of mind until the 20th century when the sensibilities of Federico García Lorca, one of Spain's greatest modern poets and playwrights, and the violent passions of the Civil War shook it out of its provincial complacency. Today, Granada's population is not much more than it was at the zenith of the Moorish kingdom but the city has a comfortable, cheerful feel to it and lives reasonably well from internal and foreign tourism, light industry and agriculture.

## THE ALHAMBRA

"To the traveler imbued with a feeling for the historical and poetical, the Alhambra of Granada is as much an object of veneration as is the Kaaba or sacred house of Mecca to all true Moslem pilgrims. How many legends and traditions, true and fabulous, how many songs and romances, Spanish and Arabian, of love and war and chivalry are associated with this romantic pile!" So wrote Washington Irving, in his florid style, on his arrival in Granada in 1829. His *Tales of the Alhambra* became a best-seller and did much to put Granada on the tourist map then and since.

Built on the top of an elongated hill that dominates the city, the Alhambra (Al Qalat Alhamra, "the Red Castle" in Arabic from

Start with the **Alcazaba**, the ninth-century fortress on the western end, which portrays the military power of the Moorish kingdom and affords spectacular views over the rest of what is worth seeing, namely the adjoining hill of **Albaicín** where the old Moorish quarter is located, **Sacromonte**, the home of the gypsies to the north, and in the distance, beyond the city, the **Sierra Nevada.** From here you can also see the **Generalife** at the other end of the Alhambra, rather like looking from prow to stern on a vast, stately ocean-going liner. The highest point

the russet colored stone that was used to build it), is a fortress, a series of palaces, gardens, and in its heyday, a small town in itself. There are a number of hotels on the hill inside and around the Alhambra (see HOTELS, page 188) so that you can walk up to its walls under a cool canopy of giant elms, planted by the Duke of Wellington when he wasn't fighting the French in the Peninsular War. Early morning is the best time for the freshness of the air and the relatively small flow of visitors, and it is a good idea to avoid the heat and the crowds of high summer altogether if you can. You do not have to — and perhaps shouldn't — see everything in one day; tickets remain valid for the following day.

is the **Torre de la Vela**, the bell tower; the bell was rung to mark the times for opening and closing the sluice gates to the intricate irrigation system that fed the vega, or vale, around Granada, and to sound the alert when enemy forces were approaching — a simple and appropriate symbol of peace and war in those distant times.

The **Royal Palace**, set in the heart of the Alhambra complex, is the main attraction and tends to be crowded no matter which time of year or day you choose. But the individual attractions are so interspersed by gardens, patios and pathways, in the

OPPOSITE and ABOVE: Interior of the Alhambra Palace.

Moorish style, that there is always room to breathe and relax before moving on to the next place. The greater part of the palace complex was built in the second half of the 14th century during the height of the Nasrid kingdom. Builders, architects, craftsmen, and artisans from all over Muslim Andalusia had found refuge in Granada and, under the direction of a dynasty that had lost much of its political power but none of its artistic drive and sensibility, painstakingly put together this masterpiece, the last and arguably the greatest of its kind anywhere in the world.

The palace, much of which has been restored in the last hundred years or so, is divided into three functional areas. First, there is the public zone where the business of government and the day-to-day dealings with the public took place. Unfortunately, Carlos V pulled down a great part of this section in the 16th century to build an impressive palace for himself. Perhaps he felt impelled as a Holy Roman Emperor to leave his Christian mark on this Islamic island. In another setting, his legacy would neither have seemed excessively egocentric nor out of place. But in the middle of the Alhambra it looks at best bizarre, at worst an outrage. To add insult to injury the **Palacio de Carlos V** was hardly ever used by the man who built it.

A fragment that remains is the **Mexuar** where the king listened to petitioners and held public audiences. This room and its adjacent courtyard give the visitor the first flavor of the palace, a foretaste of carved cedar, filigreed marble, dizzying geometric patterns of blue, green, orange, brown and mauve tiles, and everywhere cool splashing, gushing, running, trickling water.

The second area consists of the state rooms where the king and his notables did their official entertaining, and most of this is still standing. The center is the **Patio de los Arrayanes** (Courtyard of the Myrtles), which has superbly carved marble arcades at each end of a rectangular pond lined by myrtle shrubs. Connecting this courtyard with the **Sala de los Embajadores** (Hall of the Ambassadors) is the curious **Sala de la Barca**

Alhambra Palace, Granada.

(Hall of the Boat) which takes its name from its hull-shaped wooden ceiling, beautifully carved and adorned with plaster "stalactites." The Hall of the Ambassadors, where the kings of Granada received envoys from friend and foe, from Christian kings and Moorish potentates, has another marvelous view over Granada and the countryside.

The third area of the palace was where the king and his family lived and centers on the lovely **Patio de los Leónes** (Courtyard of the Lions). Surrounded by a miniature forest of key-hole arches and arcades, a

small fountain plays into a carved marble basin that in turn feeds water through the mouths of the less than life-sized lions supporting it. A well-pruned, rather short orange tree stands in each corner of the courtyard casting a modest shadow and throwing in a dash of somber green to contrast with the profusion of golds, ivories and grays. Four diminutives appear in last two sentences and perhaps sum up the feel of the entire palace. Nothing is too big, excessive or overwhelming. God and king were clearly in mind as the architects planned, the

builders built, and the craftsmen chiseled, but none of them ever seems to have lost sight of the fact that, in the end, this was a place for human beings to live in.

You can sit on the edge of the **Patio de los Leónes** in one of those traditional and stern Spanish leather chairs, and watch the smaller fountains that are built into the floor under the arcades. They throw up jets of water that catch the sunlight and toss it against the creamy filigree marble of the ceilings and walls. The royal household lived in a series of apartments around the courtyard that included the quarters of the king's harem, baths and reception rooms. The occupants of the palace, however, were never far from a garden — or a view of one — as the **Mirador de Lindaraja**, overlooking a courtyard and garden in this inner complex, illustrates.

On leaving the palace, the Alhambra opens up into a series of gardens, arbors and pathways. The gardens of the **Partal**, with their lily-ponds, canals, flowers, high hedges of clipped cypress and fir, and the tiled, cobbled and brick paths, enable the visitor to make a gentle transition from the riches of the royal palace to the Alhambra's last work of art, the **Generalife.** Built on a hill higher than the rest of the Alhambra, the Generalife was the summer palace of the Nazrid kings. It is less than a 10-minute walk from the Partal gardens but is often dropped out of the average visitor's itinerary though it does not deserve to be.

**El Generalife**, the name comes from the Arabic meaning the "garden of the architect," is older than the palace being built around the middle of the 13th century and its buildings are not as distinguished. But it has superb gardens, some charming galleries and miradors, and panoramic views. The gardens are so extensive that the head gardeners use walkie-talkies to coordinate the activities of their underlings.

Early morning is the best time to visit when everything is fresh and dewy. Wherever you turn there is the sound, smell and sight of water; even some of the connecting stairways in the gardens have water channels cut into their stone railings. The Generalife was the place where the Moorish monarchs, together with their families and friends, came to relax, enjoy themselves and, from

---

ABOVE: The summer palace of El Generalife which stands on a hill beside the Alhambra Palace, Granada. OPPOSITE: Part of the extensive gardens that surround the Generalife.

time to time, indulge in illicit romance and passion. A sense of all that remains among the flowering oleanders, roses, hibiscus, and geraniums, under the shade of ancient trees, and in the music of running water.

## THE CATHEDRAL

Granada's other attractions, through no fault of their own, tend to pale after a day or two of wandering around the Alhambra. But the **Cathedral,** locked in the tight embrace of the old town at the foot of the Alhambra's lofty perch, is worth visiting. Conceived by the Catholic monarchs, almost as soon as Boabdil left Granada, the cathedral was finished in the 17th century when the locally-born Alonso Cano added the fine main façade.

Built with Renaissance exuberance, the cathedral is barely visible from the outside, so densely packed are the surrounding streets. But inside it is rather beautiful, almost as wide as it is long, with lots of wide open spaces, white limestone pillars, and lush illuminated medieval manuscripts on display. On one wall there is a list of clerics "murdered by Marxism," recalling a much more recent and bloodier fratricidal war than the conquest of Granada by the Christian kings. Ferdinand and Isabella, having achieved their life-long dream of liberating Spain from the Moors, decided to forget about Toledo and be buried in Granada. Their remains lie in the **Capilla Real** (Royal Chapel) which is an annex to the cathedral. They lie beside their beloved son, Prince John, who died when he was a student at Salamanca University, and their sad daughter, Joan the Mad, and her husband, Philip the Fair. The chapel is richly decorated but their tombs in the crypt underneath are surprisingly simple. In the sacristy adjoining the chapel, Queen Isabella's art collection, her crown and scepter, and Ferdinand's sword are on display.

The oldest Spanish part of Granada fans out from the cathedral's precincts and is both animated and picturesque. It seems to be a custom for herb sellers to pedal their wares directly outside the cathedral. Some of the herbs and potions have a modern ring but many of them, and the ills they are re-

puted to cure or prevent such as "falling off your horse," would probably not have been out of place when the quarter was first built.

Granada, the Alhambra aside, does not make much of an impact on first acquaintance but it grows on you. With about a quarter of a million people, it is a manageable size, enough to create a lively ambience, too few and too detached from the main commercial arteries of Andalusia to suffer the ills of large modern cities. It is therefore a good place in which to stroll, eat, drink, and take it easy.

## THE ALBAICÍN

One of the best sections to pass time in that way is the Albaicín, the old Arab quarter that sits on a hill next to the Alhambra. Unpretentious, friendly and clean, this over-sized village of white-washed houses, old churches, pretty squares and remnants of Moorish fortifications, miradors and courtyards has a special charm. It also is the best vantage point for absorbing — and photographing — the classic view of the Alhambra, aglow in the setting sun with the snowy peaks of the Sierra Nevada in the background. For, while the individual pieces of the Alhambra are all exquisite, it is the whole that is so remarkable.

## SACROMONTE CAVES

For a change of pace there are the gypsy caves of **Sacromonte**, situated on another hill north of the Albaicín. Long gone are the days of spontaneous, thrilling and uncommercial flamenco among the cave-dwellers. Today, a visit may satisfy the curious who want to see it for the sake of seeing it, and who are prepared to fight off or pay off the persistent fortune-tellers and other touts. But flamenco is best seen in the orderly if

antiseptic atmosphere of a night-club or at a music festival. And Granada does not stint itself when it comes to festivals. On January 2nd every year, the Catholic monarchs conquest of the city is celebrated, followed later by Holy Week and, later still, by Corpus Christi. There are also a series of classical concerts in the Alhambra between April and October, and a major international music and dance festival in June and July.

## THE CAVE DWELLERS OF GUADIX

Another place of cave dwelling gypsies is the town of Guadix which is about an hour's drive northeast of Granada. The gypsy *barrio,* or neighborhood, is in the upper part

of the town, close to the ruined Moorish castle. Small streets run up and down a series of barren hills. The "houses" have whitewashed entrances and white conical chimneys poking out of the rock. Some have gardens and cars parked outside; most have television aerials. This is no fly-by-night group of roaming gypsies but a well-established community that has its mail delivered along streets that have names and lighting and to doors, albeit cut in the rock face, that have numbers.

If you wander around the neighborhood you are almost certain to be invited into a house. Since you are a foreign tourist and your host is a gypsy entrepreneur, business is business, so you pay a negotiated fee for the visit. The cave house I saw had the number "100" painted over the entrance and an outside privy. The surprises came inside as the lady of the household showed me round. There were eight whitewashed rooms, electricity, television, a wood burning stove for the winter, a gas cooker in the kitchen and gas-heated running water. There were the religious and family pictures on the walls that you find in most Spanish homes, painted plates over the chimney, and rugs on the stone floors.

It was cool after the heat outside and warm and cozy, the owner said, in winter. All very modern — with one exception. Standing in the kitchen, I heard rustling and snorting sounds that came from an adjoining room. The owner smiled and led me through. Two very fat and contented pigs raised their snouts to greet us in what had suddenly turned into a subterranean farmyard.

## TOURIST INFORMATION

**Provincial Area Code**   (58)
From within Spain   (958)
**Tourist Office** ( 22-59-90, Corral de Corbón, s/n.
**Airport** ( 22-64-11.
**Iberia Airlines** ( 22-14-52, Plaza Isabel la Catolica, N° 2.
**Railway Station** ( 27-12-72, Avenue Andaluces, N° 12.

### HOTELS

*Expensive* means a night's lodging costs Pts.18,000 to Pts.28,000; *moderate:* Pts.8,000 to Pts.18,000; and *inexpensive*: Pts.4,000 to Pts.8,000.

### Expensive

**Alhambra Palace** ( 22-14-68, Calle Pena Partida, Nº 2, is in the gardens near the Alhambra with a good view over the city which is cavernous with plenty of Moorish flourishes.
**Carmen** ( 25-83-00, is on Calle Acera del Darro, Nº 62.
**Melia Granada** ( 22-74-00, Calle Angel Ganivet, Nº 7, is a modern hotel centrally located.

**Parador San Francisco** ( 22-14-40, in the Alhambra, is a converted 15th-century convent in an unparalleled setting. It is necessary to book a long way in advance.

### Moderate

**Guadalupe** ( 22-34-23, Avenida Alixares del Generalife, has a nice location behind Generalife.
**Juan Miguel** ( 25-89-12, on Calle Acera del Darro, Nº 24, is old-fashioned and comfortable.
**Los Alixares** ( 22-55-06, is on Avenida Alixares del Generalife.
**Washington Irving** ( 22-75-50, Paseo del Generalife, Nº 2, has a faded charm and good location.

### Inexpensive

**Dona Lupe** ( 22-14-73, Avenida de los Alixares, Nº 15, has good location and excellent value.
**Hostal America** ( 22-74-71, in the Alhambra, is a homely place with simple rooms and good food but advance booking is essential.
**Kenia** ( 22-75-06, is an old mansion in quiet area with a garden.

### RESTAURANTS

*Expensive* represents meals costing Pts.8,000 and above; *moderate:* Pts.3,000 to Pts.8,000.

### Expensive

**Carmen de San Miguel** ( 22-67-23, Calle Torres Bermejas, Nº 3, is in an old country house five minutes' walk from the Alhambra Palace Hotel; and has marvelous view over the city from the terrace and the moon comes up over the Alhambra.
**Baroca** ( 26-50-61, Calle Pedro de Alarcon, Nº 34, International cuisine.

### Moderate

**Cunini** ( 26-37-01, Calle Capuchina, Nº14, serves good fish and seafood.

LEFT: Alcaicería shopping area, a silk market in Moorish times. RIGHT: Pottery store in Granada. OPPOSITE: The cave houses of Guadix.

**Los Manueles** ( 22-34-15, Calle Zaragoza, N°2, is an old tavern noted for its local dishes.

**Sevilla** ( 22-12-23, Calle Oficios, 12, has good atmosphere; it was opened in 1930 by Lagartijo Chico the matador.

Granada is not a particularly gastronomic city, but you can get adequate food for reasonable prices. The visual feast offered by some restaurants that have good views of the Alhambra and city helps to compensate for any culinary deficiencies. The **parador**, with its unique setting in the Alhambra, is a good place to have a drink and dinner. Like most paradors the food is good, well-served and decently priced.

## NORTHERN ANDALUSIA

Northern Andalusia is not much visited by foreigners but if you want to get a feel of the rolling countryside and ancient towns and pueblos, then a detour via **Jaén** makes sense. This is the land of the olive. Wherever you turn, legions of those strange desiccated trees, which produce such a luscious oil, march to distant horizons. Jaén sits on the side of a hill, a strategic town in the days of the Arab-Christian wars, but now something of a backwater. There is, however, a magnificent parador (**Parador Castillo de Santa Catalina** ( 23-00-00) beside the castle at the top of the hill with superb views of Jaén and the countryside.

## CÓRDOBA

Córdoba, the last of the three grand cities of Andalusia, was first in its day. Built on the banks of the Guadalquivir, the city has a low profile that allows its historic landmarks to be easily seen and recognized. There is a new Córdoba but its buildings seem to have been reined in so as not to upstage the ancient structures of the other Córdoba. The transition from the city to wheat and barley fields and country ambience is swift; Córdoba, unlike so many Spanish cities, is not confined by a straitjacket of ugly modern factories and suburbs. The city's primacy goes back to Roman times when it was the capital of what is now Andalusia. Its identification with learning and religion came during the Roman period. It was the birthplace of the philosophers Séneca, father and son, the poet Lucan, and, three centuries later, of Bishop Hosius, a fanatical Christian prelate

who led the crusade against the Arian heresy in the fourth century AD. There is no better way of entering Córdoba than walking across the Roman bridge *(Puente Romano)* that crosses the oleander-strewn banks of the Guadalquivir and leads directly into the old town.

The Visigoths, in their customary undocumented way, came and went. The Moorish conquest took place in the eighth century and the city began to flourish. It rapidly became the capital of all Al-Andalus and, by the 10th century, the seat of an independent Caliphate, its rulers having decided to renounce the suzerainty of Damascus. With Córdoba's political power consolidated, the city expanded its intellectual and artistic horizons to become the pre-eminent center of learning in Europe.

In the 10th and 11th centuries, its population rose to between half a million and a million people, it had 3,000 mosques, many libraries with vast collections of books and manuscripts, a renowned university, a bustling industrial and commercial center (Cordovan leather developed here), and 300 public baths. Like Toledo in its heyday, Córdoba was also an extremely cosmopolitan city where Muslim, Jew and Christian tolerated

each other and the human synthesis produced great people and memorable works.

The savants of Córdoba were particularly notable for consolidating and translating the knowledge of the ancient world and making it accessible to contemporary and future scholars. The Moorish scientist, philosopher and doctor, Averroäs, lived in Córdoba in the 11th century and was followed in the next by Moses Maimónides, the Jewish philosopher and physician, whose writings on the reconciliation of faith and reason greatly influenced the thinking of Thomas Aquinas.

BELOW: The Roman bridge spanning the Guadalquivir in Córdoba.

## THE MEZQUITA (MOSQUE)

The mosque of Córdoba's Ommayyad caliphs remains one of the great wonders and — because of its Christian embellishments — one of the great curiosities of Spain. It was begun by Abd ar-Rahman I, the founder of the Moorish state centered on Córdoba, and continued by his successors during the next two centuries. Built on a rectangular pattern, it was easy to expand by simply constructing more aisles on each side. Minarets and mihrabs (prayer recesses) were also added.

The forest of double horseshoe-shaped arches in red and cream striped stone is probably familiar to many people from photographs. But there is no substitute for wandering, perhaps a little mystified, beneath them. Cool and gloomy, the interior of the Mezquita seems like a purposeless maze yet, in its time, it was a place of spiritual and physical lightness. The trouble was that the Christian conquerors built a dividing wall between the mosque and its courtyard where there had been none, sealed up all but a single entrance and, after three hundred years of thinking about it, dumped a cathedral in the middle of it.

Much of the Mezquita's original beauty is thus lost, but it is still an astonishing place. A better sense of its delicacy can be seen in the mihrab that was added in the 10th century. This is an octagonal room for prayer recessed in the wall facing Mecca. It has a lovely shell-shaped ceiling where the supporting columns reach up and interlock and whose surface is a dazzling display of mosaic tiles, the gift of a Byzantine emperor.

After taking Córdoba in 1236, the Christians built two chapels — the **Capilla Mayor** and the **Capilla Real** — in the outer walls of the Mezquita. In the early 16th century, the cathedral was begun — in the heart of the Mezquita. It was a bizarre idea and it is a bizarre sight but at least they left the rest of the mosque intact. As a religious building the cathedral is neither offensive nor particularly remarkable and it would have been fine in another setting. Curiously, Carlos V was reportedly horrified when he saw the completed building although he had been

guilty of a similar architectural outrage in the Alhambra. The visual discordance is one thing — you almost stumble on the cavernous cathedral as you wend your way through the mosque — but the sounds of the Catholic liturgy, the rumble of the organ and a congregation in full voice pulsing through that vast oriental edifice is one of the strangest cultural warps Spain has to offer.

## THE OLD CITY

The old city behind the Mezquita has several

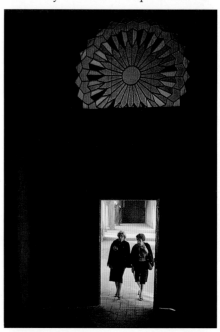

attractions, all within comfortable walking distance. There is the **Alcázar de los Reyes Cristianos**, built in the 14th century, with its tower that provides excellent views of Córdoba and its refreshing gardens that owe much to the Moorish legacy.

## JUDERÍA

The famous Judería is a jumble of cobbled streets, whitewashed houses, cool courtyards and fine mansions. The only surviving synagogue in Andalusia is here (there are only three left in the whole of Spain; the

OPPOSITE: The cathedral inside the Mezquita, Córdoba. ABOVE: The entrance to the Mezquita.

other two are in Toledo). It consists of a single high-domed room which you enter after passing through a shaded courtyard; high up on the walls there are fragments of Hebrew script and some arabesques but that is all. The Judería is swamped by tourist shops and by tourists themselves, but an early morning walk avoids both — the shops are not open and the tourists are having breakfast — and is the time to capture the flavor of the quiet, freshly watered streets and the scent of jasmine and orange blossom.

## MUSEO TAURINO

For those interested in bullfighting there is a fascinating museum (Museo Taurino) dedicated to it in the heart of the Judería. The collection of bulls' heads and hides, matadors' clothing and equipment, and some evocative art nouveau bullfight posters concentrates on local heroes who made their names in the late 19th and first part of the 20th centuries. From a later period there is a pantheon for one of the sport's greatest matadors, Manuel Rodriguez, more commonly known as Manolete, who died from a *cornada* (horn wound) in Linares in August, 1947. The skin of Islero, the bull that killed him, is stretched on the wall.

The bullfighter most closely identified with contemporary Córdoba, "El Cordobés (Manuel Benitez), is not commemorated. It is not clear whether this is because he was born in a small town some distance from Córdoba or because he is not regarded as a true artist by many experts. Judging by the purist feeling, bordering on the religious, that pervades the museum — its guardians insist on an orderly progression around the exhibits and on total silence — it could be that the dashing and daring "Córdoban" has not yet earned a place in this particular hall of fame.

Córdoba gives the impression of being less prosperous and more religious than its Andalusian sister cities, Seville and Granada. While there are pockets of affluence around the Mezquita and the Judería, where many of the large hotels and best restaurants are found, there are also many areas of decay and poverty. It is a city where you still see blind lottery ticket sellers, a symbol of an older, poorer Spain, and where a homeless man can be seen making his supper — and later his bed — at the foot of the Mezquita's walls.

To catch the religious spirit, visit Córdoba during one of its many religious festivals. At Corpus Christi, for example, priests, monks, nuns carrying candles escort the holy sacrament through hay-covered streets. Accompanied by boys in uniform and girls in white dresses carrying bouquets of flowers, the procession makes its way to the cathedral singing hymn after hymn. The smell of hay, wild herbs from the countryside, tallow from the candles, and incense blend in the warm air and float over the heads of dense crowds of people who have come to watch or join in the celebration. The cathedral-within-a-mosque is full on occasions like this, as it must have been in the 16th century when it was still being built. This is when Spain reaches back into its history and lives it without effort and without apology.

OPPOSITE: A horse-drawn carriage in Córdoba.
ABOVE: Corpus Christi procession in Córdoba.

## TOURIST INFORMATION

**Key Telephone Numbers**
**Provincial Area Code** (57)
From within Spain (957)
**Tourist Office** ( 20-05-22, Plaza de Judá
Levi, s/n.

### HOTELS
*Expensive* means a night's lodging costs
Pts.18,000 to Pts.28,000; *moderate:* Pts.8,000
to Pts.18,000.

*Expensive*
Parador La Arruzafa ( 27-59-00, Avenida
de la Arruzafa, is on the outskirts of Córdoba; modern with pool, tennis courts,
pretty gardens; a good place for rest and
recuperation.
**El Conquistador** ( 48-11-02, Calle Magistral
González Frances N° 15, is modern and
comfortable, conveniently situated next to
the Mezquita.
**Maimónedes** ( 47-15-00, Calle Torrijos, N°4,
is close to Mezquita.

**Melia Córdoba** ( 29-80-66, Jardines de la
Victoria, is functional with swimming pool,
close to the Judería.

*Moderate*
**Marisa** ( 47-31-42, Calle Cardenal Herrero,
N°6, is a modest, unpretentious place opposite the Patio de los Naranjos, the Mezquita's
courtyard.
**Hostal Séneca** ( 47-32-34, Calle Conde y
Ligue, N° 7, is not far from the northern side
of the Mezquita and has flower-filled patio
and comfortable rooms.

### RESTAURANTS
*Expensive* represents meals costing Pts.8,000
and above; *moderate:* Pts.3,000 to Pts.8,000,
and *inexpensive:* Pts.1,000 to Pts.3,000.

*Expensive*
**El Caballo Rojo** ( 47-53-75, Calle Cardenal
Herrero, N°28, touted as one of Andalusia's
best restaurants, it proved disappointing in
the flesh: undistinguished over-priced food
but good service.
**El Churrasco** ( 29-08-19, Calle Romero,
N°16, "Churrasco" is a local pork dish with
a peppery sauce; the restaurant specializes
in Andalusian cooking and has a charming
patio and a large tapas bar.

*Moderate*
**Séneca** ( 20-40-20, is on the Avenida de la
Confederación .
**Oscar** ( 47-75-17, is on Plaza de Chirinos,
N°6.

There are a many good, modestly-priced
restaurants in and around the Judería; it's
always worth taking a look at the *menu del
día* (daily menu) before ordering a la carte in
these sort of restaurants.

---

ABOVE: The Corpus Christi procession passing by
the walls of the Mezquita in Córdoba. OPPOSITE: A
water mill on the Guadalquivir, near Córdoba.

# Aragón and Northern Spain

## ARAGÓN

There is a fine highway that cuts across northern Spain from Catalonia through Aragón into Navarre and beyond to the Basque country and Galicia. The red clay, lush meadows and market gardens of Catalonia give way to the chalky gray dust of **Aragón**, and the great upland emptiness of Spain returns; and with it comes the aura of the desert and the hand of the Moor. The highway keeps company with the Ebro, Spain's largest river. Undulating irrigated fields of wheat, barley and corn, and orchards of peaches, apricots and almonds are interspersed with olive groves and copses of pine and cypress. A church tower that was once a minaret shimmers on the horizon, a punctuation mark in a vast landscape.

Aragón is a thick wedge of territory that starts in the Pyrenees and runs south to La Mancha; it separates the independent-minded Catalans to the east from the separatist-minded Basques in the west. Aragón is a crossroads rather than a destination for most visitors to Spain; it is also one of the least populated and poorest regions in the country. But it has a stark beauty, it resonates history, and there are a number of places worth visiting.

Upper Aragón includes the highest section of the Spanish Pyrenees where there are good opportunities for skiing, climbing and hiking. This region also has one of Spain's finest national parks (**Parque Nacional de Ordesa**), and offers good hunting, shooting and fishing, fortified by hearty food and wine (**Cariñena** is the best). Further south the Ebro flows across Aragón bringing fertility to a land that is for the most part rocky, barren and unproductive.

Two dynastic marriages shaped Aragón's history. The first, between Queen Petronilla (daughter of Ramiro II of Aragón) and Count Ramón Berenguer, the Count of Barcelona, in 1154, gave Aragón a window on the Mediterranean and turned it into an imperial maritime power. The second, between Ferdinand II of Aragón and Isabella of Castile in 1476, drew the kingdom into the mainstream of modern Spanish history.

Nothing of great importance, in historical terms, happened in Aragón after its absorption into the Spanish state. Francisco Goya and Luis Buñuel were born there, and during the Civil War a vast number of people died there. Aragón was one of the most bitterly contested areas and is pockmarked with battlefields. There is even a small town, **Belchite**, south-east of Zaragoza, whose ruins have been carefully preserved as a history lesson and a caution for modern Spaniards.

The attraction of Aragón is that so much of its medieval glory lives on in its churches, castles and small towns. Most notable are the Romanesque churches and monasteries in the north, many of them built along the route the pilgrims took from France to **Santiago de Compostela** in Galicia. There were two main crossing points in the Pyrenees, one at **Somport** that led the pilgrims through Aragón and the other further west at **Roncesvalles** in Navarre. The pilgrims' first stop in Aragón was the mountain town of **Jaca.** Its importance in those far off days is still reflected in the medieval buildings and most notably in the superb Romanesque cathedral built in the 11th century and one of the oldest of its kind in Spain.

Aragón is also a showcase of Mudéjar architecture and design. Following the Christian re-conquest, the kingdom was tolerant of its Moriscos — the name given to Moors who stayed on under Christian rule — and was repaid by their skill and industry. Mudéjar work can be seen in nearly every town in central and southern Aragón but perhaps the finest all-round display is at **Tarazona** 85 km (53 miles) from Zaragoza. This town also has the curiosity of a traditional bullring converted into apartment houses: a boost for those in need of housing and the anti-bullfight brigade no doubt, but a blow to lovers of the sport.

## ZARAGOZA

Zaragoza (Saragossa), the capital of Aragón, sits astride the fertile plain fed by the Ebro

OPPOSITE: Somaen, Aragon.

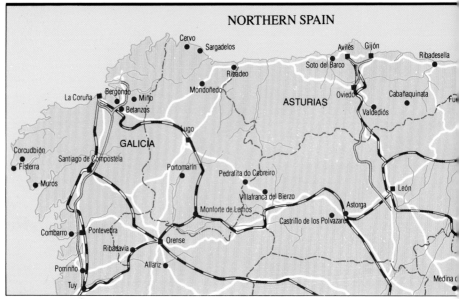

NORTHERN SPAIN

and can be distinguished from a great distance by the domes and spires of its cathedrals. (Like Salamanca, Zaragoza has two of them.) While much of the city is modern and industrial — it ranks as Spain's fifth largest — it has ancient roots and a rich history. The Romans were there and if you slur its Roman name, "Cesar Augusta," you will see why it is now called Zaragoza. Its strategic location at the center of Aragón on the Ebro made it as attractive to the Moors as it was to the Christians who later conquered them.

## SIGHTSEEING

Its cultural pleasures are dominated by the two cathedrals. The oldest, known as **La Seo**, is a mixture of practically every ecclesiastical architectural style in Spain. There is plenty of Mudéjar brick and tile work, an impressive 15th-century alabaster *retablo*, and a tapestry museum. The second cathedral, the **Basílica de Nuestra Señora del Pilar**, is newer, bigger and uglier. Built with a rather cock-eyed, almost Ottoman fervor, the Basílica has eleven domes and four towers that look like minarets but aren't; it commemorates the Virgin of the Pilar who is near the top of the list in the Spanish Marian hierarchy. Legend has it that in AD 40 the Virgin Mary appeared in an apparition before St. James the Apostle

(Santiago) on top of a stone pillar where the cathedral now stands.

Other more satisfying buildings — with less fanciful origins — include the **Lonja** or merchants' exchange, built in the 16th century, and the **Aljafería Palace**, originally the home of the Arab rulers and later the court of the Christian kings of Aragón. Zaragoza's most important fiesta commemorates the Virgin of the Pilar on October 12 each year. For those who like folk festivals, Aragón is renowned for its traditional songs and dances, particularly the jota, a lively dance performed by couples who leap high into the air and sing as they soar.

## TOURIST INFORMATION

**Provincial Area Code**  (76)
From inside Spain   (976)
**Tourist Office** ( 39-35-37, Glorieta de Pio XII.
**Airport** ( 34-90-50.
**Iberia Airlines** ( 21-82-50, Calle Canfranc, N° 22.
**Railway Station** ( 22-65-98, Calle San Clemente, N° 13.

### HOTELS

*Expensive* means a night's lodging costs Pts.18,000 to Pts.28,000; *moderate:* Pts.8,000 to Pts.18,000.

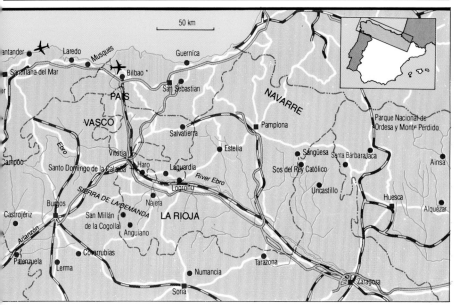

*Expensive*

**Meliá Zaragoza Aragon** ( 43-01-00, on Avenida Cesar Augusto, N° 13, is a large, modern hotel in the center of city.

**N. H. Gran Hotel** ( 22-19-01, is on Calle Joaquín Costa, N° 5.

**Palafox** ( 23-77-00, is on Calle Casa Jiménez.

*Moderate*

**Rey Alfonso I** ( 39-48-50, on Calle Coso, N° 17, is in the Central.

**Ramiro I** ( 29-82-00, Calle Coso, N° 123, is located in the old quarter.

**Zaragoza Royal** ( 21-46-00, Calle Arzobispo Doménech, N° 4, is a modern hotel.

**Don Yo** ( 22-67-41, is on Calle Bruil, N° 4.

**RESTAURANTS**

The following restaurants fall within the *moderate* price range (meals costing Pts.3,000 to Pts.8,000).

**Costa Vasca** ( 21-73-39, Calle Teniente Coronel Valenzuela, N° 13, has good Basque food and matching wine cellar.

**La Casa del Ventero** ( 11-51-87, on Paseo 18 de Julio, N° 24, is located 14 km or nine miles out of town in Villaneuva de Gallego on the Huesca road, but is worth the trip.

**La Mathilde** ( 44-10-08, on Calle Casta Alvarez, N° 10, is a good all-round restaurant with pleasant atmosphere.

**La Rinconada de Lorenzo** ( 45-51-08, Calle La Salle, N° 3, specializes in regional dishes.

**Los Borrachos** ( 27-50-36, Paseo Sagasta, N° 64, serves good game.

## NAVARRE

Another individualistic piece of the Spanish mosaic, Navarre has its head in the Pyrenees and its feet in the Ebro. An area of great physical variety, the region has a history of rugged nationalism. The Romans found it hard going and Charlemagne suffered a notable defeat at the Roncesvalles pass in the Pyrenees where his rear guard was slaughtered by the locals. This event was immortalized in *La Chanson de Roland* (the Song of Roland), the great medieval epic poem. Roland, the commander of the Franks' rear guard, was killed in the battle. In an act of literary sabotage, Roland's chronicler turned the victorious Vascons (the Basques and Gascons who inhabited Navarre), into Moors.

Navarre grew in strength in the Middle Ages and managed to preserve its independence until 1512, 20 years after the last Moorish kingdom in the south had succumbed to the Spanish crown. Even then it retained its identity and *fueros* (privileges) well into the 19th century. It supported the Carlist side in the dynastic wars of the 19th century and Franco during the Civil War in the twentieth. Although

Navarre has a large Basque population it is not technically part of the Basque country and has resisted attempts by the Basque provinces, which lie to the west, to incorporate it.

## PAMPLONA

Pamplona (Iruña in Basque) is Navarre's capital and its cultural core. The city is believed to have been founded by the Roman general Pompey, from whom its name is derived, and passed through the hands of the Moors (twice), the Franks (Charlemagne knocked its walls down and Roland and his men paid the price), and finally the Castilians. A Basque nobleman, reflecting on the meaning of his life as he lay wounded after a siege of Pamplona in the early 16th century, went on to found the Jesuits and was canonized as Saint Ignatius of Loyola.

Pamplona is a relaxed and civilized place with a quaint medieval section around the Gothic cathedral (the "ugliest beautiful church in existence," according to James Michener), some fine municipal and regional government buildings, a 16th-century citadel, and an elegant arcaded 19th-century square, the **Plaza del Castillo.** But none of this is why Pamplona has become famous and why legions of visitors are drawn to it every year. Blame it on Ernest Hemingway, if you will, but it is hard to separate Pamplona from the image of bulls charging down narrow barricaded streets as young men in white with red sashes scatter in all directions, and from days and nights of drunken carousing.

### FESTIVAL OF SAN FIRMÍN

That description does not do a disservice to the reality, but there is more to the festival of San Fermín (known locally as Sanfirmines) than that. Held from July 6 to 14, the festival celebrates the city's patron saint who was the first bishop of Pamplona and suffered a martyr's death by being dragged around the streets by a bull, or so the story goes. The irony notwithstanding, the inhabitants of Pamplona clearly love both their saint and their bulls and have no qualms risking their own lives with the descendants of the species that did in their bishop.

The running of the bulls (the *encierro* or "corralling") takes place every morning at 8 AM for six consecutive days. Originally, it was just a way of getting the bulls from their pens on the edge of the medieval quarter through the narrow streets and into the bullring for the daily *corrida*. But then it became a test of machismo and an exciting spectator event and who better to publicize it than Papa Macho himself in one of his best novels, *The Sun Also Rises* (also known as *Fiesta.*)

Pamplona showed its appreciation by erecting a statue to Hemingway, instantly

recognizable with beard and roll-neck sweater, and strategically sited under the plane trees near the point where the bulls turn off the street and into the ring. There is a short affectionate inscription saying the American writer was a true friend of Pamplona.

It is the last *encierro* of the fiesta. I awake at 6:45 AM to the sound of a brass band braying under my window. Music and singing fill the days and nights as people fill the streets. There are already large crowds moving down to the twisting corridor of cobbled streets where the bulls will run. The air is fresh and cool, the sky still gray. Spectators are positioning themselves on top of the heavy wooden posts and planks that cordon off the route.

Catching sight of a young red-headed Englishman I had talked to the day before, I climb over the fence and join him and the other runners. Many of them are standing around in small groups reading accounts of the previous day's *encierro* in the local newspapers. There are vivid photographs of youths fleeing in all directions, of hurtling bulls and fallen bodies. Those newspapers will soon be rolled up and thrown as a last resort to deflect a bull's attention should the need arise. The runners are mostly

---

The parade — a piece of 18th-century pageantry — that always precedes a bullfight. Pamplona's bullring during the feast of San Firmín in July; the bulls ran through the streets to the ring earlier in the day.

Spaniards, dressed in traditional white slacks and shirts with red sashes around their waists and red scarves around their necks.

Most of them also appear to be locals, but I spot a rather elegantly put together Madrileño whom photographer Nik Wheeler and I had seen in a fashionable restaurant the night before. The betting then was that he was all show and no go, but we were wrong. In immaculate (tailor-made?) whites, he clearly intends to run although the bravado of the night

before has been replaced by a fragility that is probably induced by a monumental hangover and pondering worst-case scenarios during the ensuing half hour or so.

The young Englishman, who is on an extended cycling tour of Europe, has run every day of the fiesta. "It's a drug," he says, "there's no way I would have missed any of it." How does he feel each morning waiting for the sound of the first rocket to go off, signaling the bulls are on their way? "Shit scared," he says laconically.

There are a few other foreigners but the big contingents, especially the Australians who come en masse every year, have already left Pamplona, burnt out after several days and nights of continuous drinking. As zero hour approaches, people converge on a small figurine of San Fermín in a niche in a church wall near the corral where the bulls are waiting. The bishop has a shepherd's crook on his arm and a red bandanna around his neck and is surrounded by candles. Starlings wheel and scream in the gray sky overhead. The crowd sings a hymn to the martyred bishop; there is a strong emotional undercurrent in the gathering as the people of Pamplona say good-bye to their bishop for another year. Red scarves flutter in a fitful breeze as the sun's rays begin to warm the slate roofs of the old town.

The ceremony comes to end and the spectators clamber back over the railings where Red Cross workers with stretchers prepare themselves for action. The runners, now alert and tensile, dance on the balls of their feet and stare down the hill which marks the first stretch of the run. Not far from where I am standing, still undecided, is a cluster of American veterans who might loosely be called the "Hemingway Brigade." Some have grizzled beards, nearly all wear red headbands, there is an odd baseball cap or two, and one of the oldest has an impressive bandage around his leg. (A knee twisted avoiding a bull in an earlier run? An old *cornada* re-opened? A misjudged cobblestone after too much red wine? It's anyone's guess.)

The red-headed Brit turns to me: "It looks like you're going to run?" he says. I nod making a mental note to stick as close to him as possible and avoid the aging, partially crippled Hemingway crowd. We are about half-way along the course, well clear of the two most dangerous spots. The first is at the beginning of the run. Freshly released, six bulls and six accompanying heifers, pound up a narrow street lined with the solid stone surfaces of churches and remnants of the city's walls. There are virtually no doorways to duck into and nothing to leap over. The second danger zone is the narrow passageway that leads into the bullring: congestion and panic there can have serious consequences. Thirteen people have been killed during the run in the last 50 years and scores injured.

The street is now jammed with runners, many of them jumping up and down and trying to see what is happening further back. The wooden fencing that seals off the side streets is festooned with spectators; more onlookers are on balconies or hanging out of windows. Conflicting emotions — anticipation, fear, excitement — pulse through the runners. There is a whoosh and a crack as the first rocket goes off and a loud cheer from the onlookers. I am suddenly aware of some very youthful runners, including a few girls. (Would Papa have approved?) My friend is leaping up and down like a leprechaun. Some runners have already taken off although the bulls are nowhere in sight. "You're not supposed to start running until you can see the tips of their horns," he says reprovingly.

A second rocket explodes indicating that all the bulls are out of the pen. There is the beginning of a mass movement. The real danger, I begin to think, is not being tossed by a bull but flattened and pounded to death by the other runners. I let my friend do the jumping. "There they are," he yells. There is an incredible stampede, feet, legs, arms and elbows flailing in all directions. I keep directly behind the young veteran and away from the center of the street. Fear truly lends wings. I turn for a fleeting second and at that moment six huge black bulls, weighing half a ton each, their horns held high, canter past at about 20 miles an hour and are gone scattering runners like raindrops. One person is down but not apparently badly hurt and the show moves on to the bullring. The running of the bulls, which lasted approximately two minutes and thirty seconds from start to finish, is over until next year.

A final rocket is fired to announce that all the bulls have reached the ring where they are guided into their pens beneath the stands. The runners, however, remain in the ring and play with the heifers that are released one by one to entertain the crowd. There is much bravado and a fair amount of tumbling as the agile little animals with blunt-tipped horns cavort about the ring running, swerving, bucking and charging as if they were fighting bulls.

The macho thing to do at this stage in the festivities is to sit or kneel in front of the gate where the heifers are released. When the gate is opened the heifer, confronted with a mass of bodies six across and as many as ten deep, is forced either to jump over or on top of the phalanx. For the spectators, the whole affair is a free show, and for the participants it's a unique opportunity to be on sacred sand and imagine what it is like to be a matador. Above all, it seems a fitting and cathartic way to recover from 150 seconds of unadul-

terated terror in the confined streets of the city.

The quality of the matadors matches the bulls during the festival and it is a good idea to buy tickets as early as possible. However, Pamplona offers more than bullfights in this heady week. You go to sleep with the sound of music in your ears and it is still there when you awake. There seem to be scores of different bands and there are also singing, dancing and street processions with costumed performers on foot and

OPPOSITE: Parade of the "giants" during the San Firmín festival. ABOVE: Façade of Pamplona's 17th-century town hall.

horseback. A favorite are the lavishly-dressed dummies that move in procession from the town hall down the church of San Fermín. These consist of the "giants," 9 m (12 ft) tall figures depicting the Catholic monarchs, Moorish princes and other historical characters, and "fat-heads," life-sized comical caricatures designed to tease and perhaps frighten the children. The giants move in as a stately fashion as their great weight allows, spinning slowly to the applause of the crowd; the fat-heads also pirouette and dart from side to side bringing

screams of delight from the children. The nicest thing about all this is the spirit and friendliness of the local inhabitants. They clearly enjoy their own show and not only tolerate the vast invasion of outsiders; they actually give them a genuinely friendly welcome.

The time to leave Pamplona is after the last *encierro,* not too late in the day — unless you want to examine the entrails of an entire city with a hangover. By Day Six, the bodies of the drunks are already scattered around the streets. A group of Brits all wearing identical T-shirts, which bear the slogans "First Annual Young Farts' Picnic" on the front, and "Old is Ugly" on the back, lurch down a side street. The ancient

cobblestones reek of stale wine and beer. And the "Hemingway Brigade's" last discussion of the finer points of the day's run has taken place, in full public view, at the Café Iruña in the Plaza del Castillo. Time to head out to the verdant valleys and clean air of Navarre.

## TOURIST INFORMATION

**Provincial Area Code**  (48)
From inside Spain  (948)
**Tourist Office (** 22-07-41, Calle Duque de Ahumada, N° 3.
**Airport** Aeroporto de Noain, **(** 31-75-12, Carreterra Zaragoza, Km. 6.5.
**Raiway Station (** 11-15-31, Calle San Jorge.

**HOTELS:**
*Expensive* means a night's lodging costs Pts.18,000 to Pts.28,000; *moderate:* Pts.8,000 to Pts.18,000.

*Expensive*
**Iruña Palace Hotel Tres Reyes (** 22-66-00, Jardines de la Taconera, is centrally located.

*Moderate*
**Maisonnave (** 22-26-00, Calle Nueva, N° 20, is confortable and close to where the bulls run.
**N. H. Ciudad de Pamplona (** 26-60-11, Calle Iturrama, N° 21, is near the university.
**Orhi (** 22-85-00, Calle Leyre, N° 7, is next to the bull ring.
**Yoldi (** 22-48-00, is on Avenida de San Ignacio, N° 11.

**RESTAURANTS**
**Josetxo (** 22-20-97, Plaza Principe de Viana, N° 1, specializes in local Navarrese dishes, both the food and decor are good.
**Las Pocholas (** 21-17-29, Paseo de Saraste, N° 6, is a charming restaurant and bar; decent food, well-priced; popular and rightly so.
**El Mosquito (** 25-50-26, Travesia de San Alberto Magno, N° 3, has good fish.
**Hartza (** 22-45-68, Calle Juan de Labrit, N° 19, near the bullring, has imaginative cooking.
**Alhambra (** 25-50-07, is on Calle Bergamin, N° 7.

## RONCESVALLES PASS

It is not a bad idea to take a trip up to Roncesvalles, the pass in the Pyrenees where the medieval pilgrims entered Spain from France on the long, dusty road to Santiago de Compostela and, of course, where Roland blew his horn despairingly for reinforcements and met his end at the hand of the local "Moors." The most attractive way — although not the shortest — is to go through Aoiz and follow the Urobi river

church built in the French Gothic style. You can eat well and inexpensively in **La Posada**, a refectory-restaurant with massive walls, flagstone floors and heavy wooden beams inside the monastery. At the pass itself, a group of French pilgrims, carrying small crosses made of pieces of wood and twigs, are kneeling on the grass close to a flock of sheep. They place bouquets of flowers at the foot of a statue of the Virgin and sing a hymn, as tens of thousands have done before them for more than a thousand years.

valley. It is rugged country relieved by fields of wheat, barley and oats ripening under the summer sun; hamlets of small stone houses, as brown as the earth itself, with geraniums on the windowsills; rows of poplar trees along the river bank, and no sound except the chatter of the birds and the babble of running water. Was it around here that Hemingway fished away a lazy afternoon and recreated it in a memorable scene in "The Sun Also Rises?"

Near the pass there is a monument to Roland, a martial figure showing him armed with a dagger and a deadly-looking mace. Underneath there is the date of the battle: 778. There is also a fine 12th-century monastery with a beautiful, restrained

## THE PILGRIMS' WAY

There were two main routes that the pilgrims followed in Spain. One, known as the **Asturian**, went along the northern coast and the other took a more southerly direction and was called the **Camino Francés** (the "French Road") on account of its popularity with French pilgrims. On foot the journey, either way, could take weeks. By car, two days is adequate whichever way you choose. Let us follow the pilgrims south

ABOVE: Traditional houses in Haro, La Rioja.
OPPOSITE: A street café in Pamplona.

through Navarre into Rioja, then westwards along the fertile Ebro valley into **Old Castile** with its cities of **Burgos** and **León,** and finally into the green hills and valleys of **Galicia** to the town that bears the Apostle's name, **Santiago de Compostela.** As Navarre gives way to Rioja, the countryside softens; expansive wheat fields the color of burnished gold await the harvester's plundering blade; vines begin to make an appearance; very old towns and a multiplicity of church towers and spires — like beacons on a rocky coast — mark the pilgrims' way;

grapes grow and the wine is made. The name comes from an elision of "Río Oja", the river valley where the vines were first planted. There are three main growing areas: **Rioja Alta** (Upper Rioja) around Haro, a moist upland region that produces the finest wines; **Rioja Baja** (Lower Rioja) east of Logroño along the Ebro Valley; and **Rioja Alavesa,** a zone north of the Ebro that borders on the Basque Country. These different areas are clearly marked on a pretty little map on the back of all Rioja wine bottles.

just before Logroño, the capital of the Rioja, a sign says "Santiago de Compostela: 666 kilometers." (414 miles.)

## RIOJA

Not so long ago Rioja did not mean much to foreigners visiting Spain. Now it is inseparable from wine, especially red wine, and rightly so. The region produces the best wine in Spain and exports it all over the world. It travels pretty well but there is no substitute for drinking it where the

The soil and the climate give Rioja wines their special flavor which is fruity and full yet light and fresh-tasting. The best reds have a wonderful color and bouquet. The wine business began in the 1880s when the railroad came to Rioja and started to boom when the phylloxera blight decimated the French vineyards. The wine was traditionally made in oak barrels but according to Felipe Nalda, the technical director of the bodegas Riojanes in Cenicero, just outside Logroño, the best wine is now made in aluminum vats. The industry is strictly controlled and the wines are on the whole, reasonably priced. They are also graded according to age. **"Crianza"** (literally, "maturation") means

ABOVE: Bridge over Arga river in Spain's most famous wine-growing region: the Rioja.

that the wine has spent at least one year in the barrel; "**Reserva**" indicates three years, and "**Gran Reserva**" means five years spent maturing.

## LOGROÑO

Logroño, is the administrative and commercial center of Rioja. Not particularly interesting in itself it is a good base for several worthwhile side trips.

### TOURIST INFORMATION

**Provincial Area Code** (41)
From within Spain (941)
**Tourist Office**, ( 29-12-60, is on Calle Miguel Villanueva, Nº 10.

#### HOTELS
All hotels listed below are in the *moderate* price range (Pts.8,000 to Pts.18,000):
**Carlton Rioja** ( 24-21-00 is on Gran Vía del Rey Juan Carlos I, Nº 5.
**Los Bracos Sol** ( 22-66-08, Calle Breton de los Herrerors, Nº 29, is a functional businessman's hotel.
**Murrieta** ( 22-41-50, is on Calle Marqués de Murrieta, Nº 1.

#### RESTAURANTS
The followings are in the *moderate* price range (Pts.3,000 to Pts.8,000):
**La Merced** ( 22-11-66, on Calle Marqués de San Nicolas, Nº 109, is an former palace in the old part of town; it has a good wine cellar.
**Meson Lorenzo** ( 25-81-40, Calle Marqués de San Nicolas, Nº 136, is another stylish restaurant in same area.
**Carabanchel** ( 22-38-83, on Calle San Agustin, Nº 2, is a reliable, long-standing establishment.
**El Cachetero** ( 22-84-63, is on Calle Laurel, Nº 3.

## HARO

Haro, 40 km (24 miles) from Longroño and in the heart of the wine-producing country, has a rather decaying charm with its medieval buildings, faded pastel walls, casement windows, and its main square on an incline that features a gazebo in the center. Bodegas abound in Haro stressing what is important in Rioja Alta, but as you move west the footprint of the pilgrim becomes clear again with the proliferation of churches, hospices, monasteries and shrines.

## ANGUIANO

Using as a point of reference the old town of **Nájera**, which was the capital of Navarre for a period before becoming part of Castile, there are some side trips worth taking on the road from Logroño to Burgos. A southerly loop will bring you into the **Sierra de la Demanda** and to the pretty mountain village of **Anguiano.** Here, every July 21 to 23, occurs a strange festival where men dressed in traditional costumes climb onto stilts and dance through the streets.

## SAN MILLÁN DE LA COGOLLA

Then there is San Millán de la Cogolla, a village that grew up around two famous medieval monasteries, **Suso** and **Yuso.** San Millán was a sixth-century hermit who picked this lovely spot to establish a religious community. In the 10th century, monks under Muslim rule built a monastery in the mountain side that later came to be known as the Monasterio de Suso (Upper Monastery). Built in the Mozarabic style, it has key-hole arches, arcades and a finely carved tomb of San Millán. A thoughtful curator has put on display a glass-fronted case that is full of bones and a skull with excellent teeth. Another tomb contains the remains of Gonzalo de Berceo who was an abbot here and the first poet to write in Castilian. He died in the middle of the 13th century. The following century, the kings of Navarre built a much more elaborate Benedictine monastery down in the valley. The Monasterio de Yuso (Lower Monastery), sometimes known as the "El Escorial" of the Rioja, is a massive, somber and strikingly beautiful pile protected by lines of poplar trees and set against a backdrop of wheatfields and copses of trees so dark that they look almost blue in the late afternoon light.

Largely rebuilt in the 16th and 17th centuries, the monastery has a vast Renaissance church, a Baroque sacristy with a painted ceiling, an alabaster floor and a Gothic cloister. There are hundreds of religious paintings, 11th-century ivory bas-reliefs, a spectacular ivory chest, and early religious texts in Latin and Spanish.

A small group of Benedictine monks now live in the monastery where hundreds used to reside. While the human factor is less in evidence than it used to be, the rural simplicity of the countryside surrounding Suso and Yuso is remarkably intact. A flock of sheep, a couple of goats, a sheep dog and a shepherd, wrapped in a blanket, move slowly across a field; on the road a mule cart with a peasant and his wife pass by. And, July or not, it is raining; steady, almost Irish rain, releasing from earth, grass, leaves and ripening wheat the freshest scent in the world.

## SANTO DOMINGO DE LA CALZADA

Returning to the main road that leads to Burgos, the pilgrims and their latter-day followers came to Santo Domingo de la Calzada. "Saint Dominic of the Road," was an enterprising and public-spirited man who, in the 11th century, built a comfortable

stopping place for the weary pilgrims, complete with a paved road, a bridge, an inn and a hospital. He was also credited, less convincingly, with clearing whole oak woods with a magic sickle. The hospital is now a parador but the cathedral, built in the 12th century, is relatively unchanged. It is worth climbing to the top of the tower, which has eight bells and a 200-years-old clock that functions with stone weights, for a splendid view over the Ebro valley and the Rioja landscape.

One of the greatest curiosities in all Christendom can be seen in the cathedral. A live cock and hen are kept in an ornate cage not far from Santo Domingo's tomb. The story that had great currency, as well as credence, in medieval Europe goes as follows. A young pilgrim rejected the advances of a local girl who, in revenge, had him unjustly accused of theft. He was summarily tried and hanged.

His parents, having completed their pilgrimage — a death in the family in those days apparently did not break a serious pilgrim's stride — were astonished and delighted to find their son miraculously alive on the gibbet when they returned to the town. They rushed to inform the judge who was sitting down to dinner. Their son, he said emphatically, was as dead as the two roast fowl on the plate in front of him awaiting his attention. The words were hardly out of his mouth when the two birds leapt up and flew out of the window. Since then a live cock and a hen have been kept in the cathedral. They are killed and replaced every year and it is supposed to bring good fortune to pluck a feather and wear it in your hat.

## BURGOS

The cradle of the Castilian Kingdom, Burgos is an elegant, manageable city packaged in coils of narrow streets, passageways and squares around a superb Gothic cathedral. There is also a fine river frontage, and the

ABOVE: Santo Domingo de la Calzada, an important stopping place for pilgrims traveling to Santiago in the Middle Ages. OPPOSITE: Burgos's massive Gothic cathedral in the heart of the city.

transition from countryside to the unspoilt heart of the city is pleasantly rapid. Burgos grew up as a frontier fortress against the Moors in the ninth century. It gained in importance as time went on because of its geographic location, its thriving Merino wool trade, and the exploits of its favorite son, Rodrigo Díaz de Vivar, more commonly known as El Cid. ("Cid" comes from the Arabic "Sidi," meaning master or leader.)

The royal court of Castile moved from León to Burgos in 1037 and the exploits of El

Cid, principally as a scourge of the Moors, unrolled during the latter part of that century. The basis of much of his reputation is contained in an epic poem, *Cantar del Mío Cid,* written about him 100 years later. In the nature of these medieval sagas there was much exaggeration, further propagated centuries later by a Hollywood film of the Spanish hero. Nevertheless El Cid seemed to be a pretty redoubtable fellow. He is greatly revered by the people of Burgos and his body, along with that of his wife, are buried in a marble tomb in the *coro* of the cathedral.

Burgos remained capital of Castile for 400 years before ceding the privilege first to Valladolid and later Toledo. With a declining wool trade, missing out on much of wealth of the New World, and no new hero to keep its name on history's map, the city

declined gracefully. It returned to prominence during the Civil War when Franco made it his headquarters from which to pursue his crusade against the less staunchly Nationalist parts of the country.

Nowhere is far from the cathedral or the river, so sight-seeing is both easy and pleasurable. There is good eating too with a rich choice of bars, cafés and restaurants. The cathedral's lacy gray limestone towers and spires dominate the center of the city and it is so centrally situated that the main door is closed to deter the populace from using the building as a convenient covered walkway.

Burgos cathedral ranks with Spain's greatest Gothic creations, along with the cathedrals of León, Toledo and Seville. Its cornerstone was laid in 1221 but the edifice was not completed until the 15th century. It is a huge place but the overall sense is of light, if not lightness, and artistry. The side chapels are as striking as the central portion of the building and there are a number of beautiful as well as bizarre things to see. The **Golden Stair** of the master carver, Gil de Siloé; the inlaid walnut choir; the **Santa Ana** chapel; the octagonal chapel of the High Constable of Castile with its star-vaulting; and the raised **Puerta Alta de la Coronería** — the best spot to view the forest of towers and spires — all fall into the first category. The light relief is provided by the 13th-century Christ-figure, made of animal skin, human hair and fingernails, and dressed in a red skirt — said to be warm to the touch — in the glass-fronted **Capilla del Santo Cristo** and the 15th-century clock across the nave known as the **Papamoscas** ("fly-catcher") where a devil-like figure strikes a device that sets the clock tower bell booming on the hour.

The military architecture that characterized the early life of the city can still be seen in the old quarter. Four towers, five out of eight gateways and stretches of the 13th-century walls survive. The 14th-century **Arco de Santa María** is the most striking gate, embellished by statues of El Cid and the Emperor Carlos V.

Down by the River Arlanzón there is the **Paseo del Espolón**, a wide avenue reserved for pedestrians that is lined with palms,

ABOVE: One of the city's medieval gates, Burgos.
OPPOSITE: The double-storied cloister at the Monastery of Santo Domingo de Silos, a classic example of the Romanesque style.

214

*Aragón and Northern Spain*

elms, chestnut trees and sculpted yews. There is a bandstand, a large open air café, and a riot of rose bushes. Through the willows that line the river bank you can catch a glimpse of waving fields of wheat in the Castilian countryside. Somebody with skill and taste has organized the night illuminations of Burgos. For that and many other reasons, try to avoid the habit of many visitors who stop only briefly in the city. Should you decide to stay overnight, you will eat well, rest well and see a great Gothic masterpiece afloat in the night sky.

**N. H. Condestable** ( 26-71-25, on Calle Vitoria, N° 8, is an elegant, well-established hotel, also centrally located.

**Landa Palace** ( 20-63-43, Carretera N-1, Km. 235, has lovely rooms and a swimming pool; part of the hotel is a medieval tower and the furnishings include many antique pieces.

*Moderate*

**Hotel Norte y Londres** ( 26-41-25, Plaza Alonso Martínez, N° 10, is a centrally positioned hotel with small, clean rooms; old-

## TOURIST INFORMATION

**Provincial Area Code** (47)
From inside Spain (947)
**Tourist Office** ( 20-31-25 is on Plaza Alonso Martínez, N° 7.

### HOTELS

*Expensive* means a night's lodging costs Pts.18,000 to Pts.28,000; *moderate:* Pts.8,000 to Pts.18,000; and *inexpensive:* Pts.4,000 to Pts.8,000.

*Expensive*

**Almirante Bonifaz** ( 20-69-43, Calle Vitoria, N° 22–24, is right in the center of the town.

fashioned with plenty of creaking polished wood.

**Corona de Castilla** ( 26-21-42, is on Calle Madrid, N° 15.

**España** ( 20-63-40, is on Paseo de Espolón, N° 32.

### RESTAURANTS

Burgos has an abundance of good eating places. In the expensive range the top spot is the restaurant in the **Landa Palace Hotel.** In town a good meal, at a moderate price (Pts.3,000 to Pts.8,000), can be had at the **Mesón del Cid** ( 20-59-71, Plaza Santa Maróa, N° 8, just opposite the cathedral in a medieval building; **Los Chapiteles**, ( 20-59-98, Calle General Santocildés, N° 7; and

**Casa Ojeda** ( 20-90-52, Calle Vitoria, N° 5, which has a good *tapas* bar in addition to its regular restaurant service.

## LEAVING BURGOS

After Burgos, the pilgrims' way leads west to León but there is a detour to the south, to the monastery of **Santo Domingo de Silos**, that is worth making. Part of the pleasure is the country road that in summer is bordered by fields of swaying grain studded with red poppies, purple lavender, pink thistles and blue cornflowers. Small farming towns, like **Covarrubias** on the River Arlanza, with their timbered houses, moldering castles and sleepy churches, break up the journey.

## SANTO DOMINGO DE SILOS

The monastery of Santo Domingo de Silos was founded in the 10th century and rebuilt in the eleventh after having been sacked by Al-Mansur Abu Jafar, the Moorish counterpart of El Cid. A monk called Domingo, later canonized, was responsible for the rebuilding. The church was replaced in the 18th century but the 12th-century cloister survives, a testament to the simplicity and beauty of the Romanesque style. It is a double cloister, the arcades and capitals made of a soft yellow sandstone, with a painted wooden ceiling and pebble patterned floors. It embraces a rose garden in which there is a fountain and a single tall cypress tree.

A small community of Benedictine monks lives in the monastery which accepts lodgers. The visitors can take part, if they wish, in the monastery's religious services and live in small cell-like rooms that are austere but not uncomfortable. The monks are famous for their performance of Gregorian chants, one of the reasons that outsiders are drawn to spend time in this tranquil corner of Spain. There is also accommodation and good food at the

nearby **Hotel de Tres Reyes** which bakes its own bread.

## LEÓN

León was a favorite stopping-place for the Santiago pilgrims because it was a hospitable, civilized city, it offered unusually lavish accommodation, and it set them on the last leg of their journey. León's symbol is a lion but the city's origins are Roman and the name comes from the Seventh Legion. After an Arab occupation it became the Visigothic capital of Astur-León, ruling over modern Asturias to the north, as well as the kingdom of León itself. León succumbed to another Moorish visitation, this time a

The Monastery of San Marcos in León, built in the 12th century for pilgrims, is now a spectacular parador.

thorough sacking, before reaching its hey-day in the 10th and 11th centuries after which its power was eclipsed by Burgos and its former junior partner, the kingdom of Castile.

## Sightseeing

León has three major architectural attractions, the last of which you can eat, drink and sleep in. The first is the magnificent Gothic cathedral, generally thought to be the finest in Spain. The difference between this cathedral and all the others of its kind is that it was built relatively rapidly — in less than 100 years in the 12th and 13th centuries — and as a result has a completeness and a unity that the others lack. Its medieval crea-

tors also seemed to have reached the zenith of their ambition and confidence as they piled stone up stone, exuberantly filling the walls with rich and expansive stained glass windows.

The moment you step inside León cathedral, the idea that Spanish churches are heavy and gloomy is swept away by the countless shafts of light from all angles that illuminate the whole structure with an incandescent glow. The *coro*, in the center of the nave, is open with a glass frontage so that there is a clear view from the entrance all the way to the altar. Huge rose windows at either end of the nave, the delicacy of the supporting columns, the fine vaulting, and above all the dancing multicolored light splashed around the interior by the 125 stained glass windows creates an unmatched feeling of lightness and beauty. The cathedral is worth visiting at different times of day to view changes in light and mood as the sun moves on its axis.

The second attraction is the **Colegiata de San Isidoro**, a fine Romanesque church founded by Ferdinand I who united the kingdoms of León and Castile in the 11th century. Originally a reliquary for the remains of San Isidoro, the church became a pantheon for the king, who was the first

addition of a Plateresque façade in the early 16th century, and the fact that a night's lodging is no longer on the house. There is a church attached to the monastery and, with a drink in your hand, you can wander around the upper level of the cloister and view the proceedings through a glass partition. Wandering around this unusual hotel at a quiet hour of the evening or morning, it is not hard to conjure up the chant of monks, the rustle of the nuns' skirts on a curving stone staircase, the smell of incense, and the silence of centuries.

to use the title "King of the Spains," and for his successors. What makes the church unique, however, are its splendidly preserved 12th-century frescoes depicting daily life through the seasons in those far-off times. There is also a fine collection of illuminated manuscripts, altar ornaments and other religious artifacts in the church's treasury.

The last delight that León has to offer is the **Monastery of San Marcos**, now a parador and a memorable place to spend a night. It was built in the 12th century expressly to house pilgrims, free of charge, as they prepared themselves for the final stretch of the journey to Santiago de Compostela. Not a lot has changed except the

## TOURIST INFORMATION

**Provincial Area Code** (87)
From inside Spain (987)
**Tourist Office** ( 23-70-82, Plaza de la Regla, Nº 3.
**Railway Station** ( 22-37-04, Calle Astorga.

### HOTELS

*Expensive* means a night's lodging costs Pts.18,000 to Pts.28,000; *moderate:* Pts.8,000 to Pts.18,000.

### Expensive
**Conde Luna** ( 20-66-00 is on Calle Independencia, Nº 7.

**Hotel de San Marcos**, ( 23-73-00, on Plaza San Marcos, N° 7, is a splendid parador converted from a 12th-century monastery.

*Moderate*

**Paris**, ( 23-86-00, can be found at Generalísimo Franco, N° 20.

**Quindós**, ( 23-62-00, is on Avenida José Antonio, N° 24.

RESTAURANTS

León has plenty of reasonably priced restaurants. The local specialty is garlic

soup while fresh trout and salmon feature on many menus.

Two good ones to go to are **Casa Pozo**, ( 22-30-39, on Plaza San Marcelo, N° 15, and **Patricio**, ( 24-16-51, on Calle Condesa de Sagasta, N° 24.

## SANTIAGO DE COMPOSTELA

### AN IMPROBABLE LEGEND

And so to Santiago de Compostela. It is hard to imagine a cathedral city, a provincial capital and a thriving university town of over 100,000 people that owes its origins and its development solely to an improbable

legend over a thousand years old. But that is what happened, and the result is a unique and peculiarly Spanish phenomenon blending myth, superstition, religious imperialism, nationalism and civic pride.

The story runs as follows. In AD 813 the locals were attracted to a meadow by a powerful supernatural light turning it into a *campus stellae*, a "field of stars." Here they found the remains of St. James the Apostle. A shrine, and later, a cathedral were built. What was he doing in a damp corner of Galicia? Well, he had apparently done some

evangelical work in Spain after the death of Christ and then returned to Jerusalem where he died a martyr's death at the hand of King Herod in AD 44.

Guided by an angel, his body was smuggled back to Spain in a marble boat by his followers. During the voyage, the apostle's remains performed a miracle by saving a man from drowning who had been carried out to sea by a frightened horse. Man and horse were covered with scallop shells which were to become the symbol of the

OPPOSITE: Interior of parador, Hotel de San Marcos, León. ABOVE RIGHT: The famous rose window in León Cathedral, and LEFT More of the Cathedral's stained glass.

apostle, his legend, and the pilgrimage. (The fame of the emblem spread: large scallops are known as Coquilles de St. Jacques and "cockle shells" feature in the anti-Popish nursery rhyme about Mary Tudor of England, *Mary, Mary Quite Contrary.*)

None of this has any historical backing. More to the point, however, was the fact that in the ninth century Christendom in general and Spain in particular needed some supernatural spine-stiffening in the bitter struggle against the Moors. Thus St. James was depicted not only as an apostle, saint, and traveler, but as a fearless soldier notably adept at smiting the Muslim invader. At the battle of Clavijo in 844, for instance, not long after his remains were discovered, he miraculously appeared in person on a white stallion and led the Christians to victory. He became known as Santiago Matamoros, St. James the Moor-Slayer, breathing fear into the Moor who, it seemed, had become overconfident about the power of the Prophet Mohammed's arm kept in the mosque in Córdoba, courage into the Spanish soldiery, and wonder into Christian minds the length and breadth of Europe.

## THE ROAD TO ST. JAMES

The myth gathered strength as time went on. Kings, popes, and powerful monastic orders approved and provided patronage; Santiago became the patron saint of Spain; and the pilgrims, dressed in their flowing cloaks and wide-brimmed hats festooned with scallop shells, began to tramp the long dusty El Camino de Santiago (the Road of St. James). In a very short time, Santiago de Compostela had joined Jerusalem and Rome as one of Christendom's holy cities, the Christian Mecca of Western Europe.

## SIGHTSEEING

The city manages to support the weight of this great myth and reward the devotion of the millions who have made such an effort to pay homage in person. Entering from the green Galician countryside, you reach the heart of Santiago in a matter of minutes. The cathedral square, **Plaza del Obradoiro**, is one of the great public spaces of Spain, a vast but finely proportioned square that gives pride of place to the cathedral itself but neither denigrates nor diminishes the other grand buildings that flank it.

Opposite the cathedral is the **Rajoy Palace**, a stately 18th-century building that houses the Town Hall and the seat of the Galician Regional Government, and the **Palacio de Gelmirez**, erected in the 12th and 13th centuries by two archbishops. On the

south side of the square stands the 17th-century **Colegio de San Jeronimo** while the north side is dominated by the **Hotel Reyes Católicos** which was built by Ferdinand and Isabella for the pilgrims at the end of the 15th century and is now an unusual and luxurious hotel.

The cathedral is both a shrine and a church. Surmounted by two great towers, the façade on the square is an 18th-century Baroque creation. The body of the cathedral, however, is Romanesque and the best way to enter it is through the **Portico de la Gloria**,

ABOVE: Façade of the Cathedral in Santiago de Compostela. OPPOSITE: A plumed functionary during the height of the pilgrimage at Santiago de Compostela.

the work of the master medieval carver, **Mateo**, who managed to sculpt more than 200 figures on the doorway. At the foot of the central column there are five well-worn finger-holds where pilgrims have for centuries placed a hand while steadying themselves to lean down and bump their foreheads against the smooth stone pate of Maestro Mateo himself. The idea, it seems, is that some of his talent will rub off.

Another line of pilgrims shuffles slowly forwards to the steps behind the altar that lead up to the statue of St. James. One by

one the pilgrims file by touching, kissing or embracing the saint's bronze garments. The south door, the **Puerta de las Platerías** is also Romanesque, and the interior of the cathedral is a treasure trove of religious paintings, statuary, carving, ancient fabrics, and relics. During the height of the pilgrimage, priests hear confessions in half a dozen languages, there is a pungent smell of wax and incense and a constant movement of people.

The central core of Santiago seemed to stop developing after the Baroque period and is a delight to wander in. The prevailing stone is granite, but it is not a somber granite. There are many golden moments as the sun touches the walls of the cathedral and other buildings, with green and copper grace notes from the lichen, moss and ivy that cover so many walls, and cheerful splashes of red from the tiled roofs.

---

ABOVE: A scene from the folk festival at the climax of the pilgrimage. OPPOSITE TOP: High mass in the Cathedral. OPPOSITE BOTTOM: Galician dancers.

## CELEBRATION OF THE LEGEND

St. James's day is celebrated on July 25th and as the climax of the pilgrimage approaches the city's program of entertainment picks up steam. There are concerts of folk music and dancing in the smaller squares around the cathedral, competitions for Galician bagpipers, a spectacular evening production of Verdi in the Plaza del Obradoiro that can be watched after dinner from a balcony of the Hostal de los Reyes Católicos, a greasy pole for young bloods to climb and win a prize, more "giants" and "fat-heads," a military parade, and even a threatened—but unconsummated — "demo" by Galician separatists. The final event on the eve of the saint's day is a huge firework display and the symbolic burning of a Moorish façade, made of painted wood, that had been erected in front of the cathedral earlier.

A solemn sung mass in honor of Santiago marks the climax of the pilgrimage. In the cathedral an eager crowd is moving down the aisles towards the high altar. Two jolly Spanish nuns whisper excitedly to each other as they mingle with the tourists and pilgrims. An old woman kneels in front of a statue of St. James on horseback, sword raised and a Moor's decapitated head at his feet. (This object will later be carried around the cathedral in procession.) A priest leans out of his confessional and blinks as the crowd becomes denser and denser and the pace slows. Thousands of candles are augmented by the glare of lights for the television cameras that are now in place near the choir stalls. The organ booms forth and the *botafumeiro* begins its slow trajectory in the cross-way behind the altar. Suspended from pulleys and ropes, the *botafumeiro* is the world's largest censer or thurible. Made in 1602, it weighs 53.6 kg (118 lbs), and needs eight sturdy men to swing it.

Pulling harder and harder, the team make it move in ever-widening arcs over the heads of the congregation. As the censer cuts through the air it spews out sparks and clouds of fragrant smoke, and draws great gasps of delight mingled with fear from the people beneath it. There is a story that when Catherine of Aragón was attending mass,

the censer parted company with its moorings and crashed through a window. The mass, which is attended by a veritable army of lay and clerical dignitaries and is nationally televised, continues. Afterwards, the crowd streams outside into the Plaza del Obradoiro where a band is playing paso-dobles in the sunshine.

## TOURIST INFORMATION

**Provincial Area Code** (81)
From inside Spain (981)

(now a parador) built by the Catholic monarchs for the pilgrims at the end of the 16th century; it shares the square with the Cathedral.
**Araguanay** ( 59-59-00, is on Calle Alfred Brañas, N° 5.
*Moderate*
**Compostela** ( 58-57-00, is on General Franco, N° 1.
**Peregrino** ( 59-18-50, is on Avenida d Rosalia de Castro.
**Gelmirez** ( 56-11-00, is on General Franco N° 92.

**Tourist Office** ( 58-40-81, Rua del Villa, N° 43.
**Railway Station** ( 59-60-50, Avenida de General Franco.

### HOTELS
*Expensive* means a night's lodging costs Pts.18,000 to Pts.28,000; *moderate:* Pts.8,000 to Pts.18,000.

*Expensive*
**Hotel de los Reyes Católicos** ( 58-22-00, Plaza de Obradoiro, N° 1, is a superb lodging

### RESTAURANTS
**Don Gaiferos** ( 58-38-94, on Rua Nova N° 23, has a sophisticated ambience and good range of dishes, including man Galician specialties.
**Anexo Vilas** ( 59-83-87, on Avenida Vila garcia, N° 21, is the city's oldest restaurar and has good Galician cuisine and atmos phere.
**Hotel Reyes Católicos** ( 58-22-00, Plaz Obradoiro, N° 1, is a great vaulted dinin room beneath the hotel supported by hand cut granite arches; excellent food and wine
**Fornos** ( 56-57-21, is located on Genera Franco, N° 24.
**Las Huertas** ( 56-19-79, on Calle Huertas N° 16 serves good Basque food.

ABOVE: Vaulted dining room in the Hotel Reyes Católicos, Santiago de Compostela. OPPOSITE: Santiago de Compostela, Galician folk dancer and bagpiper.

## THE NORTHERN COASTLINE

After the drama of Santiago, a journey along Spain's northern coastline is a soothing experience. It also has the merit of providing a sampling of three of the country's most distinctive provinces: **Galicia, Asturias, and the Basque Country**. It would be wise to set aside at least three days for this trip. The distances are not great but there is a lot to see and the roads tend to be slow with the exception of the A-9 freeway which links

Santiago with Pontevedra in the south of Galicia and La Coruña in the north.

## GALICIA

Galicia has been compared to Ireland and Brittany because of its isolation, its physical appearance, and its Celtic roots and temperament. Shut in by mountains in the northwest corner of Spain with Portugal to the south and the Atlantic Ocean to the north and west, Galicia was off history's beaten track. The Romans called its westernmost point Finisterre, Land's End.

It is a well-watered green land with a rocky coastline spliced by deep *rias*, or fjord-

like estuaries with sandy beaches, and covered with tiny fields and gardens separated by granite walls. Along the coast there are countless fishing villages whose reason for being remains the harvest of the sea, for which Galicia is famous, and not the tourist trade. Inland the scenery is essentially rural and timeless. Galicia has few large towns and farming is still primitive mainly because the parcels of land are so small and scattered. Horse and ox-drawn carts, and women with baskets — and men with small haystacks — on their heads trudging along

country lanes are common; cows, sheep, goats and conical hayricks adorn the patchwork meadows; and old-fashioned farmyards full of chickens, ducks and geese look — and smell — like old-fashioned farmyards. Galician farms also have distinctive granaries (*horreos*) that are built on stilts to protect the grain from rats and other rodents. Like much else in Galicia, the *horreos* are made out of granite and have red-tiled roofs and usually a cross at either end. In the more remote and mountainous parts of the region, shepherds still use ancient *pallozas*, circular stone huts with conical thatched roofs that have Celtic origins.

The Celts arrived about 1,000 BC and were unchallenged until the Romans invaded some 900 years later and called the locals "Gallaeci," leaving the place a name. The Suebi, from northern Europe, came next and were followed by the Visigoths. Unlike the rest of Spain, the Moors made little impact and thereafter Galicia was left largely to its own devices even though it was incorporated into the Spanish state in the late 15th century.

The local language, Gallego, is widely spoken and is closer to Portuguese than Castilian Spanish, and the region is renowned for its poetry and its folk music,

notably its bagpipes (*gaita*). Galicia is also well-known for its cuisine and vies with Basque cooking for the accolade of being the best in Spain. In most of the Galician ports along the *rias* there are colorful fish auctions every morning, except Sundays and public holidays, and the quality of the region's seafood, especially its sardines, scallops and mussels, is exceptional. Somewhat surprisingly, given its wet, cool climate, Galicia produces good white or "green" wines (similar to Portugal's *vinhos verdes*), the best being Ribero, Albarino and Condado.

Apart from Santiago, Galicia is not noted for its cities but some of the coastal towns are worth driving through and stopping for a brief visit. In the lower estuaries of the Galician coast (**Las Rias Bajas**) there is **Pontevedra**, a pretty place with arcaded streets and squares with stone crosses in them, all in Galician granite; and **Vigo**, Spain's leading fishing port. In the north (**Las Rias Altas**), there is **La Coruña**, another port and the largest industrial city of Galicia.

The harbor where the fish are brought in with its typical Galician houses and their glassed-in balconies, and the old town are worth seeing. There is also the **Torre de Her cules** ("Tower of Hercules") on the northern tip of the peninsula on which La Coruña is built and roughly 15 minutes drive from the city. Galicians proudly claim it as the only Roman lighthouse left in the world (and it works too). The claim is half true in that the lower portion of the lighthouse is indeed Roman with the architect's name still legibly inscribed on it. But the upper functional half dates from the late 18th century.

Inland, there is **Lugo**, just off the Santiago pilgrims' route but well worth a detour. It is 97 km (58 miles) from La Coruña and can be reached by taking the N-IV eastwards. Set in the mountains, Lugo is a beautiful old town that is encircled by its original Roman walls. Built of slate and granite in the third century AD, the walls are 2.4 km (1.5 miles) in extent, 9.2 m (30 ft) high, and contain four gates and 85 towers. They are the best preserved Roman walls in Spain and you can see them either by walking around the road that circles them on the outside (approximately 45 minutes), or drive around in a few minutes. You can also walk along the top with access at the **Puerta Nueva** and opposite the **Cathedral.** The Cathedral itself is a much modified 12th-century building with three great towers, richly decorated choir-stalls dating from the early 17th century, a circular 18th-century chapel dedicated to the **Virgen de Ojos Grandes** (Our Lady of the Big Eyes), a Baroque cloister, and the rare privilege of having the Host on permanent display.

## ASTURIAS AND CANTABRIA

Asturias is another green upland corner of Spain with few large towns and a fine Atlantic coastline. It is sometimes compared to Wales because of its appearance, its coal and mineral wealth, and the independent spirit of its people. In the same way that the heir to the British throne has traditionally been the "Prince of Wales," so, since the 14th century, has the heir to the Spanish throne held the title of Prince of Asturias.

Originally inhabited by a hardy Iberian tribe called the Astures, Asturias underwent Roman and Visigothic domination. The region's moment of glory came much earlier than other comparable parts of Spain. In 718, Christian forces, under a Visigothic warrior called Pelayo, defeated the Moors in a mountain valley at Covadonga, checking Muslim expansion and marking the turning of the tide from which point the **Reconquista** began. In modern times, the Asturians, particularly the miners, established a reputation for defying authority. The region

has a tradition of heroic strikes and Asturians fought hard against Franco in the Civil War and paid a heavy price. Today, however, it is a peaceful and easy-going province that has some of the most spectacular and best preserved countryside in Spain. Like its neighbor, Galicia, Asturias is known for its hearty dishes and fresh produce. It makes delicious hams and sausages and produces a tasty blue cheese called *cabrales* which is made from ewe's milk. Its tipple, however, is not wine but apple cider *(sidra)*, a deceptively smooth concoction that disguises a strong alcoholic content.

Asturias and the neighboring region of Cantabria (to the east) share a fine coast where the lush meadows break off abruptly and

give way to clean sandy beaches and small sheltered coves. But the most dramatic gift is the Cantabrian mountain range that separates the Atlantic shoreline from the Castilian plateau in the south. It is here that Spain's "Alps" are found, the snow-clad summits and verdant valleys of the Picos de Europa.

## PICOS DE EUROPA: SPAIN'S "ALPS"

There are three mountain systems, or massifs: **Andara** in the east, **Urrieles** in the

center, and **Cornion** to the west. The highest peak, **Torre Cerrado**, is 2,648 m (8,606 ft) and the range offers climbing, hiking, camping, bird-watching, horseback trekking and excursions by four-wheeled drive vehicles during the months from May through October. The town of **Potes** is the urban hub where you can obtain maps, supplies, and information about guides, itineraries and mountain *refugios* (free, overnight shelters.) Note: The best maps are published by the **Federación Española de Montañismo** and the best source of detailed mountaineering information is the **Federación Asturiana**

OPPOSITE: River bathing in the Sierra do Alba. ABOVE LEFT: Luarca, a fishing port on Spain's "Costa Verde," Asturias. RIGHT: Picos de Europa.

de Montañismo ( (942) 21-10-99, on Calle Melquiades Alvarez N° 16, Oviedo.

The easiest way for the casual visitor to get a feel for the Picos is to go up the **Deva** river valley to **Fuente Dé** by taking the N-621 from the coast road; turn right to Potes and the road ends at Fuente Dé where there is a modern parador, ( (942) 73-66-51, and a cable car up to the summit of the mountain. The car ascends 800 m (860 ft) in a dramatic ride that takes you up over the valley floor and then intimately close to the mountainside. Even in July there is often cloud over the mountain, especially in early morning and late afternoon, and the car can be enveloped by dense layers of vapor well before it arrives at the snow-covered peak.

There is a good hike back down to Fuente Dé from the top on a clearly defined path that brings you back to the main road N-621 at the village of **Espinama.** It is 11 km (6.8 miles) in all with about 3 km (1.9 miles) of that on the road. The walk takes you slowly out of the clouds and snow, through thin swirling mist, and into bright sunlight where butterflies dance, the voice of a shepherd calling his dog rises up out of the valley below, and kestrels circle overhead. Further down there are cows with bells around their necks, horses with young foals, and old men in hilly pastures cutting hay with long-handled scythes. In Espinama, a village that time forgot, smoke curls from tipsy-looking chimneys, and wild flowers sprout from the flagstones.

The Picos also offer history. There is the unusually beautiful 10th-century Mozarabic church of **Santa María** in the town of **Liebana.** The drive up the **Desfiladero de la Hermida** from Potes is slow-going but the spectacular scenery and the church bring their own reward. The church is an architectural historian's delight in that it brings together the solid pre-Romanesque vaulting of the Visigoths with the horseshoe arches and graceful use of space of Islam, all in a unique mountain setting.

Then there is the **Monasterio de Santo Toribio de Liebana**, a pleasant three kilometer (1.9 miles) walk from Potes. The original monastery dates from the eighth century but the present building is a later mixture of Romanesque and Gothic. The monastery's reputation is based on the fame of its eighth-century abbot, Beato de Liebana, whose *Commentaries on the Apocalypse* became popular scriptural texts all over Spain in later centuries, and on its claim to possessing the largest fragment of the cross on which Christ died.

Turning north and then east along the Cantabrian coast, the traveler will see a blend of a working countryside with holiday making on the beaches. There is a freshness and wholesome feeling about Spain's northern coast that contrasts favorably with

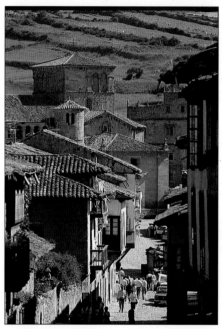

the crowded sun-baked *costas* of the south. But then the sun does not always shine here and there is a heavy annual rainfall that shows no respect for the beach-worshiper's schedule.

## SANTANDER

Santander, the capital of Cantabria, is the center of this area and functions as an important freight and ferry terminal, fishing port, and tourist attraction in its own right.

ABOVE: Santillana del Mer, reputed to be the most beautiful village in Spain. OPPOSITE: Santander's popular beaches.

Overlooking a magnificent bay, Santander has a series of sweeping interlocking beaches easily accessible from the main hotels. Rather like San Sebastián, further east, Santander established a reputation as a fashionable resort where royalty and celebrities from all over Europe spent their summers. Unfortunately, most of the city was burnt down in 1941 but some its earlier style is reflected in the northwest suburb of **El Sardinero** which escaped the conflagration. El Sardinero has two excellent beaches and its elegant boulevards, expensive shops, classy hotels and casino hark back to the Belle Epoque and to the period between the two World Wars.

## SANTILLANA DEL MAR AND ALTAMIRA CAVES

From Santander it is an easy run westwards to two places of historic and visual interest: the medieval town of **Santillana del Mar** and the prehistoric caves of **Altamira.**

Considering that Santillana del Mar has to carry the burden of being the "most beautiful village in Spain" and has been declared a national monument, it performs rather well. The time not to see it is when a dozen tourist buses descend, so the answer is an early morning or late afternoon visit or, better still, a stay overnight in the atmospheric parador or in one of the nearby hotels. The town's name comes from Saint Juliana whose remains have been there since the sixth century and are in the church. "Mar" is a bit of a misnomer because the town is just over three kilometers (two miles) from the sea.

Santillana grew up as a prosperous farming community around the monastery dedicated to Saint Juliana and attracted wealthy noblemen and clergy who built magnificent stone and timbered houses, the 12th-century Romanesque **Collegiate Church** with its lovely cloister, and the 17th-century **Convento de Regina Coeli.** All this was accomplished in a town with only one street. Its fame spread through fiction when the 18th-century French satirist, Alain-René Le Sage made it the home of his picaresque hero, Gil Blas. Local farmers still live in the town with their livestock and sell glasses of fresh milk and homemade cakes to the visitors.

The **Altamira Caves** can be reached on foot from Santillana in 20 minutes or so, but since only about three dozen people are allowed into to see the wall paintings each day, casual visitors should not expect too much. It was found that human breath caused damage to the paintings so strict limits on the number of visitors were imposed. However, the museum which provides a great deal of information, is interesting and a well-made video of the caves

can be viewed; a nearby cave of stalactites and stalagmites is open to the public. (The way to see the caves themselves is to write, preferably months in advance, to the **Centro de Investigación de Altamira**, Santillana del Mar, Santander.)

The caves are at a depth of 270 m (886 ft) and are a veritable gallery of vividly colored paintings of the bison, horses, stags and boars hunted by Paleolithic man around 13000 BC. The Altamira caves have been called the "Sistine Chapel" of primitive art and were sealed for millennia by a landslide.

Re-opened in 1868, the paintings were not noticed until more than a decade later when the nine-year-old daughter of a speliologist is reputed to have cried, "Papa, look, cows!"

## TOURIST INFORMATION

**Provincial Area Code**   (42)
From inside Spain   (942)
**Tourist Office** ( 31-23-11, Plaza Velarde, N° 1.
**Railway Station** ( 21-12-14, Calle de Rodriguez.
**Port Marítima Aucona** ( 22-72-88, at Paseo de Pereda, N° 13, is the terminal for Brittany Ferries' ships that ply between Plymouth

*Moderate*
**México** ( 21-24-50 is located on Caldeón de la Barca, N° 3.
**Roma** ( 27-27-00 is on Avenida de los Hoteles, N° 5.
**Rhin** ( 27-43-00 can be found on Avenida Reina Victoria, N° 55.

### RESTAURANTS

All the followings are in the *moderate* price range (Pts.3,000 to Pts.8,000):
**Canadio** ( 31-41-49, on Calle Gomez Orena, N° 15, is a good all-round, popular place.

and Santander — the only sea link between Britain and Spain.

### HOTELS

*Expensive* means a night's lodging costs Pts.18,000 to Pts.28,000; *moderate:* Pts.8,000 to Pts.18,000.

*Expensive*
**Real** ( 27-25-50, Paseo Pérez Galdós, N° 28, is a stylish top class hotel with great views of the bay.
**Santemar** ( 27-29-00, on Calle Joaquin Costa, N° 28, is modern and close to the beach.
**Sardinero** ( 27-11-00, Plaza Italia, N° 1, is near the casino and beach.

**Bodega Cigalena** ( 21-30-62, Calle Daoiz y Velarde, N° 19.
**La Sardina** ( 27-10-35, Calle Doctor Fleming, N° 3.
**Posada del Mar** ( 21-30-23, Calle Juan de la Cosa, N° 3.

## THE BASQUE COUNTRY

Finally, to the Basque Country. The official territory of the Basques covers the three provinces of Vizcaya, Guipuzcoa and Alava. But Basques also form the majority of the

ABOVE: : Keeping score during a pelota game in San Sebastián. OPPOSITE: Pelota players: the game, also known as "jai alai," was invented by the Basques.

population in northern Navarre and in three provinces in southwestern France, and they call the phenomenon *Euskadi* ("collection of Basques"). They are without doubt the most "different" and the most separatist-minded of all Spain's regional people.

The Basques' origins and history are shrouded in the kind of mist that often envelops their beloved valleys. They are not related in any way to the Celts and come from a pre-Indo-European people. Their fearsomely complex language (*Euskara*) is

every monarch who ascended the Spanish throne came to Guerníca, in Vizcaya, and took an oath under the Basques' sacred oak tree to uphold and protect their laws and customs.

Two critical choices in the modern period proved disastrous for the Basques. They supported the losing side in the dynastic Carlist wars of the 19th century and, as a result, lost their privileges. The Republican government restored their autonomy in the 1930s and, notwithstanding their strong Catholicism, the Basques remained loyal to the

believed to go back to the Stone Age and has no links with any European tongue. The Basques sturdily defended themselves against all-comers over the centuries. The Romans conquered them but may have regretted it; the Visigoths, Moors and early Christian kingdoms made few inroads although the Basques did adopt Christianity, embracing it with an ardor that still survives. (St. Francis Xavier and St. Ignatius of Loyola were Basques.)

They eventually accepted the rule of Castile but retained their ancient *fueros* (privileges) and made it a tradition that

anti-clerical, "Red" side during the Civil War. Franco tried to break their spirit when he sent the German Condor Legion into action over Guerníca, modern warfare's first saturation aerial bombardment. The raid was timed for market day and the high-explosive and incendiary bombs virtually leveled the town and killed a third of its population. But the Basques' oak tree and their spirit survived, and Picasso painted his famous portrayal of the attack.

Franco was singularly repressive in the Basque country after the war, a situation that led to the rise of the violent, ultra-nationalist ETA movement. Spain's new democracy has since done much to address the Basques' grievances. The region has more

ABOVE: The salon of the María Christina Hotel in San Sabastián. OPPOSITE: The port of San Sabastián.

utonomy than any other part of Spain with ts own parliament, police force (wearing distinctive red Basque berets), TV and radio stations operating in Basque, bi-lingual schools, and so on. The ETA threat remains but the organization has lost support with the majority of Basques who seem to have chosen the non-violent option for solving their political problems.

It is not surprising that the Basques cling to their culture which is full of folk-tales about genial giants who lived among them in the pre-Christian period and did marvelous things, and about heroes and acts of valor in a long turbulent history that was unrecorded. Basques love singing, especially mournful folk-songs, and dancing. Their traditional instrument is a three-holed flute, called a *txistu* that is played with one hand while the other keeps time on a small drum. Their dancing often ranks as a feat of athleticism, notably the Flying Dance *(Bolant Dantza)* and the Sword Dance *(La Espatadantza)*.

The Basques are also great sportsmen, much addicted to lifting — and tossing — weights, and they invented *pelota* or *jai alai* which is played up against two walls with a hard rubber ball hit with the hand or a basket-like racket. Basques have made their mark as Spain's gourmets (and some would add, gourmands) with the variety of their sea-food, sauces, and love of running restaurants. Cider *(sagardua* in Basque) is the main drink, although a light, tangy white wine called *txakoli* is produced in the north and Basque-produced Riojas come from the south. There is also *pacharán,* a local distilled drink of the fire-water species.

Basques have a reputation for hard work and enterprise. Their seamen roamed the world; a number were explorers, conquistadors, and colonists. Capitalizing on their ports, timber, iron ore and other natural resources, the Basques led the Industrial Revolution in Spain. **Bilbao**, for example, became famous for its shipbuilding and is the country's sixth largest city. A disproportionate number of Basques are bankers, and Basque banks control a disproportionate amount of the country's financial business.

## SAN SEBASTIÁN

San Sebastián (Donastia in Basque) is the capital of Guipuzcoa Province and Spain's classiest seaside resort. Protected by two headlands that face each other like the claws of a crab, San Sebastián is built around a superb bay that has two golden beaches (**Playa de la Concha** and **Playa de Ondar-reta**). To round it off there is an island (**Isla de Santa Clara**) in the middle of the bay and a river (**Río Urumea**) that flows through

the city under a series of picturesque bridges. Close to the French border, San Sebastián has benefited from a French connection but it is, above all, a Basque city and proud of it.

Although ancient, San Sebastián's physiognomy and demeanor are predominantly 19th century because much of the original was destroyed in the many sackings and razings that the city had endured. Fortunately, it was the last century's upper crust that patronized the place, notably the Queen Regent, María Cristina, and the Spanish court, as well as many noble and wealthy European and South American families. The result is a city full of spacious tree-lined avenues, solid town houses, elegant shops, and a large selection of fashionable hotels. Add to that the great sweep of beach — a few paces away from the hotels, restaurants and bars — a colorful fishing port where you can have lunch and watch someone else's dinner being landed, and a quaint old quarter (**La Parte Vieja**) where some of the best *tapas* and meals in Spain are served, and you have a gem of a place.

San Sebastián has established a reputation for being the gourmet capital of Spain. An indication is the presence of numerous gastronomic clubs where members (men only) prepare monumental meals and have a lot of fun devouring them with their pals. For the outsider, however, there is no shortage of places to eat and drink. The old quarter, usually full of students and the city's glitterati spilling over into the cobbled streets, is the best place to begin an evening's cruise. Local Basque specialties like *chipirones en su tinta* (baby squid cooked in its ink), *idiazabel* (ewe's cheese, cured and smoked), and a variety of shellfish can be sampled in virtually every bar. Draft beer, served in small glasses called *zurritos,* is the best thing to wash all this down before moving on to the next act in San Sebastián's nightly gastronomic extravaganza.

## TOURIST INFORMATION

**Provincial Area Code**  (43)
From within Spain  (943)
**Tourist Office (** 42-62-82, Calle Miramar.
**Fuenterrabia Airport (** 64-22-40.
**Railway Station (** 42-64-30, Camino N° 1.

### HOTELS
*Expensive* means a night's lodging costs Pts.18,000 to Pts.28,000; *moderate:* Pts.8,000 to Pts.18,000.

### Expensive
**Costa Vasca (** 21-10-11, is on Avenida Pio Baroja, N° 9.
**María Cristina (** 42-49-00, on Paseo Republica Argentina, was built at the turn of the century and has been luxuriously restored, this is *the* place to stay in San Sebastián.
**De Londres y de Inglaterra (** 42-69-89, Calle Zubieta, N° 2, overlooks La Concha Bay and is close to the beach.

**Monte Igueldo (** 21-02-11, Monte Igueldo has great views of the bay from a strategic position.

### Moderate
**Avenida (** 21-20-22, is on Monte Igueldo.
**Guadamendi (** 21-41-11, is on Monte Igueldo
**Niza, (** 42-66-63, is on Calle Zubieta, N° 56.

### RESTAURANTS
*Expensive* represents meals costing Pts.8,000 and above; *moderate:* Pts.3,000 to Pts.8,000,.

### Expensive
**Arzak (** 27-84-65, Calle Alto de Miracruz, N° 21, located a few kilometers out of town, is one of Spain's great restaurants and practitioner of nouvelle cusine with a Basque flourish.
**Akelarre (** 21-20-52, Paseo de Orkalada, is also a top level and very stylish place.
**Panier Fleuri (** 42-42-05, Paseo de Salamanca, N° 1, is a good place to go for a change to French cooking, as well as local Basque dishes.
**Casa Nicolasa (** 42-17-62, on the first floor of Calle Aldamar, N° 4, is an excellent all-round restaurant highly esteemed by the city's gourmets.

### Moderate
Three are in the old part of the town, they are: **Juanito Kojua (** 42-01-80, Calle de Puerto, N° 14; **Patxiku Quintana (** 42-63-99, San Jeronimo, N° 22 and **Kokotxa (** 42-01-73, Calle Campanario, N° 11.
**Chomin (** 21-07-05, Avenida de la Infanta Beatriz, N° 14, serves Basque and French dishes.

On the cheaper side in this gourmet city, there are many small restaurants, and countless bars, in the old town (**La Parte Vieja**) and the port. Try the local Basque cheese, *idiazabal,* when you are having a *zurrito* which is a small glass of draught beer peculiar to San Sebastián.

OPPOSITE: A street in La Parte Vieja, the old quarter of San Sabastián.

# The Balearic Islands

THE BALEARIC ISLANDS

MAJORCA (MALLORCA)

MINORCA (MENORCA)

Ciudadela
Mercadal
Mahón

Cabo Formentor

Pollensa
Alcudia

Sóller
Inca
Muro
Cala Ratjada

Valldemosa
Binisalem
Petra
Artá

Andraitx
Palma
Manacor
Felanitx

Santany

CABRERA

IBIZA

San Juan Bautista

San Antonio
Santa Eulalia del Río

San José
Ibiza

San Fernando

Santa Galdana
FORMENTERA

25 km

# SPAIN'S MEDITERRANEAN ISLANDS

pain's Mediterranean islands, which lie off he Levante coast, differ considerably from he mainland and from each other. The Balearics (Islas Baleares) have become major ourist resorts but each of the four principal slands retains a distinctive character that is he result of geography and history. The slands fall into two groups. **Ibiza** (Eivissa n the local dialect) and its smaller sister, **Formentera**, are properly called the **Islas Pitiusas** (from the Greek meaning "islands of pines"). Situated about 80 km (50 miles) from the Spanish coast, they are relatively ow-lying — most of Formentera is as flat s a Spanish omelet — and are drier and hotter than their neighbors. **Majorca** (Mallorca) and **Minorca** (Menorca), some 250 km (155 miles) from the mainland, are strictly speaking the Balearic Islands and are more mountainous with a greater climatic variety.

The islands have an interesting prehistory which can be traced in the caves and monuments scattered over Majorca and Minorca. Bronze Age people left *talayots,* ound watchtowers built with huge stone blocks, *navetas,* chieftains' stone tombs constructed in the form of upturned boats which may have later served as dwellings, and the mysterious *taulas,* T-shaped monuments with one huge slab of stone balancing on top of another and found only n Minorca. The name of the Baleares is believed to have come from a Greek or Semitic word meaning skill in throwing; the ancient inhabitants of Majorca and Minorca were apparently deadly practitioners of the slingshot.

Most of the Mediterranean's sea-faring people seem to have spent some time in the Balearics. The Phoenicians and Greeks visited and the Carthaginians turned Ibiza into a stronghold. The Romans, Vandals and Visigoths followed, and then came the Moors who left their mark in the spectacular stonewall terracing of Majorca's mountain hillsides, in irrigation systems that made extensive use of windmills, and in the cultivation of the olive. All of this can be seen today, including some of the actual olive trees planted by the industrious Moors almost a thousand years ago. The trees are gnarled, desiccated and enormously stout, yet they still flourish and bear fruit year after year.

In 1229, King Jaime I of Aragón and Count of Barcelona ("the Conqueror") seized the islands and drove the Moors out. As part of the growing Aragón-Catalonia dominion, the Balearics embarked upon a new age of prosperity and cultural achievement. Towns expanded, castles, churches, monasteries and convents were built, and maritime trade flourished. Majorca produced Ramón Llul, a polymath who wrote novels, poetry, works on mathematics, mysticism and medicine and who traveled the length and breadth of the Mediterranean. The Catalan culture and language were gradually absorbed by the inhabitants, each island developing its own dialect but none departing radically from the roots of the language.

The golden age came to an end in the early 16th century as the Ottoman Turks began to test their maritime strength in the western end of the Mediterranean, and as Spain became obsessed with the New World and neglected its Mediterranean interests. The Balearics became a happy hunting ground for foreign navies and corsairs. Watchtowers on rocky promontories, and walls around cities, villages and manor houses, many of which still exist, were a product of this period.

In the 18th century, Minorca fell under British rule giving the island a distinctive flavor, and Father Junipero Serra, who went on to found many famous Californian missions, was born in Majorca. Foreign travelers made the islands better known in the 19th century by recording their experiences and sometimes deciding to settle for good. George Sand and Frederic Chopin spent a rather miserable winter in Majorca, where he composed some lovely music and she wrote an acerbic travel book, after which they left. Archduke Louis Salvador, a scion of the Austrian Habsburgs, fell in love with

OPPOSITE: The seaview from the terrace of the Hacienda Na Xamena Hotel, Ibiza.

Majorca and with one of its peasant girls and stayed.

In the present century, more foreigners settled, attracted by the islands' natural beauty, tolerant and friendly population, low cost of living, and proximity to the rest of Europe. Robert Graves, the British poet and writer, came to Majorca in 1929 with the American poet Laura Riding after publishing *Good-bye to All That*, his moving account of life and death in the trenches during World War I. Other British, American, French, Italian and German writers, painters, and poets followed Graves' example.

The Civil War did not last long on the islands though some old scores were bloodily settled. Life went on fairly serenely until the late fifties when the hippies discovered Ibiza and millions of more conventional visitors found that the Balearics were a fine spot to indulge in some *sol, vino* and *playa* at very modest cost. Tourism expanded to what is now almost a year-round business and brought prosperity. The islands also became the home of retired expatriates, many of them on the retreat from the ebbing British empire. The Balearics were — and still are — attractive to the sailing and boating fraternity who were drawn by the indented coastlines and the numerous harbors and marinas. Spaniards from the mainland are now visiting in increasing numbers and the Spanish royal family vacations in Majorca every summer.

## MAJORCA

The largest island with over half a million people, Majorca is blessed with a varied topography that offers rugged mountains, sandy beaches, rocky bays or *calas*, and flat fertile plains. There are three distinct areas: the mountainous northwest range with its spectacular coastline; a lower range of hills in the southeast, and a broad central plain that runs between the bays of **Alcudia** and **Pollensa** in the north and **Palma's** bay in the south. Majorca has some satellite islands, mostly uninhabited like Dragonera to the west or naval stations such as Cabrera in the south. The island is a manageable size, about 90 km (56 miles) long and approximately

70 km wide (43 miles), which means you ca see much of it in a short visit yet avoid th crowds if that is your choice.

## PALMA DE MALLORCA

**Palma de Mallorca**, the capital of th Balearics, is an old city that has managed no to ruin itself as industry, mass tourism an the vulgar temptations accompanying sud den wealth have descended upon it. Since i is protected from the north winds by th mountains and faces south, Palma has milder climate than other parts of the island a fact that draws visitors throughout th year.

Built on a lovely wide bay, Palma's archi tectural treasures are best first seen from th sea, and arriving on one of the overnigh ferries from Alicante, Valencia or Barcelon provides a perfect method. The ships usu ally sail in just after dawn when everythin is fresh and glowing. On a hill above the cit stands **Bellver Castle**, palm trees and flow ering oleander and hibiscus delineate th sweep of the bay, the old quarter look peaceful as the sun warms the yellowin walls and red roofs, and on the right Palma' great Gothic Cathedral sits, the monarch o all it surveys.

### Sightseeing

The central boulevard of the city is the **Pase del Borne**, a plane tree-lined avenue with a wide central walkway similar to La Ramblas in Barcelona. It runs at right angle to the sea and is a good spot to take one' bearings for an exploration of the olde parts of Palma. The Cathedral is on the righ hand side of the Paseo del Borne as yo walk into the city from the sea. It was be gun in the 13th century, shortly after th Reconquest, but not finished until th 16th century. It has a huge airy nave an some particularly fine stained glass win dows. A curious touch is Gaudí's signatur in this otherwise strictly Gothic presenc He was commissioned to do some restora tion work in the sculptural details of th royal chapel and the canopies over the hig altar and one of the pulpits.

Next to the Cathedral is the **Almudain Palace**, which was built in the 13th century n the site of a Moorish fortress. This is another classic Gothic building but its protective cypress trees and the well-watered gardens that surround it recall its Moorish heritage. Behind the Cathedral and Almudaina are a collection of churches, squares and mansions that are well worth exploring. The **Arab Baths**, the only Moorish remnant in Palma, are in this district. There are also the Gothic churches of **San Francesc** and **Sant Eulalia**, both in squares named after them, which are fine examples of the period. San Francesc has a quiet

of **Terreno** which was fashionable in the earlier part of this century and has become the center of Palma's nightlife, and, above it all, **Bellver Castle**, built in the 13th century. There is a small museum and marvelous views from the tower.

Palma is a great yachting center — sail and motor — and there are several sailing clubs with extensive facilities. There are also colorful markets, good seafood restaurants down by the port, and plenty of *tapas* bars in the cool narrow streets behind Sa Llotja. There is a large bullring but the

loister and the tomb of Ramón Llul, Majorca's illustrious medieval scholar. There are several fine examples of Majoran domestic architecture here too, the houses of noblemen and wealthy merchants built between the 16th and 18th centuries with spacious patios, stone staircases and galleries.

On the other side of the Paseo del Borne, closer to the port, is **Sa Llotja** (La Lonja, in Castilian), an elegant 15th-century Gothic building with a crenellated tower at each corner where Palma's medieval merchants did their business; next door is the galleried **Consolat de Mar**, built in the 17th century. Continuing round the bay in a westerly direction there are many hotels, the suburb

fights are usually disappointing. Conventional wisdom faults the spectators who are largely tourists and therefore neither knowledgeable nor critical enough to keep the matadors on their toes, and seasick bulls that have had to endure a sea-crossing from the mainland. The best beaches are east of the city, in the direction of the airport, notably **Ca'n Pastilla** and **El Arenal.**

The main roads fan out from Palma to all parts of the island. There are few highways on Majorca so drive with special care, especially on the mountain roads. In addition to moving around by car and bus, there are two

ABOVE: The port of Sóller, Majorca.

quaint railroads. One goes to **Inca** in the center of the island, and the other takes you through a mountain tunnel that seems to go on forever to **Sóller** in the northwest not far from the sea. Both trains leave from a tiny station on the north side of Palma, the fares are negligible, and it is a great way to see the rural parts of the island.

## TOURIST INFORMATION

**Provincial Area Code** (71)
From within Spain (971)

**Tourist Office** ( 71-22-16, Avenida Jaime III, N° 10.
**Airport Son San Juan** ( 26-26-00.
**Iberia** ( 71-80-00.
**Port** ( 70-23-00, Calle 16 de Julio.
**Trasmediterranea Company** ( 70-23-00, Paseo Muelle Viejo.

### HOTELS

*Expensive* means a night's lodging costs Pts.18,000 to Pts.28,000; *moderate:* Pts.8,000 to Pts.18,000.

*Expensive*

**Son Vida** ( 79-00-00 FAX 79-00-17, Urban zación Son Vida, is Palma's top hotel. It is i an old castle on palatial grounds just outsid the city, with golf course and a sweepin view of Palma's bay.
**Melia Victoria** ( 73-25-42 FAX 45-08-2 Avenguda Joan Miró, N° 21, is on the sea front overlooking the port.
**Sol Bellver** ( 73-67-44 FAX 73-14-51, Pase Marítimo, is in similar position.
**San Lorenzo** ( 72-82-00 FAX 71-19-01, Carre San Lorenzo, N° 14; and **Ca Sa Galesa** ( 7 54-00, Carrer Miramar, N° 8, both are sma and charming luxury hotels in converte noblemen's houses in old Palma. Sa Lorenzo has six rooms and Ca Sa Gales eleven.

*Moderate*

**Saratoga** ( 72-72-40 FAX 72-73-12, Paseo d Mallorca, N° 6, is close to the main shoppin centre.
**Sol Jaime III** ( 72-59-43 FAX 72-59-46, Pase de Mallorca, N° 14, is only a few doors awa from the Saratoga.
**Hotel Born** ( 71-29-42, Carrer San Jaime N° 3, is centrally located in a 17th-centur building recently renovated.
**Gran Hotel Bonanza Playa** ( 40-11-1 FAX 40-56-15, Carretera Illetas, N° 21, lo cated on the coast just outside Palma; is good, unpretentious hotel with decent food

### RESTAURANTS

*Expensive* represents meals costing Pts.8,00 and above; *moderate:* Pts.3,000 to Pts.8,00C and *inexpensive:* Pts.1,000 to Pts.3,000.

The following restaurants are listed i descending order of prices — expensiv down to moderate.
**Koldo Royo** ( 45-70-21, located on Aven guda Gabriel Roca, N° 3, is run by on of Spain's top chefs serving Basque-in spired cuisine but imaginative use of loca produce and presentation of traditiona dishes.
**Porto Pi** ( 40-00-87, Avenguda Joan Mir N° 174, is the place to go for first-class cook ing in an old world setting.
**Caballito de Mar** ( 72-10-74, Paseo d Sagrera, N° 5, serves excellent fish and sea food down in the port.

ABOVE: The dramatic northwestern coastline of Majorca. OPPOSITE: The same coast near the village of Deià.

Ca'n Nofre ( 46-23-59, Carrer de Manacor, Nº 27, is a good choice for sampling Majorcan dishes.

Parlament ( 72-60-26, Carrer Conquistador, Nº 11, is where extraordinary *paella* and rice dishes are served at reasonable prices.

Two other relatively inexpensive places are worth a mention: **La Cantina**, a fish restaurant in the Club Nautico section of the port and, on the other side of the Paseo Maritimo, near the Lonja, **La Bóveda**, a charismatic *tapas* bar and small restaurant that specializes in *serrano* ham and local dishes.

## SEEING THE ISLAND

There are a number of interesting excursions and there is no need to follow a rigid pattern because distances between places are relatively short. Perhaps the best way to cover the ground is to follow the island's natural features. Let's start with the northwest mountain range and head for **Andraitx** in the southwest tip of Majorca. A new highway runs down to **Palma Nova** and then the old road continues, linking up a series of small villages that have become tourist and residential resorts. Andraitx is a typical unpretentious Majorcan farming town built, like so many towns on the island, away from the coast to avoid the attentions of pirates and other unwelcome visitors. Most of these towns, however, developed a small fishing port and Andraitx has a heavily developed one set in a perfect bay. The road then heads north and so starts the journey along one of the most glorious and unspoilt coasts in the Mediterranean. If you do nothing else in Majorca, take this drive.

After **Bañalbufar** make a short diversion to **Valldemossa**, a pretty inland town, famous (or infamous, depending on your reading of history) for being the place that George Sand and Chopin chose to stay in the bitter winter of 1838-39. They lived in the **Cartuja** (the Carthusian Monastery), which had been built 500 years earlier. Chopin managed to finish his *Preludes*, although ill with tuberculosis. The free-thinking, free-loving Sand took her revenge on what she deemed to be a primitive island, populated by boorish peasants,

and compounded by atrocious weather by letting it all hang out in a slim volume entitled *A Winter in Majorca*. It provoked an uproar among the locals. A Palma newspaper denounced her as "the most immoral of writers and the most obscene of women." (The book is available in several languages in many bookstores around the island.)

But some times a bad press turns out to be a good one. Valldemossa is full of sightseers all year round and whether or not you are intrigued by the famous lovers, the

Cartuja and its gardens repay the small effort of breaking the journey. The monastery, which overlooks a lush valley of olive groves, orchards and gardens, was built as a palace and then given to the Carthusian monks at the end of the 14th century. In 1835, during one of Spain's anti-clerical phases, it was expropriated and opened up to outsiders. Apart from Chopin and Sand, Nicaragua's national poet Rubén Darío, Argentinian writer Jorge Luis Borges, and the Spanish writer Miguel de Unamuno also stayed there. The monastery has a vast library, an 18th-century pharmacy, and some frescoes in the church painted by Goya's father-in-law. The gardens around the monastery are a delight. Valldemossa can also be reached on a more direct road from Palma that runs through almond groves, winds its way up to Valldemossa and links up with the coast road.

Returning to the coast, the next stop is **Son Marroig**, one of the homes of Archduke Louis Salvador (1847–1915) that is now a rather chaotic but charming museum displaying his house and his interests. During the summer classical music concerts are held there and the views from the house and its gardens are among the best along the coast. Turning inland and down a long hill is the village of **Deià** where Robert Graves lived for almost fifty years. He, like several other foreigners who adopted Deià, is buried in the tiny cemetery adjoining the village church that sits high on a hill overlooking the valley.

**Sóller**, further north, is a market town in the center of a fertile vale. Its plane trees and central square give it a French flavor, the result perhaps of well-established trading ties with France. The port, though encircled by hotels and modern apartment buildings, retains much of its original character and is connected to the town by a slow-moving, open-sided tram. After Sóller the road climbs out of the valley, bypassing **Fornalutx**, another picturesque mountain village much favored by expatriates; through tunnels and along the lee of the **Puig Mayor**, Majorca's highest peak at 1,445 m (4,740 ft); past **La Calobra**, a tiny village with a sandy bay at the foot of a gorge, and the **Monastery of Lluc** (museum and restaurant); to **Pollensa** and its port, and finally to the **Cabo de Formentor** (Formentor Cape) at the northernmost tip of the island.

A good way to see the central plain and the hillier eastern part of Majorca is to take the road from Palma to **Alcudia.** This passes through almond groves, olive orchards and wheat fields and links a series of small country towns that vary from the bleak to the picturesque but usually have some local product to offer the passerby. **Sant María** has hand-made fabric and antiques, **Binisalem** is the wine-making center of Majorca, and **Inca** produces leather goods as well being known for its sucking pig. At the northern end lies **Alcudia**, a town of Roman origins (there is a ruined amphitheater east of it) that has good 14th-century walls, and its port.

Turning east along the bay of Alcudia brings the traveler to **Artá** and its caves. Further south on the coast, just beyond **Porto Cristo**, there are more caves, the **Cuevas de Drach** (Dragon's Caves) and underground lakes that can be toured by boat to the music of a floating chamber ensemble.

**Manacor**, the second largest town on the island but still pretty small, is where most of Majorca's cultured pearls come from, and pottery is the specialty of **Felanitx.** There are some attractive seaside resorts and small bays with sandy beaches strung out along the eastern coast from **Cala Ratjada** in the north to **Cala Figuera** in the south. And in the center there is **Petra** where Father Junipero Serra, the missionary who made such an impact on California, was born.

## MINORCA

Minorca is poorer and less visually impressive than Majorca and not as hip or trendy as Ibiza. It has been described as the plain Jane of the Balearics and is often the island travelers choose to skip. Therein lies its charm. Minorca does not offer sophisticated nightlife, palm court orchestras, flamenco or bullfights. Instead, there are sandy coves and an azure sea — often without another human being in sight — Bronze Age monuments clearly visible from the main roads, two architectural urban gems (Mahón and Ciudadela), enough history to satisfy an historian, and festivals in unspoilt market towns where you might well be the only foreigner present.

Minorca has not, of course, escaped mass tourism but the invasion came later than on the other islands. The tourist armies, led by the British and followed by the Germans, have confined themselves to specific parts of the coast and usually stay in small hotels, apartment complexes and villas. There are no large hotels in Minorca, not even in the two main towns, and this has helped to separate tourism from the island's natural rhythm and lifestyle.

Minorca is not as well connected to the mainland — or, for that matter, to Majorca and Ibiza — as its sister islands, and the best way to approach it is by air from Palma which is a 20-minute flight. There is also an infrequent car ferry service between Palma and **Mahón**. But once there, it is easy to get around though you do need to rent a car which can be done inexpensively at the airport. The island is only 48 km (30 miles) long and 16 km (10 miles) wide and has a serviceable main road linking Mahón in the east with Ciudadela in the west. The other roads are not as good but in three days you can cover much of the island.

The island's profile consists of a low plateau with some broken hills and one high peak (**Monte Toro**) roughly in the center. It has countless coves, bays and inlets making it specially attractive to sailors and windsurfers. Inland, Minorca is still rural, its small fields separated by dry stone walls interspersed by contorted outcrops of rock. V.S. Pritchett, the English writer and critic, described the island as having "the toughened look of a Mediterranean Cornwall."

While the stony fields, the prehistoric artifacts and the peasant farming conjure up Celtic lands farther north, the Mediterranean character of Minorca is all pervasive. You see it on the hilltops in the brilliantly whitewashed farmhouses with their ivy green shutters (in a passion for whitewash some Minorcans whiten their tiled roofs as well), you smell it in the scent of pine and thyme, you hear it in the howl of the *tramontana* wind that sweeps across the island from north to south, permanently bending the wild olive trees in that direction so that no one is ever at a loss over where the points of the compass lie.

So much of the land is covered with barren rock, wild olives, pine trees and a succulent called *mata*, whose red berries the partridges love, that agriculture appears a foolhardy pursuit. Yet, it remains a major industry and Minorca is a significant producer of dairy produce, notably a fine cheese with a golden rind and a robust flavor that you can buy directly from the cooperatives which produce it. (There is one in Alayor in the center of the island.)

The Mediterranean marrow in Minorca's ancient bones is nowhere more evident than in its history. Believed to have been inhabited since the early Bronze Age (2000 BC), its population was probably larger in 1000 BC than it is today. This was the great age of the talayots, the best preserved being **El Tudons** which can be seen and easily reached from the Mahón-Ciudadela road. There are also many distinctive T-shaped *taulas* and some spectacular prehistoric caves on the south coast at **Cala Covas**

where modern man, in the shape of several hippie families, has taken up residence in his troglodytic ancestors' dwellings.

## CUIDADELA AND MAHON

Minorca may have become a backwater but it was a prize plum throughout most of its history. Phoenicians, Greeks, Carthaginians, Romans, Vandals, Byzantines, Moors, Spaniards, the British and the French all pounced on the island at one time or another. Minorca's history can best be seen in its two contrasting principal towns. **Ciudadela**, the former capital and still the religious center, is a lovely town with old faded pastel palaces, generous squares, narrow curving streets, and a cozy port nestled at the foot of towering battlements. Sacked by the Turks in the 16th century, Ciudadela rose to glory in the 17th century and retains an aristocratic, almost Italianate air and an intensely private sense of place.

**Mahón**, by contrast, is much more down to earth with the imprint of the 18th century British occupation clearly displayed in its terraced houses, steep cobbled streets, sash windows and Georgian doors with heavy brass knockers. The British, during almost a century's residence, gave Minorca good roads, a number of enduring words (bow window, clover and pudding remain, albeit accented in the Minorcan dialect of Catalan, which is the language of the island) and gin. They also planted the seeds of gossip about Admiral Horatio Nelson and his passionate affair with Lady Emma Hamilton. The claim that "Nelson and Emma slept here" is made by a number of owners of fine old houses. The prosaic truth, however, is that Emma never came to the island and Nelson always slept on board his ship.

The Moors left their mark in place names like Alayor and Binibeca, and the French governor of Minorca is reputed to have been suitably inspired by his stay to introduce mayonnaise into French cuisine. Even distant America has some Minorcan connections. Many American sailors, who fought the Barbary pirates in the 19th century, found a final resting place in the military cemetery on an island in Mahón's much-coveted, fjord-like harbor. And the father of Admiral David Farragut came from Ciudadela. Farragut, a veteran of the American Civil War, made the famous remark: "Damn the torpedoes, full steam ahead," and now has a statue commemorating his renown in his father's birthplace.

## MINORCA'S FESTIVALS

Minorca has several lively festivals throughout the summer months. Ciudadela celebrates the feast of **San Juan** on June 23 and 24 with horsemen dressed in medieval costume and with some vigorous jousting; Mahón goes to town on September 8; and in between, the smaller places have their own events. One of the main features of most of these celebrations is a challenge for the young bloods who try to distract the horses by pushing them round in circles. The riders' task is to remain calm and, above all, in control of their steeds.

## TOURIST INFORMATION

**Provincial Area Code** (71)
From inside Spain (971)
**Tourist Office** ( 36-37-90, plaça de S'Esplanada, N°40.
**Aiport** ( 15-70-00.

### HOTELS
*Expensive* means a night's lodging costs Pts.18,000 to Pts.28,000; *moderate* Pts.8,000 to Pts.18,000.

### Expensive
**Port Mahón** ( 15-46-46 Avda Fort de L'eau, s/n, Mahón, is probably the island's best address. 74 rooms.
The **Audax** ( 15-46-46 on the coast at Cala Galdana, is a good hotel with 244 rooms.
South of Mahón, in Es Castell, the **Agamenón** ( 36-21-50 is smallish but good while the **Rey Carlos III** ( 36-31-00 has enjoyed a good reputation for a long while.

### Moderate
**Son Blach Cottage** ( 38-55-86, is in the Urb. Caleta Sant Andria, Arc. 4-7. There are plenty of hotels, mostly large, in Cala Galdana. Try the large 250-room hotel of the same name, **Cala Galdana** ( 37-42-09.

### RESTAURANTS
**Pilar** restaurant ( 36-68-17, Forn N°61, Mahón, still enjoys an excellent reputation (meals from Pts.3,000 to Pts.8,000). Reservation advisable.

## IBIZA

Ibiza lies southwest of Majorca, closer to the mainland, and is both warmer and drier than its more northerly sisters. It can be easily reach from Palma by a 30-minute flight or roughly four hours ride on a car ferry. There are also regular connections by sea and air with the mainland. Like Minorca, Ibiza is hilly but not mountainous and is generously endowed with long sandy

beaches and rocky bays, all of which are easily accessible by bus, car, moped or small boat. The island is 41 km (25 miles) long and 20 km (12 miles) wide.

The first impression of Ibiza brings Greece to mind. The whitewashed houses that climb the hillside around the port, the unpretentious, unadorned churches, and the quality of the light — purer and more luminous than in Majorca and Minorca — are particularly striking. But then the embattled history of Spain makes itself felt in the great walls that were built to defend Ibiza town from pirates in the 16th century and in the severe countenance of the Cathedral that presides over it.

The town was founded by the Carthaginians in the seventh century BC and the island prospered under their rule. The Phoenicians, Greeks, Romans and Moors followed each other and evidence of all these occupations can be seen in the **Museo Arquelógico**, which is opposite the Cathedral, and in the necropolis of **Puig des Molins** (Windmill Hill) at the foot of the hill on Vía Romana. The museum has an impressive collection of Punic art and pottery including a terra-cotta bust of the Carthaginian goddess Tanit. The necropolis has hundreds of tombs cut into the rock and many artifacts from the Carthaginian and later periods.

---

Another view of the Hacienda Na Xamena Hotel, Ibiza.

## THE OLD TOWN

The best way to see **d'Alt Villa**, or old town, is to enter through the 16th-century gateway, the **Puerta de las Tablas**, and wind your way up the steep streets, past many fine mansions as well as more cramped quarters, until you reach the Cathedral, the Citadel and the archaeological museum. From that point there are unparalleled views over the busy harbor and out to sea. While you're up there, have a drink, meal, even a bed if they have one, at **El Corsario**. Once one of the grand houses, the hotel with its terrace restaurant is perfectly sited for observing the town and bay below.

## AROUND THE ISLAND

The rest of the island offers little of historic interest. The main towns, **San Antonio Abad** and **Santa Eulalia del Río**, grew rapidly to cope with the booming tourist trade. But there are a number of small villages and hamlets that have character and give the visitor a sense of what the real Ibiza was like before the latest invaders hit the beaches. **San Miguel** and **San Juan Bautista**, at the north end of the island, are good examples; there are also a number of small churches, built on unusually simple lines and immaculately whitewashed, that enliven the landscape.

Ibiza, traditionally poorer than either Majorca or Minorca, has passed through different phases of the tourist phenomenon. It began as a place for writers and painters and then the hippies discovered it. Later, the beautiful people came, many staying and opening boutiques, bars, restaurants, hotels and antique shops. And throughout there was the steady throb of jet engines as the package tourists poured in.

All these elements are present today, and during the seven month season (May through October) it is sometimes hard to find a local inhabitant. You can still occasionally see old peasants in traditional dress but the suspicion is that they, like almost everyone else, have a commercial motive in mind. What draws people to Ibiza is that dazzling sun, which seems to bestow a specially dark tan as if the skin's pigment has been permanently changed, the marvelous turquoise sea, and the evening parade down in Ibiza port, followed by a wild nightlife.

## TOURIST INFORMATION

**Provincial Area Cod**e (71)
From inside Spain (971)
**Tourist Office** ( 30-19-00, Paseo Vara de Rey, N°13.
**Aiport** ( 30-03-00.

### HOTELS
*Expensive* means a night's lodging costs Pts.18,000 to Pts.28,000; *moderate* Pts.8,000 to Pts.18,000.

*Expensive*
**La Hacienda** ( 33-45-00, on Na Xamena, Afores S/N, San Miguel, is the island's most expensive and beautiful hotel. Set high up in the mountains overlooking the sea, it has panoramic views and full facilities. Like many hotels, it is not open in winter.
**La Ventana** ( 39-08-57, Sa Carrosa N° 13, Dalt Vila is a small hotel in the old part of town. Each room is decorated differently.
**Royal Plaza** ( 31-00-00, Pere Frances 27–29, is comfortable with full facilities but lacks charm.

*Moderate to expensive*
**Las Brisas del Mar** (mobile phone) ( 908-534-467 ( 802193 FAX 802308, Porroig, Cala Jondal, San José (one of the most exclusive districts of the island) is a small charming Moorish-style hotel.

### RESTAURANTS
*Expensive* represents meals costing Pts.8,000 and above; *moderate*: Pts.3,000 to Pts.8,000.

*Expensive*
**Sa Tasca** (no phone) in Can Gazuet S/N, San José, set in a an old country house, offers good food in a lovely setting at rather high prices.
**Sa Capella** ( 34-00-57, Puig den Basora, San Antoni is set in a deconeacrated church and is noted for its good food, folk dance show and unusual ambiance.
**El Faro** ( 31-75-78 in the heart of Ibiza town, proves popular with the tourists who want to see and be seen.

OPPOSITE: Popular beach in Ibiza.

*Moderate*
**Casa Victoria** ( 34-09-00, Ctra San Agustín, Cala Tarida, San José and **Sa Soca,** Ctra San Jose, San Antonio Km20, are renowned for their menus. The latter is popular with locals.

## FORMENTERA

Formentera, seven kilometers (four miles) from Ibiza, is easily accessible by boat and makes a pleasant diversion from the tempo of life on the larger island. Known as the

a lighthouse, some high cliffs and a great panoramic view over land and sea.

## TOURIST INFORMATION

**Provincial Area Cod**e (71)
From inside Spain (971)
**Tourist Office** ( 332-20-57, La Savina.

### HOTELS

*Expensive* means a night's lodging costs Pts.18,000 to Pts.28,000; *moderate* Pts.8,000 to Pts.18,000.

"wheat island" to the Romans, Formentera is the least developed of the Balearics and is still largely rural in character producing wheat, almonds, figs and grapes. Its lakes and salt flats attract many birds, including flamingos, it has a Bronze Age megalithic monument near **San Ferrán**, and five fortified watchtowers built in the 18th century.

The best way to move around is by moped or bicycle, both of which can be rented at the port of **La Sabina.** The "capital" of the island is **San Francisco Javier** (population 800 souls) which has an 18th-century church. There are a number of beaches, the best being **Es Pujols**, a long stretch of fine sand in the north. On the far side is **La Mola**, the highest point of Formentera, that offers

*Moderate*
**Hostal Entrepinos** ( 32-70-19 Playa Es Caló. A pretty spot and decent hotel.

### RESTAURANTS

*Expensive* represents meals costing Pts.8,000 and above; *moderate*: Pts.3,000 to Pts.8,000.

*Expensive*
**Es Molí de Sal** ( 13-67-73, at Ses Illetes, was an old salt mill and now a fashionable restaurant.

*Moderate*
**Restaurante Le Cyrano** on the paseo Maritimo at Playa de Pujols is a French-owned restaurant with good food.

# Travelers'
# Tips

# GETTING THERE

## BY AIR

Iberia Airlines is the national carrier and has regular flights from the United States to Spain (non-stop to Madrid and Barcelona and, via Madrid to Málaga.) From the United Kingdom, Iberia operates direct flights to those cities plus Alicante, Bilbao, Palma de Mallorca, Santiago de Compostela, Seville and Valencia. American Airlines and TWA fly from the United States to Madrid and British Airways offers regular flights to a number of Spanish cities as well as a daily run to Gibraltar. Since the re-opening of the Spanish border, visitors to Gibraltar can cross easily into Spain.

## BY SEA

The only sea connection between Britain and Spain is from Plymouth to Santander, a modern car ferry service operated by Brittany Ferries which goes twice a week and takes 24 hours.

## BY TRAIN

It takes about 24 hours by train to reach Barcelona from London with changes in Paris, and Port Bou at the eastern end of the Pyrenees. The way to San Sebastián is through the French frontier town of Hendaye at the western extremity of the Pyrenees. A more central route goes through Toulouse and Pau and enters Spain at Somport-Canfranc in Aragón.

## BY CAR

There are a number of alternative routes if you travel by car. The most direct one frm London is via Calais, Paris and meeting other routes at Bordeaux, and entering Catalonia at La Jonquera and then leading down to the Mediterranean coast. For Spain's Atlantic seaboard the best way is via Hendaye. There are also a number of lovely scenic mountain roads through the Pyrenees. Roncesvalles and Somport are the old pilgrim entry points and the Puigcerda

entry point leads to Andorra. An international driving license and car insurance are needed to enter Spain with your own vehicle.

## FRONTIER TOWNS

Many visitors to Spain drive there, the vast majority coming through France. Apart from the natural inclination to get across any frontier as fast as possible and into the heart of the destination country, there is not much along Spain's frontiers to delay the motor-borne traveler. In the northeast, **Girona** is the first town of any consequence, and the temptation to press on to the Costa Brava or Barcelona usually proves overwhelming. In the Pyrenees, there are no towns of any size close to the border, but on the Atlantic end there is the elegant city of **San Sebastián** which is well-worth spending at least a night in.

## VISAS

American, Canadian, British and Irish passport holders do not need visas to go to Spain and can stay up to three months. Australians, New Zealanders and South Africans do require visas but they can easily be obtained from the nearest Spanish embassy or consulate. Customs formalities at all entry points are usually pretty relaxed and Spain has adopted the "green" door for people with nothing to declare, and the "red" one for those with something on their minds.

## SPANISH NATIONAL TOURIST OFFICES

Even when Spain had a reputation for a top-heavy bureaucracy and Latin inefficiency, its tourism operation was both professional and effective. There are Spanish National Tourist Offices in a number of countries and are invariably staffed by high-grade officials. They speak the necessary languages and offer a wide range of brochures, booklets, travel information and maps — all free. The material, glossy and well-produced, will weigh your luggage down a bit but it's worth the effort. Some addresses:

CANADA

**Toronto:** ( (1-416) 961-3131 FAX (1-416) 961-1992, 102 Bloor Street West, 14th Floor, Toronto, Ontario M5S 1M8, Canada.

UNITED KINGDOM

**London:** ( (44-171) 499-1169 FAX (44-171) 529-4257, 57–58 St James Street, London SW1A 1LD.

UNITED STATES

**Chicago:** ( (1-312) 642-1992 FAX (1-312) 642-9817, Water Tower Place, Suite 915 East, 845 North Michigan Avenue, Chicago, Illinois 60611.

**Los Angeles:** ( (1-213) 658-7188 FAX (1-213) 658-1061, 8383 Wilshire Boulevard, Suite 960, Beverly Hills, California 90211.

**New York:** ( (1-212) 265-8822 FAX (1-212) 265-8864, 666 Fifth Avenue, 35th Floor, New York, NY 10103. New York, NY 10022.

**Miami:** ( (1-305) 358-1992 FAX (1-305) 358-8223, 1212 Brickwell Avenue, Miami, Florida 33131.

## TRAVEL IN SPAIN

### INTERNAL FLIGHTS

Internal flights are operated by Iberia and Aviaco, are frequent between most cities, and are well-run. There is an "air bridge," or "shuttle," between Madrid and Barcelona that goes each way hourly through the day. Some flights to popular resorts — Málaga, Palma de Mallorca, and Ibiza, for example — can become heavily booked in the summer months, so make reservations as far ahead as possible. The same principle applies to the car ferries that ply between the coastal ports of Barcelona, Valencia and Alicante and the Balearic Islands. The company that operates these ferries (Trasmediterranea) has offices in Madrid and the main Mediterranean ports.

### TRAINS

Spanish trains tend to be slow but are a good way of getting around, mixing with the locals and seeing the countryside change with a drink in your hand and your feet up.

The pride of the Spanish fleet is not slow at all. This is the **AVE**, the new highspeed train that was developed to link Madrid to Seville in time for Expo 92. A new terminus was built in the capital for the AVE next to the old Atocha station which has been turned into a travel center arranged around a delightful tropical garden. There are plans to expand the AVE service to other parts of Spain.

In a category of its own is **Al-Andalus**, the luxury sightseeing train that takes its pampered occupants at a leisurely pace through the main cities of Andalusia. You join the train in Madrid or Seville for a week's tour, sleeping on the train and having most of your meals in smart restaurants and hotels en route. The Al-Andalus is designed for that special occasion and priced accordingly.

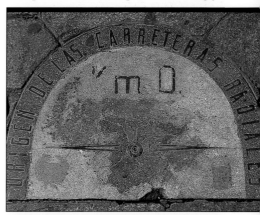

The **Talgo** is the country's fastest general service, linking Madrid to all the major centers. It has airconditioned cars, restaurants, bars and comfortable seats.

The next best are the **TER** trains and slowest, ironically, is the **Expreso**. Discounts are give on the **días azules** ("blue days"); the amount is 20 percent for roundtrips only. There are also two special excursion trains, one that runs along the Cantabrian coast and the other that does a circuit of the main cities in Andalusia. Eurorail and Interail passes are accepted though a small supplement levied on presenting the ticket at the station. Train travel can be complicated, so seek clarity from a travel agent or the local tourist office.

### CAR HIRE

It is easy and relatively cheap to hire cars in Spain. The large American companies — Hertz and Avis — have branches in most of

ABOVE: Km 0, Plaza Mayor, Madrid.

the major cities and there are a number of good Spanish rental companies, notably Atesa and Marsans. If you are coming from the United States or the United Kingdom, make the reservation before leaving; there are often better rates offered at that end. Speed limits are 120 kph (75 mph) on the expressways *(autopistas)*, 100 kph (62 mph) on other roads, and 60 kph (37 mph) in built-up areas. Seat belts are compulsory. Take extra care on the two or three lane national highways *(carreteras nacionales)*, prefixed by the letter N, where the heavy trucks belt

and are the most efficient way of getting around these two large cities. Taxis are plentiful in most cities and relatively cheap, and although their drivers do not believe in dawdling, they usually drive well. They are also polite and do not expect large tips (5% to 10% of the fare is normal.)

## ACCOMMODATION

It is always a good idea to reserve your accommodation well in advance when planning a

along and sometimes overtake when they shouldn't. Also remember that traffic coming from the right has priority on traffic circles. Gasoline and tolls (on the fancy new highways) are expensive, but if you choose a small car and stay on the older roads, where there are no tolls, you can cut your costs.

### BUSES AND URBAN TRANSPORT

Spanish buses are clean and functional, and cover the ground well in the major cities. Madrid and Barcelona have good subway systems with excellent directions and maps and cost very little, especially if you buy a book of ten tickets at a time. The subways are less complicated to use than the buses

trip to Spain, especially in the summer and during the popular festival seasons. A good travel agent can do it all for you without any difficulty. The paradors have their own central reservation system (see below). If, however, you do not want to structure your travel too precisely, you can usually find a comfortable and affordable bed wherever you go, especially out of season and away from the heavily traveled tourist tracks.

All Spanish hotels are graded and regulated by the government. Hotels **(H)** are rated by stars, one to five in ascending quality. A one-star hotel will not be inexpensive and should be counted in the "moderate" price range. *Hotel Residencias* **(HR)** have similar ratings but do not have restaurants,

*Hostales* (Hs) and *Pensiones* (P) are more modest lodgings and are rated by one to three stars. Then come *fondas* or inns (F) and *casas de huespedes* (CH), similar to one star *ostals*. The grade of each establishment is identified outside the building on a pale blue plaque.

In this guide hotels classed as *deluxe* means a nights' lodging costs Pts.28,000 and above; *expensive*: Pts.18,000 to Pts.28,000; *moderate*: Pts.8,000 to Pts.18,000; and *inexpensive*: Pts.4,000 to Pts.8,000.

Hotels usually ask for your passport on registering and return it the next day. If it is not waiting for you at the reception desk, don't forget to ask for it. It is not amusing to find yourself at your next destination, reaching for the precious document, and having to slog back to retrieve it.

## PARADORS

In 1926, the Marquis of Vega-Inclán, Spain's Royal Tourist Commissioner, came up with the idea of establishing a chain of state-run inns based on the tradition of the *parador* literally, "stopping-place"), the upscale inns of the past where the better kind of traveler lodged for the night while his servants and horses went to the local *posada* or coaching inn. The first parador was opened in 1928 in the Sierra de Gredos mountains and since then 85 more have opened their doors.

The marquis's concept was not just a way for the state to cash in on the tourism business, but to take Spain's surplus antique housing stock — castles, palaces, monasteries, convents and so on — and put it to good use. It was a brilliant and innovative idea, and there is still nothing quite like the paradors anywhere else in the world.

The chain includes thirteen medieval castles, nine Gothic or Baroque palaces, and six monasteries or convents.

The most spectacular are the **Hotel de los Reyes Católicos** in Santiago de Compostela, built as a hostel for the pilgrims by Ferdinand and Isabella in 1499 ("the world's oldest hotel," according to the brochure); the **Hotel de San Marcos** in León, a stunning 16th-century convent; the **Parador de San Francisco** in the Alhambra, another convent,

founded by the Catholic Monarchs after the capture of Granada, with splendid views of the Alhambra; the **Fernando II de León** in Benavente, a 12th-century castle on a hill where the court of the King of León often met; and the **Marqués de Villena**, at Alarcon, another medieval castle in a dramatic setting, this time in La Mancha.

Not all paradors are as attractive, or as old. Many are modern buildings, functionally designed with touches of tradition such as antique furniture and rugs and old paintings. Some of these compensate by being located in such a position that guests can see something interesting from their bedroom windows or balconies. The modern paradors of **Toledo** and **Salamanca** are good examples, each having superb views over its parent cities.

Paradors are no longer inexpensive, most falling into the three- or four-star hotel category, but they invariably have good food and service and are worth stopping at for a meal or a drink if the cash flow does not permit an overnight stay.

Further information and reservations can be made at the following addresses. **Madrid:** Central de Reservas de Paradores, ( 435-9700, Calle Velázquez, 25, Madrid. **New York:** Marketing Ahead ( (1-212) 686-9213, 433 Fifth Avenue, New York, NY 10016. **London:** ( (44-171) 402-8182, Keytel International, 402 Edgware Road, London W2 1ED.

## EATING AND DRINKING

Spaniards eat late, very late. Hotels usually serve breakfast from 8 to 10:30 AM (a generous self-service, buffet-style spread is becoming more and more common, following the lead of the paradors); lunch runs from 1:30 to 4 PM; and dinner starts at 9 PM and goes on until 11:30 PM (later in many restaurants.)

All hotels and restaurants must, by law, serve a "menu of the day," *(menu del día)* which is a three-course meal that includes bread and wine and is always modestly priced. It is worth asking about and the menu is available at both lunch and dinner.

OPPOSITE: Hostal de San Marcos, León: this 16th-century convent is now a parador.

In this guide meals listed as *expensive* cost Pts.8,000 and above; *moderate*: Pts.3,000 to Pts.8,000, and *inexpensive*: Pts.1,000 to Pts.3,000.

Drinking tap water in the larger hotels is fine but not advisable in the smaller places when bottled mineral water is safer. Ask for *agua mineral con* (or *sin*) *gas*. (Mineral water with or without fizz). It is a good idea to take plenty of fluids and fruit with you when driving in Spain during the summer months. Mild dehydration can set in on the *meseta* or driving through Andalusia under

the constant glare of the Spanish sun. An airconditioned car makes a great difference.

When you stop for refreshment, you will find that Spanish coffee is the best in the world, whether taken black (*café solo*), with milk (*café con leche*), or black with just a dash of milk (*café cortado*). Spanish beer is also good, especially the draft beer. The best brand is a matter of taste, but my preferences are **Estrella Dorada** in central and northern Spain and the rich, creamy **Cruzcampo** of Andalusia. There are plenty of cooling soft drinks in Spain but good fruit juice is surprisingly rare.

Buy and develop your film at home if you can, and keep it out of the sun as much as possible. There is no shortage of film in

Spain but it tends to be expensive. Batteries and other electrical accessories are plentiful and cost much the same as they do in the rest of Europe and in the United States.

## TOURIST OFFICES

Every town has at least one tourist office, run either by the national organization or the municipality, and it should be your first port of call. These offices will provide you with all the maps and general information you will need, plus a good idea of what fiestas and other cultural events are going on in the town and the surrounding area. The offices are usually open Mondays to Fridays, 10 AM to 1 PM and 4 to 7 PM, and Saturday mornings. They are closed on Sundays and public holidays.

## DRESS

Spaniards are remarkably informal when it comes to dress, especially in the summer months. The Ritz Hotel in Madrid seems to be the only exception where an iron-fisted dress code is in operation at all hours of the day and night. The manager of the best hotel

n San Sebastián, a five-star gem, tried to
nstitute a dress code of jacket and tie for
dinner when he first came to the hotel.
"After one night I gave up," he told me
uefully. "They just came along in open-
necked shirts and casual slacks and ignored
ny little rule."

## CURRENCY

The peseta comes in coins of 1, 5, 10, 25, 50,
00, 200, and 500 pesetas and in notes of
,000, 2,000, 5,000 and 10,000 pesetas. *Duro*,
t means a 5 peseta piece. Travelers' checks
nd foreign currency can be changed at all
banks and at money exchanges — look out
or the **Cambio** (Exchange) signs.

## PUBLIC HOLIDAYS

New Year's Day
January 6, the Epiphany
Holy Thursday and Good Friday
May 1, Labor Day
Corpus Christi (late May or early June)
July 25, the Feast of Santiago (St. James)
August 15, the Feast of the Assumption
November 1, All Saints' Day
December 6, Constitution Day
Christmas Day

As you can see, the Spaniards are generous to themselves when it comes to holidays. But keep an eye open for even more
since many regions and municipalities take
additional days off to celebrate some local
event or saint.

## POST OFFICES AND TELEPHONES

ost Offices *(Correos)* are plentiful although
you can also buy stamps in shops that sell
tobacco *(tabacleras or estancos)*. Mailboxes
are painted yellow though there are not
many around and it is usually easier to mail
your letters and postcards from the hotel
where they often sell stamps too.

The Spanish telephone system has been
modernized and works well. You will see
plenty of public call booths on the streets but
you can also make local calls from any bar.

The public telephones have a little chute on
which you put your coins and they roll
down into the box as you speak. If you get
cut off you can grab the coins and stop them
from disappearing. Five peseta pieces will
handle local calls but have plenty of Pts. 25
and Pts. 50 pieces if you are making long
distance calls from one of these public booths.
There are no public telephones in the post
offices but there are central telephone offices
called **Telefonicas** where you can place
international calls. Avoid making international calls from the hotel — there is invari-

ably a huge surcharge. Dial "9" before the
area code for out of town calls within Spain.

## ELECTRICITY

Electric current is 220–225 volts and plugs are
the round, two-pronged variety. Many modern hotels have special 110–125 volt circuits
in the bathrooms for electrical appliances.

## HEALTH

Spain has a social security system for its
citizens but no reciprocal arrangement with
other countries.

Health insurance for travel in Spain can
usually be obtained through a travel agent
before you leave.

OPPOSITE LEFT: Pastry shop on Las Ramblas,
Barcelona. OPPOSITE RIGHT: An animated bar in
Seville's old quarter. ABOVE: Mobile snack vendors
in Retiro Park, Madrid.

Most Spanish hotels, even some of the smaller ones, have a "house doctor," whose services can be obtained through the hotel staff. Pharmacies *(farmacias)*, indicated by a green cross on a white background, work on a rotation system so that there is at least one open 24 hours a day.

## TOILETS

Spain is not a place where public toilets flourish outside of train and bus stations and airports. However, every bar, café and restaurant has them and Spaniards use them as if they were public property, whether they are buying a drink or not. The phrase is: *"Dónde estan los servicios, por favor?"*

## WEATHER

The best times to visit Spain are in the spring (mid-March to June) and the fall (mid-September to November). Summer is fine if you want to spend a lot of time on the beach but be ready for consistently hot days and warm nights. The exception is the northern coast which has cooler weather and some rainfall during the summer months. Spain's central plateau, the *meseta*, has a typical continental climate, that is hot, dry summers and bitterly cold wet winters. The Mediterranean coastline and the Balearic Islands also have hot, dry summers but milder winters with a considerable amount of rain. The saving grace of the Spanish weather is that, on the whole, the humidity is low, with the exception of the northwest where constant moisture produces the lush greens and mists of an Ireland or Wales. While winters can be cold in central Spain, there are many sunny days and, if beaches and sunbathing are not your thing, this is a good time to visit the cities and monuments of Castile and other areas of the Spanish heartland.

## EMBASSIES AND CONSULATES

UNITED STATES:
**Barcelona**: ( 280-2227, Reína Elisenda de Montcada, N° 23.

**La Coruña**: ( 21-32-33, Canton Grande, N° 1(
**Madrid**: ( 577-4000, Calle Serrano, N° 75
Consular office for passports is around th corner at Paseo de Castellana, N° 52.
**Malaga**: ( 247-4891, Centro Comercial La Rampas, Planta I, Fuengirola.
**Palma de Mallorca**: ( 72-26-60, Avengud Jaime III, N° 26.
**Seville**: ( 423-1885, Paseo de Delicias, N° 7
**Valencia**: ( 351-6973, Calle de la Paz N° 6.

GREAT BRITAIN:
**Alicante**: ( 26-66-00, Plaza Calvo Sotelo.
**Barcelona**: ( 419-7600, Diagonal, N° 477.
**Bilbao**: ( 415-7600, Alameda Urguijo, N° 2.
**Madrid**: ( 319-0200, Fernando el Santo, N° 1(
**Málaga**: ( 221-7571, Duquesa de Parcent, N° 8
**Palma de Mallorca**: ( 71-24-45, Plaza Mayo: N° 3D.
**Seville**: ( 422-8875, Plaza Nueva, N° 8.
**Tarragona**: ( 20-12-46, Calle Satran, N° 4.
**Vigo**: ( 43-71-33, Plaza de Compostela, N° 2:

CANADA:
**Barcelona**: ( 410-6699, Vía Augusta, N° 12!
**Madrid**: ( 431-4300, Nuñez de Balboa, N° 3!
**Málaga**: ( 222-3346, Plaza de la Malagneta N° 3.
**Seville**: ( 422-9413, Avenida de la Consti tución, N° 30.

## SPORTS

Spain, without exaggeration, is a sportsman' paradise. Its natural features facilitate ever imaginable kind of outdoor activity. The tou ist boom, growing prosperity, the automobil( and more time for leisure have combined t produce a huge growth in resorts, equipmen and facilities for the sports enthusiast. Her is a bird's eye view of the sporting scene.

### GOLF

Spain's sunshine and the abundance c water have produced perfect conditions fo the pursuit of the small white ball over th fairway. There are now over two hundre( and sixty golf courses in the country an( golfing holidays have become a regular fea ture for foreigners and Spaniards alike. Th game has been greatly popularized by Span sh prowess in international competitions with Severiano Ballesteros leading the way.

Madrid has eleven courses of which **Golf La Moraleja** and the **Real Club Puerta de Hierro** (created by the British in the 19th century) are probably the finest. Barcelona's top club is the **Real Club de Golf El Prat,** there is the **Club de Golf de Pais** in Girona province, and there are another seven courses in Catalonia. Further south, in the Levante, there is a fine course next to the parador just outside Valencia (**El Saler**) and the **Torrevieja** course in Alicante. In northwest Spain, Santander has the classy club, **Real Golf de Pedrena,** and there is the pretty **La Toja** course, on an island of that name, close to Pontevedra in Galicia. The Balearic Islands, a favorite spot for golfers, have eight courses, with the top three in Majorca (**Son Vida, Magalluf** and **Santa Ponsa).**

The mecca for golfers, however, is the Costa del Sol or, as some people now call it, the "Golf Coast." There are fifteen well-designed courses along the coast, dovetailed with all the other resort facilities such as hotels, restaurants, health spas, marinas and nightclubs. The greatest advantage is the weather, virtually a hundred percent predictable sunshine throughout most of the year. **Marbella,** as the swankiest spot on the coast, has five courses with the **Golf Río Real** at the head of the list. There are other courses at **Estepona, Benalmadena** and **Torremolinos,** all in the province of Málaga; in **El Ejido** to the north in Almeria province; and in **Sotogrande** further south in **Cádiz** province. A useful source of information is the **Real Federación Española de Golf** (Royal Spanish Golf Federation) ( (91) 455-682, Calle Capitán Haya, Nº 9, Madrid.

## HUNTING, SHOOTING AND FISHING

Spaniards love hunting and go after anything from wild boar that have a sporting chance to rather tame and tiny birds that have virtually none. Licenses are required and can be obtained from local government offices and there is a national hunting organization that can provide full details: **Federación Española de Caza** (Spanish Hunting Federation) ( (91) 253-9017, Avenida Reina Victoria, Nº 72, Madrid.

Spanish waters, fresh and salt, contain a great abundance of fish, as you will see from a visit to any fish-market. The Mediterranean is the least fecund due to pollution and overfishing, but the Atlantic coast, north and south, and the country's rivers, lakes and dams provide plenty of sport. Freshwater fishing permits, usually valid for two weeks at a time, can be obtained from local authorities and deep sea permits from the provincial port commissioners. For more details contact Spanish tourist offices and the **Federación Española de Pesca y Casting** (Spanish Fishing and Casting Federation) ( (91) 232-8352, Calle Navas de Tolosa, Nº 3, Madrid.

## WATER SPORTS

**Sailing, windsurfing, scuba diving** are all readily available in most resorts along the Spanish coast and in the Balearic Islands. There has been a great growth in marinas in recent years. Some of them, notably on the Costa del Sol and in parts of the Balearics, cater for the stratospheric reaches of the international yachting crowd (for example, Puerto Banus on the Costa del Sol and Palma's Club de Mar), but many others are designed for the ordinary sailor and are both well-equipped and affordable. For information contact the **Federación Española de Vela** (Spanish Sailing Federation) ( (91) 233-5305, Calle Juan Vigon, Nº 23, Madrid.

Windsurfing can be done off almost any beach in Spain and most resorts rent boards. The best general area with constant yet not too boisterous winds are the southern Atlantic beaches between Gibraltar and the Portuguese frontier, with Tarifa generally regarded as the best beach of them all. Scuba diving has also become a popular sport in Spain, especially in the warmer waters of the southern Mediterranean coastline and the Balearic Islands. There is a national organization, based in Barcelona: **Federación Española de Actividades Subacuaticas** (Spanish Federation of Subaquatic Activities)( (93) 200-6769, Carrer Santalo, Nº 15, Barcelona.

## SKIING

Spain is not usually thought of as a place to go skiing yet it is the most mountainous country in Europe after Switzerland and has twenty-seven ski resorts. The best are in the Pyrenees, especially **Bequiera-Beret** (Lerida province) and (ski resort, Huesca Province **Candanchú** (Huesca Province), and the **Solynieve** ski station in the Sierra Nevada in Andalusia, which is little more than two hours' drive from the Costa del Sol. The ski season normally runs from Christmas to early May. For details contact: **Federación Española de Deportes de Invierno** (Spanish Winter Sports Federation) ( (91) 275-8943, Calle Claudio Coello, N° 32, Madrid.

## SOCCER

Finally, it would be criminal not to mention soccer *(futbol)*, the Spanish passion which outranks bullfighting and all other sports in popularity. However, there is not much to be said except try to see a big match in a stadium. Real Madrid and Barcelona, inveterate rivals, are usually at the top and you cannot do better than catch one of their games. Hotel concierges will normally be able to obtain last-minute tickets for soccer matches (and bullfights) if you have not made earlier reservations.

## SHOPPING

Shops generally open at 10 AM, close for lunch at 1:30 PM or 2 PM, and reopen from 4 PM or 5 PM until about 8 PM. (Banks run a tighter ship, with opening hours from 9 AM to 1:30 PM and 3 to 5 PM. Museums have similar hours to shops and are nearly always closed on Mondays.) There is an enormous amount of junky tourist stuff for sale in places like Toledo (swords, armor, daggers etc.), and in coastal resorts (silly straw hats, phony bullfight posters where you can have your name inscribed alongside Paco Romero and El Cordobés, and cheap castanets.) But there are also good things, traditional and modern, if you are patient and prepared to look.

Leather goods are well-known, no longer the bargain they once were, but there is a huge selection of fine leather products at the upscale Loewe stores and other more modestly priced shops. Strong and macho-looking hunting boots are sold in Seville and other southern cities, as well as Salamanca. Hand and machine made lace — table linen, clothes and shawls particularly — are good buys in Andalusia and the Levante. Furniture fabric, handmade, can be found in Almeria and Majorca. Pottery and ceramics are sold almost everywhere but the best tiles come from the south and the Valencia region. Jet jewelry is a specialty of Galicia and Asturias; cultured pearls of Majorca; and wineskins of Navarre.

One way of making sure you cover the ground, at least in the preliminary "window-shopping" stage, is to visit the **Artespana** stores. This a government-sponsored cooperative designed to preserve traditional craft skills and sell the products. The stores stock a wide range of furniture, fabric, pottery, ceramics, and rugs, all based on traditional Spanish designs. Here is a short list:

**Barcelona:** Rambla Catalunya, N° 75.
**Bilbao:** Colon de Larreatgui.
**Caceres:** San Anton, N° 17.
**Granada:** Corral de Carbon.
**Madrid:** Gran Vía, N° 32; Ramón de la Cruz N° 33; Hermosilla, N° 14; Plaza de las Cortés, N° 3.
**Marbella:** Ricardo Soriano, N° 54.
**Seville:** Rodriguez Jurado, N° 4.

Spain's largest department store is E Corte Inglés. There is no special area for antiques, although the towns of **Old Castile** have more than their fair share of shops. You just have to keep your eyes and ears open but, bear in mind, the days of the bargain 16th-century chest or the medieval tapestry disappeared a long time ago.

## KEEPING IN TOUCH

Tourism and the embrace of the European Common Market have opened Spain up to the outside world in no uncertain manner One glance at a newspaper stand, or kiosk will confirm this: newspapers, magazines periodicals and books, in half a dozen different languages, are abundantly available Most British newspapers arrive the day they appear in Britain. The *International Herald .Tribune* and the European version of the *Wall Street Journal*, both printed in Paris, are on sale the day they are published in France

*Time, Newsweek, The Economist,* and most of the glossy magazines that you find in Britain and the United States are also available. They can cost double of what they would on their home turf.

There are an increasing number of English-language publications produced in Spain that include a monthly called *In Spain* containing general information about hotels, restaurants and so on, *Guidepost,* a weekly aimed at the American community, and *Lookout,* another monthly produced on the Costa del Sol but full of general articles and useful information for anyone visiting or living in Spain. There is a good English-language bookshop in Madrid called **Booksellers** ( (91) 442-7959, Calle José Abascal, Nº 48, Madrid.

The BBC's World Service programs can be picked up around the clock on the 19 m, 25 m and 49 m wave bands. Voice of America broadcasts can also be heard.

In popular tourist areas, such as the Costa del Sol and Majorca, there are English-language radio stations playing music and broadcasting local news. Pan-European television programs are reaching Spain with films, sports events and news in several different languages. CNN and other satellite programs are available in the better hotels.

## TIPPING

Most hotels and restaurants include a five-percent service charge on their bills, on top of the "value added tax," known as IVA in Spain, which is seven and a-half percent. It is customary, however, to add a tip of between five and ten percent depending on the service you received and on the size of the bill. (The higher the bill the smaller the tip.) Taxi-drivers usually get a tip worth five percent of the fare shown on them, and in bars some small change is adequate. Watch Spaniards closely; they nearly always tip, but modestly.

## SPANISH: A SAMPLER

Spanish is one of the easier languages to learn as well as the most useful after English. Any knowledge of a Latin-based Romance language (French, Italian or Portuguese)

will help. Pronunciation is phonetic and regular and the rules are simple. The most difficult aspects are the verbs, the different accents encountered in many parts of the country, and the speed with which most Spaniards talk. (Andalusia is notorious for its tricky accent where, as in many Latin American countries, consonants disappear and unfamiliar words and phrases intrude. It is worth remembering that the Spanish of Spain is usually known as castellano, or Castilian, and that Catalan is spoken in Catalonia, Valencia and the Balearic Islands, Basque or euskera in the Basque Country, and Galician or gallego in Galicia.

a little    *poco*
a lot    *mucho*
all    *todo*
before    *antes*
big    *grande*
bill/check    *cuenta*
cheap    *barato*
closed    *cerrado*
cold    *frio*
do you speak English    *habla usted inglés*
down    *abajo*
excuse me    *perdón/disculpe*
expensive    *caro*
fast    *rápido*
good afternoon    *buenas tardes*
good morning    *buenas días*
good night    *buenas noches*
goodbye    *adiós*
hello hi    *olá*
hot    *caliente*
how are you    *cómo está usted*
how much is that    *cuánto es*
how much    *cuánto*
I am hungry    *tengo hambre*
I am sorry    *lo siento*
I am thirsty    *tengo sed*
I am tired    *estoy cansado*
I don't understand    *no comprendo/entiendo*
it doesn't matter    *no importa*
it's all right    *está bien*
later    *después*
left    *izquierda*
madame    *señora*
menu    *carta*
miss    *señorita*
month    *mes*
never    *nunca*
no    *no*

nothing    *nada*
now    *ahora*
OK    *vale*
open    *abierto*
please    *por favor*
right    *derecha*
sales (in shops)    *rebajas*
see you later    *hasta luego*
sir    *señor*
slow    *despacio*
small    *pequeño*
speak slowly please    *hable despacio por favor*
straight ahead    *todo derecho*
thank you    *gracias*
today    *hoy*
toilets    *servicios/aseos*
tomorrow morning    *mañana por la mañana*
tomorrow    *mañana*
up    *arriba*
wait a moment, please    *espere un momento, por favor*
waiter    *camarero*
week    *semana*
what is that    *qué es eso*
what is your name    *cómo se llama usted*
what    *qué*
when    *cuándo*
where    *dónde*
who    *quién*
why    *por qué*
year    *año*
yes    *sí*
yesterday    *ayer*
you're welcome    *de nada*

*Buen víaje.*

## FURTHER READING

BRENAN, GERALD: *Spanish Labyrinth (Cambridge, 1943)*. A classic study of Spain up to the Civil War.

BURKHARDT, Titus: *Moorish Culture in Spain* (Allen and Unwin). Good general work on Andalusia.

CERVANTES, Miguel de: *Don Quixote* The Penguin Classics edition, translated by J.M. Cohen, is the best.

GARCIA LORCA, Federico: *Three Tragedies & Five Plays: Comedies and Tragedicomedies* (Penguin)

GRAHAM, Robert: Spain: *A Nation Comes of Age* (St. Martin's Press, New York). Best account of post-Franco political, economic and social developments.

HEMINGWAY, Ernest: *The Sun Also Rises* (sometimes called *Fiesta*). All about Pamplona, bullfighters, fishing and frustrated love. *Death In the Afternoon*. Papa's classic on the art of tauromachy.

HOOPER, John: *The Spaniards* (Viking). New survey of Spain and its people clearly written and insightful.

IRVING, Washington: *Tales of the Alhambra Fanciful Stories*; fun to read when you are in Granada.

LEE, Laurie: *As I Walked Out One Midsummer's Morning, A Moment of War* and *A Rose for Winter* (Penguin). Spain seen through the eyes of a young wanderer, with notebook and violin, just before the Civil War, during it and then two decades later. Lovely read.

MITCHELL, David: *Here in Spain* (Lookout Publications, Fuengirola, Malaga). A witty sampling of how travelers to Spain, from the 17th century to the present, saw the country.

MICHENER, James A: *Iberia* (Fawcett Crest). Massive rambling but full of good information and observations.

MORRIS, Jan: *Spain* (Penguin Travel Library). Marvelously written in the romantic tradition in the early Sixties, although marred by inaccuracies and some sweeping generalizations.

ORWELL, George: *Homage to Catalonia* (Penguin). Not only was he in Barcelona at a critical time during the Civil War but he fought on the Aragon front. Vintage Orwellian clarity combined with feeling.

THE POEM OF THE CID, translated by *R. Hamilton* and *Janet Perry* (Penguin).

THOMAS, Hugh: *The Spanish Civil War* (Penguin) Still the best general history of the conflict.

## PHOTO CREDITS

# Quick Reference A–Z Guide
## to Places and Topics of Interest with Listed Accommodation, Restaurants and Useful Telephone Numbers

**A** accommodation
*check under place names* 254
*general information* 254
*paradors*
booking information 255
booking in London ( (01) 042-8182 255
booking in Madrid ( 435-9700 255
booking in New York ( (212) 750-8682 255
*rating system in this guide* 254
airlines 252-253
*domestic flights* 253
shuttle service between Madrid and Barcelona 253
*Iberia*
reservations in Barcelona ( (3) 412-5667 135
reservations in Granada ( (58) 22-14-52 188
reservations in Madrid ( 329-5767 102
reservations in Palma de Mallorca ( (71) 271-80-00 242
reservations in Seville ( (5) 422-8901 158
reservations in Zaragoza ( (67) 21-82-50 202
reservations in Valencia ( (6) 325-0500 144
*Al Andalus* luxury train 18, 253
**Albacete** 123
**Alcalá de Henares** 117
**Alpujarra mountains** 180-181
*attractions*
Bubión 180
Capileira 181
Pampaneira 181
Trevelez 181
**Andalusia** 147
*history* 149
**Andorra** 143
**Andraitx** 243
**Anguiano** 211
**Aragón** 199
*attractions*
Parque Nacional de Ordesa 201
*history* 201
**Aranjuez** 117
*attractions*
palace and gardens 117
architecture
*Baroque* 84
*Gaudí* 84
*Gothic* 83
*Moorish* 81
*Mudéjar* 83
*Neo-classical style* 84
*Roman, in Spain* 81
*Romanesque* 83
**Arcos de la Frontera** 37, 165-166
*accommodation*
Parador Casa del Corregidor ( (56) 70-00-05 166

*attractions*
Parador Casa del Corregidor 165
ruined castle 165
Ruta de los Pueblos Blancos (Route of the White Towns) 165
sixteenth century church 165
arriving in Spain 252
*by air* 252
*by car* 252
*by sea* 252
*by train* 252
*frontier towns* 252
*visas* 252
arts
*literature* 86
*Spain's master painters* 84
**Asturias** 226-227
**Ávila** 35, 45, 104, 115-116
*accommodation*
Palacio de Valderrábanos Hotel ( (20) 21-10-23 116
Parador Raimundo de Borgoña ( (20) 21-13-40 115, 116
*attractions*
medieval walled fortress town 115
*restaurants*
Mesón del Rastro ( (20) 21-12-18 116
**B** **Badajoz** 122
**Balearic Islands** 237-249
*history* 239, 240
**Bañalbufar** 243
**Barcelona** 127-136
*accommodation*
Avenida Palace Hotel ( (3) 301-9600 135
Balmes ( (3) 451-1914 136
Claris ( (3) 487-6262 135
Colon Hotel ( (3) 301-1404 135
Hotel Arts ( (3) 221-1660 41, 135
Le Meridien ( (3) 318-6200 136
Princess Sofia Hotel ( (3) 330-7111 136
Regina ( (3) 301-3232 136
Ritz ( (3) 318-5200 41, 135
Wilson ( (3) 209-8911 136
*attractions*
Ajuntament (City Hall) 130
Aquarium 42
Avinguda Diagonal 132
Barri Gotic 130
Barrio Chino (red light district) 132
Barrio Santa María del Mar 131
beaches and esplanades 129
Calle Montcada 131
Columbus's Column 132
Ensanche (Eixample) 132
Fundació Joan Miró (Miró museum) 45, 135
Gothic cathedral 130
Gran Teatre de Liceu 132
La Pedrera 132

Mercado de la Boquería   *132*
Montjuïc   *135*
Museo d'Historia   *131*
Museu Maritim   *42*
Museu Picasso   *45*
Olympic Stadium   *135*
Oriente Hotel   *132*
Palacio Guèll   *132*
Palau de la Generalitat   *130*
Palau de la Musica Catalana   *132*
Palau de Llonctinent   *131*
Parc de la Ciutadella   *135*
Park Guèll   *134*
Passeig de Gracia   *132*
Picasso Museum   *131*
Plaça de Catalunya   *132*
Plaça del Rei   *131*
Plaça Real   *132*
Ramblas   *130, 132*
Sarrià   *134*
Templo de la Sagrada Familia   *132*
Tibidabo   *135*
Underground Museum   *131*
Vía Laietana   *130*
*Eixample (see under Ensanche in this guide)*   *132*
*environs*
 Montserrat   *137*
 Sitges   *138, 139*
*general information*
 brochures from tourism authorities listing
  accommodation   *136*
 El Prat Airport, Terminal A
  (international) ( (3) 478-4704   *135*
 El Prat Airport, Terminal B (national)
  ( (3) 478-0565   *135*
 Iberia ( (3) 412-5667   *135*
 radio taxis ( (3) 357-7755 and 358-1111   *135*
*history*   *130*
*nightlife*
 El Cordobés ( (3) 317-6653   *13*
 El Otro ( (3) 323-6759   *137*
 El Patio Andaluz ( 209-3378   *13*
 La Cava del Palau   *41*
 Metro Disco ( (3) 323-5227   *137*
 Nick Havanna ( (3) 215-6591   *137*
 Satanassa ( (3) 451-0052   *137*
 Trauma ( (3) 487-9447   *137*
*public transport*
 subway system (Metro)   *135*
*restaurants*
 Botafumeiro ( (3) 218-4230   *41, 136*
 Chicoa ( (3) 253-1123   *136*
 Els Quatre Gats ( (3) 302-4140   *137*
 Los Caracoles ( (3) 302-3185   *137*
 Reno ( (3) 200-9129   *136*
 Salamanca ( (3) 221-5033   *137*
 Vía Véneto ( (3) 200-7024   *41, 136*
*tourist information*
 Carrer de Tarragona   ( (3) 423-1800   *135*
 El Prat Airport   ( (3) 325-5829   *135*
 free maps from El Corte Inglés   *135*
  ( (3) 301-7443   *135*
Basque country   *231*
**Belchite**   *201*
**Bequiera-Beret** (ski resort, Pyrenees)   *260*
**Bilbao**   *233*
bird watching in Spain   *30*
**Blanes**   *141*
**Bocairente**   *50*

*festivals*   *50*
**Bubión**   *180*
**Burgos**   *210, 212, 215-216*
*accommodation*
 Almirante Bonifaz Hotel ( (47) 20-69-43   *215*
 Condestable Hotel ( (47) 26-71-25   *215*
 Corona de Castilla ( (47) 26-21-42   *215*
 España ( (47) 20-63-40   *215*
 Hotel Norte y Londres ( (47) 26-41-25   *215*
 Landa Palace Hotel ( (47) 20-63-43   *215*
*attractions*
 Arco de Santa María   *214*
 Gothic cathedral   *212, 214*
 old quarter and thirteenth century walls   *214*
*environs*
 Covarrubias   *216*
 Santo Domingo de Silos   *216*
*general infomation*
 Tourist Office ( (47) 20-31-25   *215*
*restaurants*
 Landa Palace ( (47) 20-63-43   *215*
 Los Chapiteles ( (47) 20-59-98   *215*
 Mesón del Cid ( (47) 20-59-71   *215*
bus services in Spain
 *general*   *254*

**C**   **Cáceres**   *121*
**Cadaqués**   *141*
**Cádiz**   *171-172*
*attractions*
 festivals   *53*
 old town   *172*
*history*   *171*
*restaurants*
 El Faro ( (56) 21-10-68   *172*
 Mesón del Duque ( (56) 28-10-87   *172*
**Candanchú**   *260*
**Cantabria**   *226, 229*
**Capileira**   *181*
car hire   *253*
**Casares**   *177*
**Catalonia**   *125*
 *Catalan language*   *127*
 *Catalan wines*   *128*
 *Catalonian dances*   *128*
 *history*   *127*
**Chinchón**   *117*
*attractions*
 Plaza Mayor   *117*
climate   *63*
**Consuegra**   *123*
*attractions*
 ruined castle   *123*
 windmills   *123*
consulates   *258*
**Córdoba**   *36, 190-196*
*accommodation*
 El Conquistador ( (57) 48-11-02   *196*
 Hostal Séneca ( (57) 47-32-34   *196*
 Maimónedes Hotel ( (57) 47-15-00   *196*
 Marisa Hotel ( (57) 47-31-42   *196*
 Melia Córdoba Hotel ( (57) 29-80-66   *196*
 Parador La Arruzafa ( (57) 27-59-00   *196*
*attractions*
 Judería   *193*
 Mezquita (Mosque)   *193*
 Museo Taurino (Bullfighting Museum)   *195*
 the Old City   *193*
*general information*
 tourist information   *196*

history   191
restaurants
　El Caballo Rojo ( (57) 47-53-75   196
　El Churrasco ( (57) 29-08-19   196
　Oscar ( (57) 47-75-17   196
　Séneca ( (57) 20-40-20   196
**Costa Brava**   127, 141
Blanes   141
Cadaqués   141
Figueres   142
Port Lligat   142
**Costa del Sol**   175–80
attractions
　Adra   179
　Almeria   179
　Estepona   175, 177
　Fuengirola   177, 179
　Málaga   175, 176, 179
　Marbella   176
　Mijas   177
　Motril   175, 179
　Nerja   179
　Puerto Banus   177
　Punta de la Chullera   177
　San Pedro de Alcántara   176
　Sotogrande   177
　Tarifa   177
　Torremolinos   179
**Costa Dorada** 127, 141
**Covarrubias**   216
**Cuenca**   123
attractions
　"hanging houses"   123
　Museo de Arte Abstracto Español   123
**Cuidad Real**   123
**Cuidadela**   245
cuisine courses in Spain   59
cuisine in Spain   55
currency   256

D **Doñana National Park and Wildlife Reserve**   160
dress code   256

E eating and drinking in Spain
general   255
**El Escorial**   36, 104, 109
attractions
　Monastery of San Lorenzo del Escorial   22
**El Rocío**   160
attractions
　pilgrimage to Nuestra Señora del Rocío   160
electricity   257
embassies   258
Canada (in Madrid) ( (1) 431-4300   258
Great Britain (in Madrid) ( (1) 319-0200   258
United States (in Madrid) ( (1) 577-4000   258
**Estepona**   177
accommodation
　Stakis Paraíso Hotel ( (5) 278-3000   177
attractions
　all-year nudist colony   177
environs
　Casares   177
**Extremadura**   118, 121-122

F festivals
April Fair, Seville   156
Bocairente mock battles, February   50
Cádiz Carnival, February   53
Carnival, February or March   53
Christmas   50

Ciudadela, Minorca, high summer   54
Corpus Christi, May   54, 109
Epiphany   50
Fallas, Valencia, March   50, 53, 144
Feria, Seville, April   50, 156
Fiestas de Virgen de Pilar, Zaragoza, October   55
Holy Week in Málaga   53
Holy Week in Seville   53
Horse Fair, Jerez de la Frontera, April   54, 166
Los Magos   50
Music Festival, Toledo, October   109
New Year's Eve   50
Pedro Manrique, Soria Province, high summer   54
pilgrimage to Nuestra Señora del Rocío, Doñana
　Wildlife Reserve, May   160
pilgrimage to Nuestra Señora del Rocío, Doñana
　Wildlife Reserve, May   158, 160, 162, 163, 164
San Antonio, January   50
San Fermín, Pamplona,
　July   50, 204, 205, 206, 207
San Isidro, Madrid, May   54
San Juan, June   246
San Sebastián, January   50
Santiago de Compostela, July   222
Semana Santa, Seville March   50
Semana Santa, Seville, March   155
Sitges Carnival, February   53, 139
Villanueva Carnival, February   53
wine festivals in autumn   55
Wine Harvest, Jerez de la
　Frontera, September   50, 166
Zamarramala, February   50
**Figueres**   142
attractions
　Dalí Museum   142
flamenco   12, 159
**Formentera**   249
accommodation
　Hostal Entrepinos ( (071) 32-70-19   249
attractions
　Es Pujols beach   249
　La Sabina   249
　San Francisco Javier   249
general information
　Tourist Office ( 332-20-57   249
getting around   249
restaurants
　Es Molí de Sal ( (071) 13-67-73   249
　Restaurante Le Cyrano   249
**Fuengirola**   177-179
attractions
　zoo and aquatic park   179
environs
　Lew Hoad's Campo de Tenis
　　( (5) 247-4858 177, 179
　Mijas   179
**Fuente Dé**   229
attractions
　cable car to Picos   229

G **Galicia**   210, 225, 226
geography   63
**Gibraltar**   172
attractions
　English nostalgia   172
　views of the Straits   172
**Girona**   142
accommodation
　Ultonia Hotel ( (72) 20-38-50   143

attractions
  Cathedral   *142*
  El Call (Jewish Quarter)   *143*
  Old Quarter   *142*
restaurants
  Cal Ros ( (72) 20-10-11   *143*
  Rosaleda ( (72) 21-36-68   *143*
golfing   *32, 176, 177, 258*
  general information
    Real Federación Española de Golf
     ( (91) 455-2682   *32*
**Granada**   *37, 181-89*
  accommodation
    Alhambra Palace Hotel
     ( (58) 22-14-68   *189*
    Carmen Hotel ( (58) 25-83-00   *189*
    Dona Lupe Hotel ( (58) 22-14-73   *189*
    Guadalupe Hotel ( (58) 22-34-23   *189*
    Hostal America ( (58) 22-74-71   *189*
    Juan Miguel Hotel ( (58) 25-89-12   *189*
    Kenia Hotel ( (58) 22-75-06   *189*
    Los Alixares Hotel ( (58) 22-55-06   *189*
    Melia Granada Hotel ( (58) 22-74-00   *189*
    Parador San Francisco ( (58) 22-14-40 *19*
    Parador San Francisco ( (58) 22-14-40   *189*
    Washington Hotel ( (58) 22-75-50   *189*
  attractions
    Albaicín, (old Arab quarter)   *187*
    Alcazaba in the Alhambra   *183*
    Alhambra   *19, 182*
     Royal Palace   *184*
    Cathedral   *187*
    El Generalife palace in the Alhambra   *183, 186*
    gardens in the Alhambra   *186*
    Royal Palace in the Alhambra   *183*
    Torre de la Vela in the Alhambra   *183*
  environs
    El Suspiro del Moro   *181*
    Guadix cave dwellers   *188*
    Sacremonte caves   *188*
  general information
    airport ( (58) 22-64-11   *188*
    Iberia ( (58) 22-14-52   *188*
    Railway Station ( (58) 27-12-72   *188*
    tourist information ( (58) 22-59-90   *188*
  history   *181-182*
  nightlife
    El Curro ( (58) 28-35-37   *14*
  restaurants
    Baroca ( (58) 26-50-61   *189*
    Carmen de San Miguel
     ( (58) 22-67-23   *189*
    Cunini ( (58) 26-37-01   *189*
    Los Manueles ( (58) 22-34-15   *190*
    Sevilla ( (58) 22-12-23   *190*
Greeks   *67*
**Guadalupe**   *122*
  attractions
    Monastery of Guadalupe   *122*
**Guadix**   *188*
**Guerníca**   *232*
 H  **Haro**   *12, 211*
  attractions
    Rioja wine *bodegas*   *211*
    Santo Domingo de la Calzada   *12*
health matters   *257*
hiking in Spain   *30*
history of Spain   *76*
  *Andalusia*   *149*

Catholic Monarchs   *70*
earliest times   *67*
Moors   *69*
Phoenicians   *67*
the Franco years   *74*
the Inquisition   *71*
the monarchy in decline   *72*
the Spanish Civil War   *74*
horseback riding   *177*
 I  **Ibiza**   *246-249*
  accommodation
    La Hacienda ( (071) 33-45-00   *248*
    La Ventana ( (071) 39-08-57   *248*
    Las Brisas del Mar ( 908-534-467
     FAX 802193   *248*
    Royal Plaza ( (071) 31-00-00   *248*
  attractions   *247, 248*
    D'Alt Villa (old town)   *248*
    Museo Arqueológico   *247*
    San Juan Bautista   *248*
    San Miguel   *248*
    Santa Eulalia del Río   *248*
  general information
    Aiport ( (071) 30-03-00   *248*
    Tourist Office ( (071) 30-19-00   *248*
  restaurants
    Casa Victoria ( (071) 34-09-00   *249*
    El Faro ( (071) 31-75-78   *248*
    Sa Capella ( (071) 34-00-57   *248*
    Sa Soca   *249*
    Sa Tasca   *248*
Inca   *242*
 J  **Jaca**   *201*
  attractions
    medieval buildings   *201*
    Romanesque cathedral   *201*
**Jaén**   *38, 190*
  accommodation
    Parador Castillo de Santa Catalina
     ( (53) 23-00-00   *190*
  attractions
    Parador Castillo de Santa Catalina   *190*
**Jerez de la Frontera**   *37, 166-168*
  accommodation
    Ávila Hotel ( (56) 33-48-08   *167*
    Jerez Hotel ( (56) 30-06-00   *167*
    Mica Hotel ( (56) 34-07-00   *167*
  attractions
    Alcázar   *166*
    equestrian activities   *166*
    fine aristocratic mansions   *166*
    Horse Festival, May   *54*
    Royal Andalusian School of Equestrian
     Art   *37, 168*
    sherry bodegas *166, 167, 168*
  environs
    Los Alburejos ranch,
     Medina-Sidonia   *169*
  festivals   *50, 54, 166*
  restaurants
    Gaitán ( (56) 34-58-59   *167*
    Tendido ( (56) 34-48-35   *167*
 L  **La Coruña**   *226*
  attractions
    old town   *226*
    Torre de Hercules   *226*
**La Mancha**   *118, 122-123*
**Lanjarón**   *180*

*accommodation*
Miramar Hotel ( (5) 77-01-61   *180*
*attractions*
spa   *180*
**Las Lomas**   *180*
**León**   *210, 216-219*
*accommodation*
Conde Luna Hotel ( (87) 20-66-00   *218*
Hotel de San Marcos ( (87) 23-73-00   *219*
Paris ( (87) 23-86-00   *219*
Quindós Hotel ( (87) 23-62-00   *219*
*attractions*
Colegiata de San Isidoro   *218*
Gothic cathedral   *217*
Monastery of San Marcos   *218*
*general information*
Railway Station ( (87) 22-37-04   *218*
Tourist Office ( (87) 23-70-82   *218*
*restaurants*
Casa Pozo ( (87) 22-30-39   *219*
Patricio ( (87) 24-16-51   *219*
**Léon**   *38*
*attractions*
Santo Domingo de Silos monastery   *39*
**Levante**   *125, 143*
**Liebana**   *229*
*attractions*
Santa María church   *229*
**Logroño**   *211*
*accommodation*
Carlton Rioja Hotel ( (41) 24-21-00   *211*
Los Bracos Hotel ( (41) 22-66-08   *211*
Murrieta Hotel ( (41) 22-41-50   *211*
*environs*
Haro   *211*
Nájera   *211*
*general information*
Tourist Office ( (41) 29-12-60   *211*
*restaurants*
Carabanchel ( (41) 22-38-83   *211*
El Cachetero ( (41) 22-84-63   *211*
La Merced ( (41) 22-11-66   *211*
Meson Lorenzo ( (41) 25-81-40   *211*
**Lugo**   *45, 226*
*attractions*
old town and Roman walls   *226*
twelfth century cathedral   *226*
M | **Madrid**   *91-104*
*access*
Barajas airport ( (1) 305-8345 to 47   *92, 102*
*accommodation*   *102*
Alcázar Regis Hotel ( (1) 247-9317   *102*
Balboa Hotel ( (1) 563-0324   *102*
Europa ( (1) 521-2900   *102*
Gran Hotel Velázquez
   ( (1) 572-2800   *102*
Gran Vía Hotel ( (1) 522-1121   *102*
Hostal Delfina ( (1) 522-2151   *102*
Mora ( (1) 420-1569   *102*
Palace Hotel ( (1) 429-7551   *102*
Principe Pio Hotel ( (1) 247-8000   *102*
Ritz ( (1) 521-2857   *102*
Ritz ( (1) 521-2857 *41*
Villa Magna Hotel ( (1) 576-7500   *102*
*attractions*
Alcalá   *98*
Aquarium in Caso del Campo Zoo   *42*
Archaeological Museum (Museo
   Arquelógico)   *96*

Army (Museo del Ejército)   *96*
Atocha Railroad Station
   (Estación de Atocha)   *92*
Ayuntamiento (City Hall)   *100*
bullring (Plaza de Toros)   *92*
Calle Alcalá   *91*
Calle Arenal   *100*
Casa de Lope de Vega   *100*
Caso del Campo Zoo and Aquarium   *42*
Convento de las Descalzas Reales   *100*
Cortés, the Spanish parliament   *100*
Main Post Office (Correos)   *92*
Mercado de San Miguel   *100*
Museo Centro de Arte Reína Sofía   *19*
National Museum of Decorative Arts
   (Museo de Artes Decorativas)   *96*
nightlife   *104*
Old Madrid   *92, 98*
Opera   *100*
Palacio Real   *42, 100*
Paseo de la Castellana   *91*
Paseo del Arte   *19*
Plaza Cibeles   *92*
Plaza de España   *98, 100*
Plaza de Oriente   *100*
Plaza Mayor   *98*
Prado Museum   *19, 91, 93*
Puerta de Toledo   *98*
Puerta del Sol   *98*
Rastro market   *101*
Real Madrid's soccer stadium
   (Estadio Bernabéu)   *92*
Retiro Park   *92, 96*
Royal Palace (Palacio Real)   *92*
Salamanca   *101*
Thyssen collection in Palacio Villahermosa   *19*
Torre de Madrid   *100*
*environs*   *104*
Aranjuez   *117*
Ávila   *104*
Chinchón   *117*
Consuegra   *123*
El Escorial   *104*
Segovia   *104*
Sierra Guadarrama   *104*
Toledo   *104*
Valle de los Caídos   *115*
*festivals*   *54*
*nightlife*
Archy   *104*
Bar Chicote ( (1) 462-3875   *41, 104*
Café Central   *104*
Café de Chinitas ( (3) 548-5135   *13, 104*
La Peña Flamenca La Carcelera   *104*
Pacha   *104*
Salon del Prado   *104*
*public transport*   *92, 102*
buses   *92*
Metro (subway)   *92*
radio taxi ( (1) 547-8200   *102*
rail, Chamartin Station ( 323-2127   *102*
*restaurants*
Alkalde ( (1) 276-3359   *103*
Cabo Mayor ( (1) 250-8776   *103*
Café Gijón ( (1) 531-0548   *103*
Casa Botín ( (1) 266-4217   *103*
El Bodegón ( (1) 262-3137   *102*
Jockey ( (1) 419-1003   *103*
La Dorada ( (1) 270-2004   *103*

La Fuencisia ( (1) 221-6186   *103*
La Trainera ( (1) 576-8035   *41, 103*
Viuda de Vacas ( (1) 366-5847   *103*
Zalacaín ( (1) 561-4840   *41, 103*
*shopping*
 Calle Serrano   *101*
*tourist information*
 Tourist Offices at:
 Barajas Airport ( (1) 305-3656   *102*
 Calle Señores ( (1) 242-5512, 248-7426   *102*
 Chamartin Railway Station
  ( (1) 315-9976   *102*
 Duque de Medinaceli( (1) 429-4487   *102*
 Plaza España ( (1) 541-2325   *102*
 Plaza Mayor ( (1) 366-4874 or 366-5477   *102*
**Mahón**   *244-245*
**Majorca**   *240-244*
 *see also under* Palma de Mallorca *240-243*
*attractions*
 Alcudia ruined amphitheater   *244*
 Andraitx   *243*
 Artá   *244*
 Bañalbufar   *243*
 Cabo de Formentor   *244*
 Cala Figuera   *244*
 Cala Ratjada   *244*
 Cartuja (Carthusian Monastery)   *243*
 Cuevas de Drach (Dragon's Caves)   *244*
 Deià   *244*
 Felanitx   *244*
 Inca   *241*
 La Calobra   *244*
 Manacor   *244*
 Monastery of Lluc   *244*
 Palma de Mallorca   *240-243*
 Palma Nova   *243*
 pearl cultivation   *244*
 Petra   *244*
 Porto Cristo   *244*
 Sóller   *242, 244*
 Son Marroig   *243*
 Valldemossa   *243*
**Málaga**   *38, 179*
*attractions*
 Alcazaba (fortress)   *179*
 Gibralfaro Castle   *179*
 Holy Week festival   *53*
 La Manquita Cathedral   *179*
*festivals*   *53*
**Manacor**   *244*
**Marbella**   *37, 176-177*
*accommodation*
 Andalusia Plaza Hotel ( (5) 278-2000   *176*
 Del Golf Plaza ( (5) 281-1750   *176*
 Don Carlos Hotel ( (5) 823-1140   *41, 176*
 Los Monteros ( (5) 277-1700   *176*
 Marbella Club ( (5) 282-2211   *41, 176*
*attractions*
 beaches   *177*
 casino   *176*
 Marbella Club   *177*
 Puerto Banus marina *38*
*environs*
 Las Lomas   *180*
*restaurants*
 Marbella Club ( (52) 77-13-00   *38*
**Medina-Sidonia**   *169*
*attractions*
 Los Alburejos ranch   *169*

**Mérida**   *45, 122*
*attractions*
 Roman architecture   *122*
*meseta* (central plateau)   *63*
**Mijas**   *41, 179*
*accommodation*
 Byblos Andaluz ( (5) 247-3050   *41*
**Minorca**   *244-246*
*accommodation*
 Agamenón ( (071) 36-21-50   *246*
 Audax ( (071) 15-46-46   *246*
 Cala Galdana ( (071) 37-42-09   *246*
 Port Mahón ( (071) 15-46-46   *246*
 Rey Carlos III   *246*
 Son Blach Cottage ( (071) 38-55-86   *246*
*attractions*
 Cala Covas pre-historic caves   *245*
 Cuidadela   *245*
 Mahón   *245*
 San Juan festival, Ciudadela   *246*
*general information*
 Aiport ( (071) 15-70-00   *246*
 Tourist Office ( (071) 36-37-90   *246*
*restaurants*
 Pilar restaurant ( (071) 36-68-17   *246*
**Monastery of Guadalupe**   *122*
money matters   *257*
**N Nájera**   *211*
*attractions*
 Santa María la Real monastery   *12*
national parks in Spain   *27, 201*
 *Coto Doñana*   *27*
 *Covadonga*   *27*
*general information*
 contact ICONA (Instituto Nacional para la
  Conservación de la Naturaleza)
  ( 266-8200   *27*
**Navarre**   *203*
**Northern Andalusia**   *190*
**O Old Castile**   *118, 210*
**P Palma de Mallorca**   *50, 240-242*
*accommodation*
 Ca Sa Galesa ( (71) 71-54-00   *242*
 Gran Hotel Bonanza Playa ( (71) 40-11-12   *242*
 Hotel Born ( (71) 71-29-42   *242*
 Melia Victoria ( (71) 73-25-42   *242*
 San Lorenzo ( (71) 72-82-00   *242*
 Saratoga ( (71) 72-72-40   *242*
 Sol Bellver ( (71) 73-67-44   *242*
 Sol Jaime III ( (71) 72-59-43   *242*
 Son Vida Sheraton Hotel
  ( (71) 79-00-00   *242*
*attractions*   *240*
 Almudaina Palace   *240*
 Arab Baths   *241*
 Bellver Castle   *241*
 Ca'n Pastilla and El Arenal beaches   *241*
 Consolat de Mar   *241*
 Gothic Cathedral   *240*
 Marineland   *42*
 Paseo del Borne   *240*
 Sa Llotja   *241*
 San Francesc and Sant Eulalia churches   *241*
 yachting marina   *241*
*general information*
 airport   ( (71) 26-26-00   *242*
 Iberia ( (71) 71-80-00   *242*
 Port ( (71) 70-23-00   *242*

shipping line, Trasmediterranea Company
  ( (71) 70-23-00  242
Tourist Office ( (71) 71-22-16  242
*restaurants*
  Ca'n Nofre ( (71) 46-23-59  243
  Caballito de Mar ( (71) 72-10-74  242
  Koldo Royo ( (71) 45-70-21  242
  La Bóveda  243
  La Cantina  243
  Parlament ( (71) 72-60-26  243
  Porto Pi ( (71) 40-00-87  242
**Pampaneira**  181
**Pamplona**  38, 204-208
*accommodation*
  N. H. Ciudad de Pamplona
    ( (48) 26-60-11  208
  Nuevo Hotel Maisonnave Hotel
    ( (48) 22-26-00  208
  Orhi Hotel ( (48) 22-85-00  208
  Tres Reyes Hotel ( (48) 22-66-00  208
  Yoldi Hotel ( (48) 22-48-00  208
*attractions*
  Gothic cathedral  204
  Plaza del Castillo  204
  San Firmín festival, July  16
  16th century citadel  204
*festivals*  204
  San Fermín  50
*general information*
  airport
    ( (48) 31-75-12  208
  Tourist Office ( (48) 22-07-41  208
*restaurants*
  Alhambra ( (48) 24-50-07  208
  El Mosquito ( (48) 25-50-26  208
  Hartza ( (48) 22-45-68  208
  Josetxo ( (48) 22-20-97  208
  Las Pocholas ( (48) 21-17-29  208
**paradors**  11
*general information*
  history and description  255
  reservations in Madrid
    ( (1) 435-9700  11, 255
  reservations in London
    ( (01) 042-8182  255
  reservations in New York
    ( (212) 750-8682  255
**Parque Nacional de Ordesa**  201
*pelota*  233
**Peñaflor**  37
**Penedés** (wine growing region)  128
**pharmacies**  258
**Picos de Europa**  227
*attractions*
  Fuente Dé  229
  Liebana  229
  outdoor sports  227
  Potes  27, 229
**pilgrim routes through Spain**  38
**Pontevedra**  226
**Port Lligat**  142
**post offices**  257
**Potes**  227
*attractions*
  Monasterio de Santo Toribio de Liebana  229
**public holidays**  257
**Puerto Banus**  38, 177
*accommodation*
  Atalaya Park Hotel ( (5) 288-4801  177

*attractions*  177
  yacht marina  177
**Pyrenees**  127, 201

R  **railways**  253
**Rioja**  38, 210
**Romans**  67
**Roncesvalles**  201
*attractions*
  Roncescalles Pass  209
*restaurants*
  La Posada  209
**Roncesvalles Pass**  209
**Ronda**  37, 172-173
*accommodation*
  Parador ( (5) 287-7500  175
  Polo Hotel ( (5) 287-2447  175
  Reina Victoria Hotel ( (5) 287-1240  175
  Royal Hotel ( (5) 287-1141  175
*attractions*
  bullfight museum  173
  bullring  173
  Puente Nuevo (New Bridge)  173
*restaurants*
  Don Miguel ( (5) 287-1090  175

S  **sailing**  241
**Salamanca**  118, 119, 120
*accommodation*
  Gran Hotel ( (23) 21-35-00  120
  Monterey Hotel ( (23) 21-44-00  120
  Parador de Salamanca ( (23) 22-87-00  120
  Residencia-Albergue Juvenil Salamanca
    (the YHA) ( (23) 26-91-41 and 21-31-93  120
*attractions*
  Parador de Salamanca  119
  Plaza Mayor  120
  Roman bridge  119
  Salamanca University  120
  Salamanca's Cathedrals  120
*restaurants*
  Chez Victor ( (23) 21-90-27  120
  El Candil Nuevo ( (23) 21-90-27  120
**Salou**  42
*attractions*
  Port Aventura  42
**San Ildefonso de la Granja**  116
**San Lorenzo del Escorial**  109-110
*attractions*
  Monastery of San Lorenzo del Escorial  109
**San Millán de la Cogolla**  211-212
*attractions*
  medieval monastries  211
  Suso and Yuso, Benedictine
    monasteries  12
**San Pedro de Alcántara**  176
*accommodation*
  Golf Hotel Guadalmina ( (5) 278-1400  176
*attractions*
  golf  176
**San Sebastián**  41, 233-234
*accommodation*
  Avenida Hotel ( (43) 21-20-22  234
  Costa Vasca Hotel ( (43) 21-10-11  234
  De Londres y de Inglaterra Hotel
    ( (43) 42-69-89  234
  Guadamendi Hotel ( (43) 21-41-11  234
  María Cristina Hotel ( (43) 42-49-00  41, 234
  Monte Igueldo Hotel ( (43) 21-02-11  234
  Niza Hotel ( (43) 42-66-63  234

attractions
  Basque cuisine  234
  La Parte Vieja (old quarter)  234
general information
  Fuenterrabia Airport
    ( (43) 64-22-40  234
  Tourist Office ( (43) 42-62-82  234
restaurants
  Akelarre ( (43) 21-20-52  234
  Arzak ( (43) 27-84-65  234
  Arzak ( (43) 27-84-65  41
  Casa Nicolasa ( (43) 42-17-62  234
  Chomin ( (43) 21-07-05  234
  Juanito Kojua ( (43) 42-01-80  234
  Kokotxa ( (43) 42-01-73  234
  Panier Fleuri ( (43) 42-42-05  234
  Patxiku Quintana ( (43) 42-63-99  234
**Sanlúcar de Barrameda**  171
attractions
  Doñana National Park and Wildlife
    Reserve  171
  wine-making  171
**Santander**  229, 231
accommodation
  México ( (42) 21-24-50  231
  Real Hotel ( (42) 27-25-50  231
  Rhin Hotel ( (42) 27-43-00  231
  Roma Hotel ( (42) 27-27-00  231
  Santemar Hotel ( (42) 27-29-00  231
  Sardinero Hotel ( (42) 27-11-00  231
general information
  Port ( (42) 22-72-88  231
  Railway Station ( (42) 21-12-14  231
  Tourist Office ( (42) 31-23-11  231
restaurants
  Bodega Cigalena ( (42) 21-30-62  231
  Canadio ( (42) 31-41-49  231
  La Sardina ( (42) 27-10-35  231
  Posada del Mar ( (42) 21-30-23  231
**Santiago de Compostela**  12, 39, 210, 219-224
accommodation
  Araguanay Hotel ( (81) 59-59-00  224
  Compostela Hotel ( (81) 58-57-00  224
  Gelmirez Hotel ( (81) 56-11-00  224
  Hotel de los Reyes Católicos
    ( (81) 58-22-00  39, 224
attractions
  cathedral  221
  Colegio de San Jeronimo  221
  Hotel de los Reyes Católicos  221
  one of Christendom's holy cities  221
  Palacio de Gelmirez  221
  Plaza del Obradoiro  221
  Rajoy Palace  221
festivals  222
general information
  Railway Station ( (81) 59-60-50  224
  Tourist Office ( (81) 58-40-81  224
pilgrims' route  12
restaurants
  Anexo Vilas ( (81) 59-83-87  224
  Don Gaiferos ( (81) 58-38-94  224
  Fornas ( (81) 56-57-21  224
  Hotel de los Reyes Católicos
    ( (81) 58-22-00  224
  Las Huertas ( (81) 56-19-79  224
**Santillana del Mar**  230
attractions  230
  Altamira Caves  231

  Convento de Regina Coeli  230
  Romanesque Collegiate Church  230
**Santo Domingo de la Calzada**  212
attractions
  cathedral  212
**Santo Domingo de Silos**  216
accommodation
  Hotel de Tres Reyes  216
attractions
  Romanesque monastery  216
**Segovia**  36, 116
accommodation
  Los Linajes Hotel ( (21) 46-04-75  116
  Parador de Segovia ( (21) 44-37-37  116
attractions
  Alcázar  116
  Gothic cathedral  116
  Roman Aquaduct  116
environs
  Alcalá de Henares  117
  La Granja (royal palace)  116
  Riofrio Royal Hunting Lodge  117
  Zamarramala  50
restaurants
  Casa Amado ( (21) 43-20-77  116
  Mesón de Cándido
    ( (21) 42-59-11  116
  Mesón Duque ( (21) 43-05-37  116
  Mesón José María ( (21) 43-44-84  116
**Seville**  14, 36, 150-159
accommodation
  Alfonso XIII Hotel ( (5) 422-2850  41, 158
  Doña María Hotel ( (5) 422-4990  41, 158
  Fernando III Hotel, ( (5) 421-7307  158
  Inglaterra Hotel ( (5) 422-4970  158
  Macarena Sol Hotel ( (5) 437-5700  158
  Monte Carmel ( (5) 427-9000  158
  Reyes Católicos Hotel, ( (5) 421-1200  158
  Simon Hotel ( (5) 422-6660  158
attractions
  Alcázar  151, 152
  Barrio de Santa Cruz  154
  Barrio de Santa Cruz
    (old Jewish
    quarter)  151
  Casa de Pilatos  154
  Cathedral  151
  Feria  50
  Giralda  150
  Guadalquivir (River)  151
  Holy Week festival  53
  Jardines de Murillo  154
  La Maestranza bullring  151, 156
  Los Remedios  156
  Museo Arquelógico  155
  Museo de Bellas Artes  155
  Parque de María Luisa  154
  Parque María Luisa  151
  Patio de Banderas  154
  Patio de los Naranjos  151
  Plaza Alfaro  154
  Plaza de España  151, 154
  Semana Seville
    festivals  50
  Semana Santa (Holy Week) festival  23
  Torre del Oro  151
  University  151
environs
  Isla de Cartuja  155

Itálica   155
Rocío annual pilgrimage   158
Santiponce (Itálica)   155
*festivals*   53, 155-156
*general information*
  airport (San Pablo) ( (5) 451-0677   158
  Iberia reservations in Seville
    ( (5) 422-8901   158
  Railway Station ( (5) 423-1918   158
  tourist information ( (5) 422-1404   158
*history*   150
*nightlife*
  Tablao de Curro Velex ( 21-64-92   14
*restaurants*
  (flamenco) La Trocha
    ( (5) 435-5028   160
  (flamenco) Los Gallos
    ( (5) 241-6981   159
  (flamenco) Tablao de Curro Velez
    ( (5) 421-6492   159
  Don Raimondo ( (5) 422-3355   159
  Enrique Becera ( (5) 421-3049   159
  La Dorada ( (5) 445-5100   159
  La Judería ( (5) 421-4338   159
  Oriza ( (5) 427-9585   159
  Rio Grande ( (5) 427-8371   159
  San Marco ( (5) 421-2440   159
*where to eat*
  tapas bars and tavernas   159
shopping
*antiques*   260
*Artespaña*   46, 260
*bedspreads and rugs from Galicia*   46
*Calle Serrano, Madrid*   46
*El Corte Inglés*   46, 260
*furniture and fabrics in Almería*   46
*general information*   260
*glassware, La Granja, near Segovia*   46
*pearls in Majorca*   46
*Ramblas, Barcelona*   132
*Zara, stores throughout Spain*   46
**Sierra de la Demanda**   211
**Sierra de Montserrat**   138
**Sierra Guadarrama**   104, 109
*attractions*
  Ávila   109
  El Escorial   109
  Segovia   109
  skiing   109
  Valle de los Caídos   109
**Sierra Nevada**   180-181
*attractions*
  Mulhacen peak   181
  Solynieve (ski resort)   181, 260
  Veleta peak   181
**Sitges**   139
*accommodation*
  Hotel Romantic ( (3) 894-0643   139
  Hotel Terramar ( (3) 894-0500   139
*attractions*
  beaches and nudist beaches   139
  palm tree fringed promenade   139
  picturesque Baroque church   139
*festivals*   53, 139
*restaurants*
  La Masia ( (3) 894-1076   139
  Mare Nostrum ( (3) 894-3393   139
skiing 30, 31, 109, 260
**Sóller**   244

**Solynieve** (ski resort, Sierra Nevada)   181, 260
*attractions*
  ski resort   181
**Somport**   201
**Son Marroig**   243
**Soria Province**   54
*festivals*   54
Spanish courses   59
Spanish vocabulary   257
sport   109, 227, 233, 258
*fishing*
  contact Federación Española de Pesca y
    Casting (Spanish Fishing and Casting
    Federation) ( (1) 232-8352   259
*golf*
  contact Real Federación Española de Golf
    (Royal Spanish Golf Federation)
    ( (1) 455-2682   259
*horseback riding*   177
*hunting*
  contact Federación Española de Caza
    (Spanish Hunting Federation) ( (1) 253-
    9017   259
*sailing*   259
  contact Federación Española de Vela
    (Spanish Sailing Federation)
    ( (1) 233-5305   259
*skiing*   260
  contact Federación Española de Deportes de
    Invierno (Spanish Winter Sports
    Federation) ( (1) 275-8943   260
*soccer*   260
*windsurfing*   177, 259

**Tarazona**   201
*attractions*
  Mudéjar architecture   201
**Tarifa**   177
*attractions*
  Hurricane Beach   177
  windsurfing   177
**Tarragona**   140, 141
*accommodation*
  Imperial Tarraco ( (77) 23-30-40   141
*environs*
  Monasterio de Santa María de Poblet   141
  Monasterio de Santes Creus   141
  Port Aventura   42
*restaurant*
  Sol Ric ( (77) 23-20-32   141
telephones   257
tennis   177
tennis coaching in Spain   31
tipping   256
toilets   258
**Toledo**   35, 104
*accommodation*
  Alfonso VI Hotel ( (25) 22-26-00   109
  Cardenal Hotel ( (25) 22-49-00   109
  Carlos V Hotel ( (25) 22-21-00   109
  María Cristina Hotel ( (25) 21-32-02   109
  Parador Conde de Orgaz ( (25) 22-18-50   109
*attractions*
  Alcantará bridge   109
  Alcázar   105
  Casa del Greco   108
  cathedral   108
  Church of Cristo de la Luz   108
  Church of Santo Tomé   108
  Holy Week festival   109

Judería  *108*
Music Festival  *109*
Parador Conde de Orgaz  *105*
San Martin bridge  *109*
*festivals  109*
*history  104, 105, 108*
*restaurants*
Asador Adolfo ( (25) 22-73-21  *109*
Cardenal Hotel ( (25) 22-49-00  *109*
El Abside ( (25) 21-26-50  *109*
Hierbabuena ( (25) 22-34-63  *109*
Parador ( (25) 22-18-50  *109*
**Torremolinos**  *179*
tourist information (on Spain)
*Chicago* ( (312) 944-0215  *253*
*general  252*
*London* ( (0171) 499-1095  *253*
*Toronto* ( (416)  961-3131  *253*
*tourist offices  256*
**Trevelez**  *181*
**Trujillo**  *121*

**V** **Valdepeñas**  *123*
**Valencia**  *143, 144, 145*
*accommodation*
Astoria Palace Hotel ( (6) 325-6737  *144*
Dimar Hotel ( (6) 334-1807  *144*
Expo Hotel ( (6) 347-0909  *144*
Feria Sol Hotel ( (6) 364-4411  *144*
Inglés Hotel ( (6) 351-6426  *144*
Lehos Hotel ( (6) 334-7800  *144*
Reina Victoria Hotel ( (6) 325-0487  *144*
Rey Don Jaime Sol Hotel ( (6) 360-7300  *144*
*attractions*
festivals  *50*
Museo Nacional de Cerámica  *144*
Palacio de la Generalidad  *144*
Palacio del Marqués de los Dos Aguas  *144*
*festivals  50, 53, 144*
*general information*
airport (Manises) ( (6) 370-3408  *144*
Railway Station ( (6) 231-0634  *144*
tourist information ( (6) *315-0417*  *144*
Trasmediterranea (Shipping Company) (
(6) 367-6512  *144*
*restaurants*
Commodoro ( (6) 321-3815  *145*
Condestable ( (6) 369-9250  *145*
El Plat ( (6) 334-9638  *145*
La Hacienda ( (6) 373-1859  *145*
Ma Cuina ( (6) 341-7799  *145*
**Valladolid**  *118*
*accommodation*
Felipe IV Hotel ( (83) 30-70-00  *118*
Imperial Hotel ( (83) 33-03-00  *118*
Olid Meliá Hotel ( (83) 35-72-00  *118*
*attractions*
Church of San Pablo  *118*
Colegio de San Gregorio  *118*
Museo Nacional de Escultura  *118*
*restaurants*
La Fragua ( (83) 33-71-02  *119*
La Goya ( (83) 23-12-59  *118*
Mesón Panero ( (83) 30-16-73  *119*
Mesón ( (83) 30-16-73  *119*
**Valldemossa**  *243*
**Valle de los Caídos**  *114*
**Vigo**  *226*
Visigoths  *68*

**W** weather  *258*
windsurfing  *177*
wines and wine production  *12, 57, 128, 137, 141, 210*
**Y** yachting  *177*
**Z** **Zamarramala**  *50*
**Zamora**  *118, 120, 121*
*attractions*
Romanesque cathedral  *121*
**Zaragoza**  *201, 202, 203*
*accomodation*
Corona de Aragon Hotel ( (67) 43-01-00  *203*
Don Yo Hotel ( (67) 22-67-41  *203*
Gran Hotel ( (67) 22-19-01  *203*
Ramiro I ( (67) 29-82-00  *203*
Rey Alfonso Hotel ( (67) 39-48-50  *203*
Zaragoza Royal Hotel ( (67) 21-46-00  *203*
*attractions*
Aljafería Palace  *202*
Basílica de Nuestra Señora del Pilar  *202*
Fiestas de Virgen del Pilar, October *55*
fifteenth century alabaster retablo  *202*
La Seo Cathedral  *202*
Lonja (merchants' exchange)  *202*
tapestry museum  *202*
*festivals  55*
*general information*
airport ( (67) 34-90-50  *202*
Iberia ( (67) 21-82-50  *202*
Railway Station ( (67) 22-65-98  *202*
tourist information ( (67) 39-35-27  *202*
*restaurants*
Costa Vasca ( (67) 21-73-39  *203*
La Casa del Ventero ( (67) 11-51-87  *203*
La Mathilde ( (67) 44-10-08  *203*
La Rinconada de Lorenzo ( (67) 45-51-08  *203*
Los Borrachos ( 272(67) 27-50-36  *203*